NU
OPENING

BLACK&DECKER®

WITI

D0580424

THE COMPLETE GUIDE

MAINTAIN YOUR POOL & SPA

Repair & Upkeep Made Easy

Rich Binsacca

Creative Publishing
international

CHANHASSEN, MINNESOTA
www.creativepub.com

**Creative Publishing
international**

Copyright © 2007
Creative Publishing international, Inc.
18705 Lake Drive East
Chanhassen, Minnesota 55317
1-800-328-3895
www.creativepub.com

Printed at R. R. Donnelley

10 9 8 7 6 5 4 3 2 1
Library of Congress Cataloging-in-Publication Data

Binsacca, Rich.
  The complete guide : maintain your pool & spa : repair & upkeep made easy / by Rich Binsacca.
      p. cm.
   At head of title: Black & Decker.
   Summary: "Includes information on basic maintenance, water quality, seasonal upkeep, and routine repairs. Provides everything needed to keep water features in good operating condition"-- Provided by publisher.
   ISBN-13: 978-1-58923-286-0 (soft cover)
   ISBN-10: 1-58923-286-0 (soft cover)
   1. Swimming pools--Maintenance and repair. I. Title. II. Title: Black & Decker the complete guide, maintain your pool & spa.

   TH4763.B56 2007
   643'.5560288--dc22

2006029242

THE COMPLETE GUIDE - Maintain Your Pool & Spa
Created by: The Editors of Creative Publishing international, Inc., in cooperation with Black & Decker.
Black & Decker® is a trademark of The Black & Decker Corporation and is used under license.

President/CEO: Ken Fund

Home Improvement Group
Publisher: Bryan Trandem
Senior Editor: Mark Johanson
Managing Editor: Tracy Stanley

Senior Design Manager: Brad Springer
Design Managers: Jon Simpson, Mary Rohl
Art Director: Dave Schelitzche

Director of Photography: Tim Himsel
Lead Photographer: Steve Galvin
Photo Coordinators: Julie Caruso, Joanne Wawra
Shop Manager: Randy Austin

Production Managers: Laura Hokkanen, Linda Halls

Author: Rich Binsacca
Page Layout Artist: Joe Fahey
Illustration: Dave Schelitzche, Earl Slack
Photographers: Joel Schnell, Aaron Parker

Contents

Maintain Your Pool and Spa

Introduction

Owning a swimming pool or spa is part of the American Dream of homeownership. Who hasn't envisioned lounging by the pool, splashing in the water on a hot summer day, or enjoying a relaxing soak in a bubbling outdoor tub? Once we attain the goal of owning our own home, the next logical thought is to improve it. Pools and spas often top the wish list.

If you currently own a swimming pool or spa, or are hoping or planning to add one (or both) somewhere in your yard, this book is for you. While there is significant value in the pure pleasures of owning and using a pool or spa, their benefits extend into achieving better fitness and enhancing property value, among others.

In turn, it makes sense to understand the inner workings of a pool and spa and how to maintain them to retain their myriad benefits. Whether you plan to tackle the bulk of the maintenance chores or hire a service technician to take care of some or all of them, being an educated pool or spa owner is a cornerstone for long-lasting enjoyment.

This book encompasses everything pool or spa owners need to gain that knowledge and apply it to their particular circumstances, skill level, and comfort zone. In addition to a comprehensive overview of the different types and styles of pools, spas, and accessories available today, this book provides detailed information about proper cleaning, routine and seasonal maintenance, achieving healthy water quality, and ensuring pool safety. You'll learn about the complete set of equipment for both a pool and spa, from heaters and filters to pumps and skimmers and—perhaps most important—troubleshooting tips for their maintenance and repair.

This introduction provides an overview of what to expect from this book. It also adds some depth to the various (and often combined) benefits of owning a pool and/or spa, the reasons to properly maintain those features, and tips for lowering ongoing operating costs and energy consumption. There's also a glossary of the basic pool and spa terms you'll come across as you read each chapter.

Types of Pools & Spas

Beyond the basics of defining the differences between an in-ground and an above-ground pool, as well as a spa and hot tub, this chapter illustrates and explains the various materials and methods used to build and finish pools and spas. You'll also gain insight into increasingly popular infinity-edge pools, integrated pools and spas, and indoor facilities.

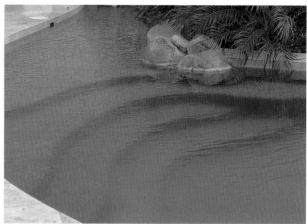

Water Quality

As with regularly scheduled cleaning, it is essential to the operation and enjoyment of a pool or spa to keep the water clean and chemically balanced. This chapter translates water chemistry into practical terms and tasks, from the chemicals and organic treatments to various delivery systems, so that you can achieve safe and healthy water quality.

Cleaning and Maintenance

This is the stuff most pool and spa owners tackle on their own: the daily, weekly, monthly, and annual routine chores associated with properly keeping a pool or spa clean of debris and other hazards that can hinder its optimal operation and your enjoyment. This chapter shows you the basic set of tools and equipment needed to do the job and offers a handy calendar for cleaning and other fundamental maintenance.

Systems and Repairs

This chapter is the heart of this book, providing—in both text and photos—the inner workings of pools and spas. Divided into five subchapters, it's an exhaustive treatment that not only covers the equipment set that every pool and spa relies on for its operation, but also the various components and materials of each piece within the set, including basic information about how to maintain and repair them. Included in this section are several fully photographed examples of some fairly advanced projects, such as replacing the element of a spa heater or replacing a leaking spa jet. Even if you never plan to lay a hand on the equipment set, this chapter will give you a solid base of knowledge to work efficiently with a pool or spa professional.

Seasonal and Special Maintenance

For most pool owners, winterizing and reopening is a necessary rite of seasonal passing and a critical process in protecting and maintaining the value of a pool. In addition to an illustrated, step-by-step guide to winterizing and reopening a pool, this chapter provides tips for the proper care and seasonal storage of outdoor furniture.

Pool Safety

Normally, the rule is "safety first," but this chapter is placed at the end in hopes it will leave a lasting impression on the importance of keeping your pool and spa, above all else, safe and hazard-free.

According to the Consumer Product Safety Commission, more than 250 children under the age of five drown every year, among thousands of accidents and deaths related to residential swimming pools. This chapter offers a comprehensive approach to pool and spa safety, including the latest regulations and advice from industry trade associations, watchdog groups, and government agencies.

Glossary of Basic Pool & Spa Terms

In-ground—A pool or spa built into the property as a permanent fixture or feature

Above-ground—A freestanding pool or spa constructed on the surface of the property, often (but not always) so that it can be removed or placed elsewhere, if necessary.

Hot tub—A freestanding, non-jetted, above-ground tub of heated water, primarily for relaxation.

Spa—An in-ground or freestanding/above-ground jetted tub of heated water, designed either for hydrotherapy, relaxation or both; most modern freestanding/above-ground units feature a self-contained equipment set for mobility and ease of service or maintenance.

Equipment set—The essential works of a pool or spa, including the heater, pumps and motors, valves, and filters, among other components.

Skid pack—The equipment set for a free-standing spa, contained within the unit.

Pool deck—The area surrounding the pool or spa, constructed of various materials including concrete, tile, paving stones, or wood, among others.

Solar—Heating and lighting systems that utilize or rely upon the sun for their operational power.

Winterizing (or Closing)—The process of preparing and protecting a swimming pool during long stretches of non-use, typically during extreme cold or other winter season conditions.

Service professional (or Technician)—A licensed, certified, and/or professionally trained expert in the proper maintenance and repair of pools and/or spas. Also called a service provider or contractor.

Infinity-edge—A design technique that makes the outer edge(s) of a pool or spa appear to have no discernible stop or coping treatment to contain the water.

Integrated pools and spas—Pools that feature a spa as part of their design, effectively creating two temperature zones (the higher temperature in the spa) within the same footprint.

The World of Pools and Spas

I f you're shopping for a house with a pool or spa, or both, or if you're thinking of adding a pool or spa to your current home, it's important to define why and how you'll use these lifestyle assets.

Without a doubt, pools and spas offer a variety of benefits, often in combination. For instance, they can serve a personal need for relaxation while enhancing the resale value of your home. Defining and prioritizing the importance of a pool or spa as a component of your lifestyle will help refine your plans, and the decision to add or remodel one or both and gain a better understanding and appreciation for taking care of that investment. Consider the following benefits of a pool or spa:

Entertainment. Most pools and spas for private home use are built and used for entertainment, whether alone, as a couple, as a family, or with friends, neighbors, and extended family. Like the kitchen inside the house, a pool is a natural and popular gathering place, even if no one is swimming or relaxing in the water. Add some patio furniture and perhaps an outdoor kitchen setup, and a pool or spa becomes an oasis for entertaining.

Relaxation. Coupled with entertainment, there's the benefit of relaxation, of cooling off in the water on a hot summer day or enjoying a soak in the evening. Sometimes, you're not even in the water, but instead floating on top of it on an inflatable raft or buoyed lounger, enjoying the gentle and soothing movement of the water beneath you, easing the tensions and cares of the day.

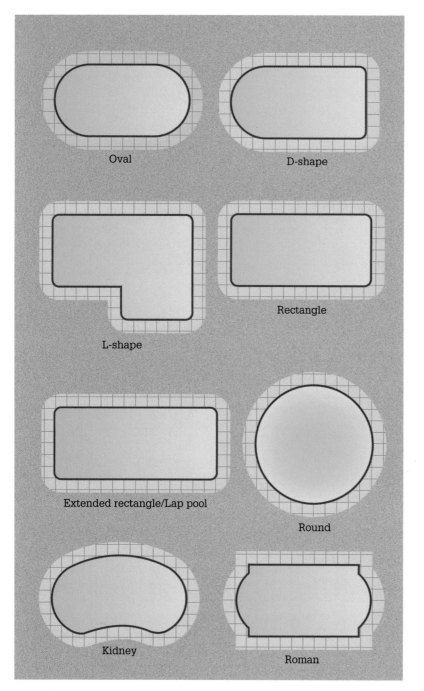

Typical swimming pool shapes give you several recognizable design options, but if you're using a vinyl liner or concrete pool walls and floor, the design possibility are practically limitless.

Housing value. Homes with an in-ground pool add about 8 percent to the value of a residential property, according to a recent study by the National Association of Realtors; adding an in-ground pool to a $200,000 home, for instance, appreciates its value by $16,000 as soon as you fill it with water and fire up the pumps. That's more than the estimated impact of an indoor whirlpool bathtub, hardwood floors, or a view of a natural water feature, such as a lake or pond, among several other household features and amenities. (The same study found that above-ground pools add no discernible value to a home, while spas and hot tubs were not part of the survey.)

Status. No question, a swimming pool or spa is a status symbol, representing a summit of success, wealth, and leisure. One or both are often on the wish lists of people shopping for a home, looking to improve their current home, or simply as a dream they one day hope to realize. To be sure, adding a pool or spa has become more affordable as new and more cost-efficient materials and methods come to the fore; still, less than 7 percent (or nearly 8 million) of the estimated 121 million homes in the United States boast a swimming pool, and an even smaller share enjoy a spa or hot tub, so owning one—and certainly both—puts you in fairly exclusive company.

Exercise. Aquatic centers like those found at a YMCA or fitness club are often geared toward the health benefits of swimming, one of the best

Key Considerations for Building a Pool or Spa

- Available space and access from the house.
- Budget and affordability.
- Type of construction.
- Personal taste.

- Primary purpose.
- Style of the house and garden.
- Current versus future lifestyle wants and needs.

low-impact aerobic exercises you can get. Only recently have individual homeowners realized and planned for that same value in their private pools. While a private pool may lack lanes painted along the bottom or can accommodate an Olympic-like length (25 meters or about 82 ft., usually too long within a standard home lot), a 4-ft. deep, 45-ft. long pool provides plenty of space to get a good workout at your convenience. For smaller yards, swim spas measuring 10-ft. to 14-ft. long replicate lap swimming by generating a constant, artificial current that allows you to swim in place in much the same way that treadmills simulate jogging.

Hydrotherapy. Self-contained fiberglass spas, specifically, can be designed to deliver hydrotherapy benefits beyond simply soaking in hot water, helping their owners ease daily aches and pains or recover from more serious injury or surgery. With adjustable, air-forced water jets strategically placed in and around molded seats, hydrotherapy spas enable multiple therapy sessions at the owner's convenience, supplementing or perhaps even replacing an offsite therapy regimen.

Design element. While this book focuses on swimming pools and spas for a homeowner's use and enjoyment, some pools are designed and built simply as water features in the garden. Whether still or with movement facilitated by a pump and filter system, decorative pools bring the soothing and attractive element of water to the garden and become places to reflect alone or gather as a group.

Relaxation is one of the principal reasons for installing a pool or spa. That might mean a leisurely swim or a therapeutic soak, or it could even be achieved simply by reclining on the pool deck and admiring the sumptuous surroundings.

Maintaining a swimming pool or spa involves plenty of old-fashioned work, but the benefits of keeping everything in ship-shape more than outweigh the labor for dedicated pool and spa enthusiasts.

Making Good Decisions for Your Underwater Experience

It may seem obvious, but with such a wide variety of real and perceived values associated with owning a pool and/or spa, it is your responsibility to care for and maintain them to retain whatever you derive from your ownership of these amenities.

The most important decision to make is whether you think you have, or want to develop, the skills and knowledge (and find the time) to maintain a pool or spa yourself, or hire a service professional to conduct some or all of the work. This book is intended to help you make that decision by giving you a basic understanding of all that's involved and required to properly care for a swimming pool or spa.

Throughout the book, you'll learn a few tips about how to make cleaning your pool or spa and maintaining balanced water quality an easier and more efficient process. Simply put, staying on top of the chores makes more sense than letting work build up.

It's the same basic principle that's behind house cleaning. You'll also gain insight into lowering the operating costs of a pool or spa, either by shutting it down ("winterizing") during long stretches of non-use, or selecting or retrofitting systems, including solar power, that conserve and reuse heat and/or use less energy for heating and operating the pumps of your pool or spa. Owning a pool or spa should not be a burden, but both carry essential and important responsibilities for their owners. Even if all you choose to do is contract with a pool service, at least educate yourself about and appreciate the value of keeping your pool or spa operating at peak efficiency.

A jetted spa that can accommodate four or more people can provide a great volume of entertainment for your family and friends, whether the spa is located indoors or outside on a deck or patio.

Whether you inherited a pool or spa with a house purchase or are thinking of adding one or both to your property, it's important to know the basics about how they are made so you can properly maintain and enjoy them. It will also let you tackle everyday repair jobs and perhaps even embark upon a pool or spa remodeling project.

Pools and spas are available in two fundamental types: those built into and flush to the ground (or "in-ground") and those built or installed partially or entirely above ground (including "self-contained" or "portable" units). Within those two types are myriad choices of shapes and styles, construction methods and materials, surface finishes, and ancillary amenities. Narrowing those choices, or figuring out why certain choices were made in the construction of an inherited pool or spa, is a formula of available space, budget, personal taste, and lifestyle wants and needs, among other considerations.

For instance, if your lot or tastes lean toward a "natural" pool featuring an asymmetrical shape, sculptured rock edges, and extensive surrounding landscaping, an in-ground concrete pool with an aggregate interior surface treatment is a likely choice.

If you're unsure about whether a pool or spa is right for you and your family, or you need to stick to a smaller budget, an above-ground, vinyl-lined pool package or inflatable unit might be a better option. If your climate limits outdoor swimming to less than half the year, perhaps an indoor pool or spa is most appropriate. If all you need is a rigorous workout, swim spas can fill the bill, or if hydrotherapy is prescribed for a chronic health condition, a molded, jetted fiberglass spa can help ease your pain.

No matter what you choose to build, you'll likely rely on a professional pool builder or retailer/installer to help determine what's best for your circumstances and guide you through the entire design and construction process. In the case of an existing pool or spa, a professional service technician can help identify the type of pool or spa you own, explain the intricacies of its construction and operation, and instruct you about how best to care for it. In this chapter, you'll gain insight into finding and selecting a pool builder or technician for your project, one that will work with you to satisfy your needs, ensure a smart investment, and comply with regulatory standards for your area.

Climate is an important consideration when planning a pool or spa. But keep in mind that even if your area has four distinct seasons, some kinds of spas and even pools can be enjoyed winter, spring, summer or fall.

A formal yard demands a formal pool (at least that's what the designers are likely to tell you). Formal elements include dedicated dining areas and classical ironwork. Regular bond brickwork always has a formal appearance, even if a few curves are used in the design.

To say that there are no limits to the style and shape of pool and spas is too simplistic. As you plan a new project or consider what you have inherited on your property, it will be clear what you can do and what limitations, if any, exist. Once you map that landscape, you can more easily navigate it to arrive at a pool or spa project and long-term maintenance, repair, and remodeling schedule that best meets your goals and circumstances.

While it's true that you can build whatever you can imagine in a pool or spa shape and style, such design flexibility depends on a variety of other factors, most notably your budget, the available area and topography of your property, and your choice of pool or spa construction.

Concrete in-ground pools and spas offer the most choices of shape, size and features, simply because the excavation process literally forms the pool or spa. Other construction methods and mate-rials are less flexible in their available designs, albeit constantly expanding in their options, from vinyl-lined, in-ground pool packages to gel-coated fiber-glass shells and portable, self-contained spas.

When considering a shape for your pool or spa, or trying to determine why a previous owner selected a certain design, consider not only the layout and available space on the property, but also the intended or prevailing purpose of the pool or spa. Also evaluate how the pool or spa design complements the architectural forms and details of other built structures, such as the house, a covered porch, an existing deck, or a nearby water feature.

A long, narrow pool with a consistent (if slightly sloping) depth, for instance, is clearly designed for a lap swimmer; a pool with a diving board, meanwhile, requires a particular design and shape to maintain safe use and overall recreation. A free-form shape, especially one finished with materials designed to

Prioritizing Wants and Needs

As you consider a new pool or spa project, or perhaps a remodeling job for an existing one, it's important for the planning and design process to create a "wants and needs" list. Simply, over the course of a few weeks, keep a running tab of the reasons you want or need a pool or spa, from recreation to exercise. There are no "wrong" answers, simply an honest brainstorming of ideas. Once you have a complete list, separate wants and needs and prioritize them. With those lists as a foundation, you can more easily make choices and consider trade-offs when confronted with practical issues of available space and budget.

simulate a natural setting, might complement a more rustic or asymmetrical home and garden style, while a rectangular pool or spa with clean lines and perhaps an infinity edge indicates a more formal and contemporary style shared by the entire property.

There are other factors at work that direct the design and construction of new pools and spas. Simply, lots for new homes are getting smaller, while the square footage of new homes continues to increase. As a consequence, new homeowners typically have less available outdoor space within their property lines to add a pool, or at least one as large as

they might want or would have been able to build a decade ago.

Concurrently, today's pool design trends support more specific uses, such as relaxation, exercise, or simply aesthetics, compared to traditional or multipurpose recreational activities, resulting in smaller pools.

The upside of this downsizing trend is that smaller pools (and certainly spas) are less expensive to build, cost less to maintain in terms of the water volume and chemicals they require, and take less time to care for than larger vessels—something the owner

Building an in-ground pool is an ambitious project that requires a professional builder. From a homeowner's standpoint, your main job is to make sure you're prepared for the mess and disruption.

A poured concrete pool with concrete coping can take on just about any shape you please. Although concrete is more common in nonresidential pools and in areas with a warmer climate, the only good reason not to consider one is that they cost at least 50% more to install than a vinyl-lined pool of the same size.

of a large, inherited pool might ultimately appreciate and try to rectify in a remodeling project.

As mentioned earlier, there are several ways to build a pool or spa, each with its own limitations and considerations. Some methods, like vinyl-lined and fiberglass, can be used for in-ground and above-ground pool or spa projects; others, such as concrete or inflatable, are strictly one or the other.

Concrete Pools and Spas

For most of the country, the image of a private residential pool is one that is dug into the ground and cemented in place with concrete. An in-ground pool or spa offers the most design flexibility because the shape, size, depth, slope, and any integral seating, steps, or other features are created during the excavation and preparation for concrete. What you dig into the ground is generally the pool or spa you'll get.

Because in-ground pools and spas, and specifically concrete units, rely heavily on the soil to provide stability and, in large part, contain the shell they

form, the surrounding soil should resist compression and expansion, and ideally drain water away from the structure. Concrete and other in-ground and above-ground pools and spas can be built on any type of soil, but those set in or on expansive or unstable soils need to be specially engineered and built (at higher expense) to avoid potentially significant structural problems and expensive repairs later. Conducting a soil test is a key step in any new pool or spa project.

Assuming stable (or stabilized) soil conditions and a creative design that prescribes a concrete pool or spa, the excavated hole and integral features will need to be reinforced with steel bars, or re-bar, to further support the concrete shell. When finished, the web of vertical and horizontal re-bar resembles a metal cage in the same shape as the excavation, held about 4" out from the dirt sides and bottom of the pool. Other features, such as steps or integral seating, might be formed with plywood or re-bar in preparation for concrete. In addition, a thicker "bond beam"

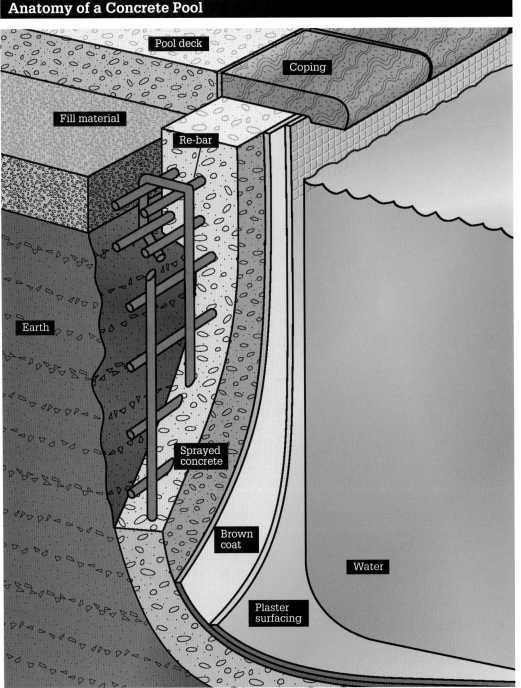

Pool deck

Coping

Fill material

Re-bar

Earth

Sprayed concrete

Brown coat

Plaster surfacing

Water

A concrete pool is built much like a building foundation, with reinforced concrete walls and floors. Most concrete pools are coated with a surface layer of gunite or shotcrete.

along the top of the walls is formed with re-bar to support the pool deck and coping.

Concurrently, the contractor will install (or "rough in") the pool or spa's recirculation system behind and within the re-bar cage, including skimmer openings, the main drain, suction valves, and any automated cleaning, water feature, and/or lighting conduits that are to be run underground from the pool or spa structure to the equipment set nearby. Once properly installed, the pipes, wires, and other conduits are

located or "stubbed up" near the location of the equipment set, to be connected later; their openings in the pool shell are covered or otherwise protected during the construction process to keep dirt, construction debris, trash, pests, and concrete from clogging the system.

For several years, pool builders have relied on one of two spray-applied methods and materials to create the shell of a concrete pool, all but replacing standard poured concrete (as you might see for a patio or sidewalk) and concrete masonry units (or preformed, rectangular concrete blocks, which offer less design flexibility) in pool and spa construction.

These two spray-applied methods, gunite and shotcrete, are more time-efficient and appropriate for concrete pool and spa building because they are easier to control, faster to apply, adhere better to the excavated and reinforced sidewalls without significant sloughing (compared to traditional poured concrete methods), and enable the greatest amount of design flexibility.

Specifically, gunite is a dry mixture of cement and sand that is blended with and applied to the walls and floor with pressurized water, resulting in a stiff but workable mortar. Shotcrete is a similar wet mortar formula applied with pressurized air. It's important for the contractor to mix and apply the materials properly: wet enough to adhere to the walls and get completely behind and a few inches out from the re-bar cage, but also dry enough to hold and stiffen quickly against the sidewalls and other reinforced forms.

The resulting concrete shell is about 6" thick (usually thicker, and with more re-bar, in cold climate areas). While the mortar is still wet, workers smooth and sharpen the surfaces and remove excess material, refining the pool or spa shape and formed features.

Because of the thickness of the walls, bond beam, and floor, the structure requires several yards of concrete to complete, and thus a week or more to dry or before the application of a watertight finish coat completes the pool or spa shell.

Of course, the same method can also used to build short, above-ground walls of an integral spa during construction of a concrete pool, but usually only when a pool and spa are designed and built together; rarely, if ever, would a pool or spa builder suggest or advocate a concrete structure for a truly above-ground pool or spa, if only because more cost- and time-efficient (not to mention less permanent) alternatives exist to achieve a comparable result.

Once the concrete shell is properly cured and any slight cracks properly patched and allowed to dry, there are a dizzying array of finishes that provide a watertight seal and contribute to the aesthetic quality of a pool or spa.

Once dominated by white plaster, a mix of marble sand and white cement applied evenly in a thin, somewhat rough-textured coat over the concrete shell, the industry for pool and spa finishes has exploded into a variety of specialty materials. The most notable of these new finishes are pebbled aggregates, quartz plaster, and ceramic tile. As a result,

Color Keys

When pool builders and plaster companies began adding colors to their white plaster finishes for concrete pools and spas, they soon discovered that dark-color pigment additives and paint coatings could not withstand the variety of chemicals and ultraviolet light exposure of a pool's environment, resulting in uneven and streaky finishes over time. Earth tones held up better, but pool owners asked for more variety and customization. The advent of specialty finishes in the early 1990s, including quartz plaster (in which quartz sand replaces marble sand in the plaster mix), pebble aggregates, and glass beads, ushered in a new era of deep, rich color choices to satisfy consumer demand. Though commanding a price premium of perhaps 50 percent compared to white plaster, specialty finishes are not only colorfast but also considered more durable than traditional plaster, and are also easier to keep clean.

More color choices, however, requires a higher level of understanding. In addition to a pool's or spa's depth and shape, its finish coat color helps determine how the water looks when exposed to sunlight and the reflection of landscape features; even if the water is clear and clean, it might appear colored and thus less attractive depending on the plaster or aggregate finish color. For instance, white-dominant mixes elicit blue hues (hence the prevailing use of white plaster), while brown tints can result in greener-looking water; pool builders often replace brown pebbles or quartz with purple, for instance, to create a more natural look once the pool or spa is filled with water. When considering a specialty or colored finish, visit your pool builder or remodeler's recent projects and perhaps consult a color specialist to determine the right blend for your tastes and circumstances.

One advantage of building a concrete pool is that you can design and build a spa and integral pool deck from the same material for a seamless appearance.

concrete pool and spa owners have almost endless options for colors and textures, especially when specialty finishes are mixed and matched.

Most cement-based finishes are spray- or trowel-applied to the raw concrete surface; pebble aggregate finishes are usually thicker (about ¾", or up to four times that of a traditional plaster application) to make sure the material adheres to the sidewalls and pool bottom.

Ceramic tile is often applied along the top several inches of the sidewalls as a decorative feature and as an easy-to-clean material at the waterline in plaster-finished pools and spas. It requires a longer, manually-set installation, especially if tile, usually in 1"- or 2"-mosaic pieces, is used to finish the entire shell rather than as simply a perimeter accent detail. That's a function not only of ceramic tile applications, in general, but also because the tiles must lay perfectly level to deliver a safe, smooth surface. Installed and

cared for properly, however, a ceramic tile finish should last for the life of a pool or spa.

Beyond traditional plaster and specialty finishes, as well as ceramic tile, concrete pools can be completed with spray-applied liquid vinyl or acrylic gel-coat, or covered with a reinforced PVC membrane. Such finishes offer fewer color and texture options (if typically more colorfast than plaster paints or pigments), but are also more affordable, easier to clean, more resistant to algae growth, and longer lasting than traditional plaster.

Once the finish is cured (requiring perhaps another week), the pool or spa builder or equipment installer finishes the systems rough-in with skimmer flaps, drain covers, outlet fittings, and, of course, the equipment set nearby. Once the deck and any other landscape or integral water features and finishes are completed, the pool or spa can be filled with water, cleansed and balanced, and enjoyed.

Vinyl-Lined Pools and Spas

In-ground and above-ground pools built using a vinyl liner are less expensive and faster to build than a concrete pool. Often called "packaged" pools, they are available in a limited—if increasing—variety of shapes and sizes, and are typically delivered with all the necessary components to complete the project.

Instead of reinforced concrete, an interlocking system of support members creates the structure of a vinyl-lined pool, whether in-ground or above-ground. These usually L-shaped components are engineered and made of aluminum, steel, plastic, or stainless steel; a contractor may also use concrete blocks or treated wood for below-grade projects. Regardless, these structural components create a solid shell for a thick, watertight vinyl membrane.

For in-ground, vinyl-lined pools and spas, the excavation phase of the project is similar to that of a concrete pool, except that the hole must be dug large enough to accommodate the buttresses of the sidewall components, as well as the rough-in of the recirculation system and any accessory features serving the pool.

The pool bottom, meanwhile, is leveled and covered (and leveled again) with sand, cement, or vermiculite, the latter a fine mix of lightweight, spongelike shale granules with water-absorbing qualities. This soft bottom helps reduce the chance of small tears in the liner, something even a smooth concrete slab might eventually cause.

For above-ground, vinyl-lined pools, the excavation process is eliminated, or at least significantly less than an in-ground project. At most, the area needs to be made stable and level—again, with enough clearance for the pool's or spa's structural sidewall members. As the sidewalls are fitted together, the contractor may use flat, wide concrete paving stones under a few of the supports to achieve precise level. Above-ground pools also feature a frame for the bottom of the pool, which is covered with a 3" to 4" layer of sand or similar base for the liner.

With the structure secure and level, the system's rough-ins in place, and the pool or spa bottom ready, the liner is carefully unfolded and/or unrolled and gently pulled to the sides. Most liners are drawn (or draped) over the sidewalls and attached behind

Vinyl pool liners are taking over much of the residential pool market because they are the least expensive systems and they offer low maintenance. Because the pressure from the weight of the water maintains the pool shape, in-ground vinyl pools cannot be drained.

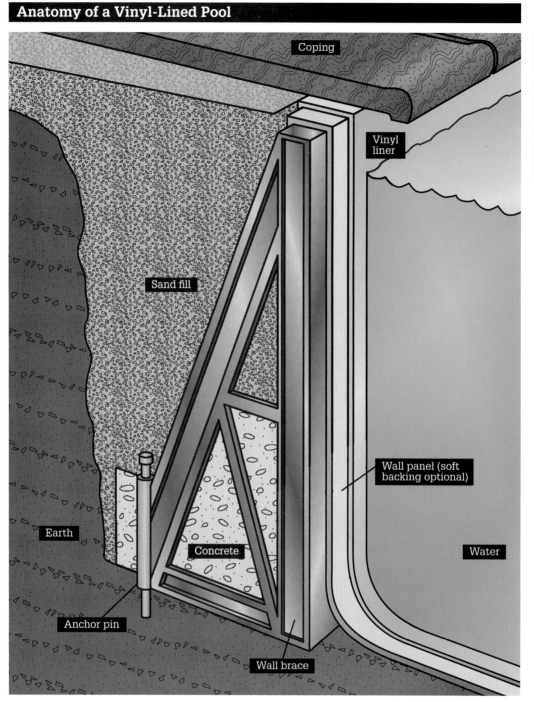

Coping

Vinyl liner

Sand fill

Wall panel (soft backing optional)

Earth

Concrete

Water

Anchor pin

Wall brace

In-ground pools with a vinyl liner are low in maintenance, but the liners usually require replacement after 15 years or so.

them; some, however, are drawn up to the top of the structural members and fitted (or beaded) at or near the top.

Regardless, the process is arduous, requiring several people and, especially toward the end, a good deal of strength to forcibly but still carefully stretch and attach the liner over the last bit of the pool or spa's structural shell. Folds, if any, are spread out or cut away, the latter requiring the cut edges of the liner to be fused together. With packaged pools,

especially, the material is cut very precisely in the factory to fit exactly to the shell's design and thus mitigate such circumstances.

With the liner securely in place and molded to any steps, seating, or other integral features (typically accommodated in the factory to maintain the liner's structural integrity), a contractor installs and connects the plumbing and lighting finishes and the equipment set, making the pool or spa ready for water.

At the same pace as the in-ground shell fills with water, the contractor fills in the excavated area behind the structural members with dirt (called backfill) to balance the pressure on both sides of the pool or spa. The fill dirt, usually derived from the pool or spa's excavation, is ideally cleaned of any sharp rocks and debris, conditioned with non-expansive or compressive soils, if necessary, and compacted behind the sidewalls to create a stable support system that sheds or drains water (and thus relieves hydrostatic pressure) away from the structure. The backfill also forms the base for the deck and coping material surrounding the pool or spa.

For above-ground, vinyl-lined pools and spas, the sidewalls are self-supporting or bolstered by the surrounding deck structure (often part of the pool package), which provides the counter-pressure required as you fill the pool or spa with water.

While it's true that vinyl-lined pools and spas cannot accept the myriad finishes available to concrete vessels, the membrane can be manufactured to a particular color or pattern, including simulated aggregate pebbles, ceramic tile, or some other custom design or image—while still providing a smooth, easy-to-maintain pool surface that better resists algae growth and bacteria than plaster-finished pools and spas. Darker colored liners, however, have been known to fade eventually from exposure to pool or spa chemicals and the sun's ultraviolet light.

The main concern about vinyl liners, in fact, is their structural resistance to chemicals and UV rays, especially if the water chemistry is chronically unbalanced and unsanitary. Dry chlorine, for instance, must be completely dissolved in the pool water, perhaps mixed in a separate, non-metal bucket of water beforehand; even so, it's prudent to brush the interior surface thoroughly after a dry chlorine application.

Similarly, a regularly low pH level can cause the liner to wrinkle or become brittle over time, while a too-high pH level might result in scaling or calcium build-up that is difficult to remove and can bake onto the surface from the sun, permeating the material and causing cracks. Too much total alkalinity, meanwhile, can also cause a vinyl liner to lose elasticity, and cleaning tools not specifically designed for a vinyl surface can tear the material.

As with any pool or spa, a regular schedule of careful and appropriate maintenance goes a long way to preserving the integrity and value of your investment. Care for it correctly, and a vinyl liner can last up to 15 years before it needs to be replaced from normal wear and tear.

Underground plumbing lines are run from the pool drain and skimmer locations to the intended location of the equipment set.

Vinyl liners are made in a dizzying array of colors and patterns that you may choose from when ordering your new pool or a replacement liner.

Installation of a Vinyl-Liner Pool

A swimming pool with a vinyl liner is a relatively fast pool type for professionals to install.The hole that is excavated for the pool has very low tolerance, however, so great pains are taken to get the shape leveled and finished. Any imperfections in the excavation will show through on the finished product.

Once the pool installation is complete, the pool deck is added. Often, the deck is made of poured concrete with integral coping that covers the tops of the pool support walls. Other materials, such as flagstone or concrete pavers, also may be used for the deck surface.

1

The site is excavated to the sidewall depth, then the walls are positioned and braced.

2

The excavation is completed to final depth at the deep end, usually with a backhoe.

Plumbing and equipment are hooked up and the shape of the excavation is refined. A concrete footing is poured around the perimeter of the pool wall.

Soft wall panels are installed on the excavation walls to provide cushion so the vinyl is less likely to tear. An additional cushion layer may be installed between the wall and the vinyl liner.

The vinyl liner is placed into the pool excavation and attached to the tops of the support walls. The area behind the walls is backfilled once all of the pool connections are made.

Fiberglass pools are installed as a single preformed shell, making them the easiest type of pool to install (but not the cheapest). They tend to be made in simple geometrical shapes.

Fiberglass Pools

The third most-popular type of pool or spa construction method is fiberglass; in fact, the material is by far the most common for above-ground, self-contained (or portable) spas, discussed later in this chapter.

The term "fiberglass" is a bit of a misnomer; in fact, fiberglass (an inorganic composite of long, thin glass strands) is mixed with resin to create the structural material for this type of pool or spa, forming a molded, one-piece shell that is finished on the inside with a smooth, permanently bonded gel-coat or quick-setting resin material applied during the manufacturing process. The result is a hard (though certainly not inflexible) vessel that can be used for in-ground or above-ground pool or spa projects.

Even more so than vinyl-lined packages, fiberglass pools are limited in their available sizes and shapes.

As factory-completed (if lightweight) one-piece shells, they must be built within certain dimensions to be transported from the factory to your house safely. That being said, the manufacturing process is evolving to offer a wider variety of fiberglass pool and spa shapes (or molds), if not necessarily larger vessels.

For in-ground pools, the excavation process for a fiberglass pool is similar to concrete and vinyl-lined projects; as with the latter, the contractor digs a hole a bit larger than the shell to accommodate the system rough-in components and to allow the installation crew to properly level the bottom and backfill against the outside of the pool walls.

Once the excavated area has been prepared and its bottom leveled or shaped to match that of the pool shell as close as possible, the pool is hoisted with a crane from the delivery truck and carefully placed in the hole. Rarely will the first placement be perfect; more likely, the crew (using the crane) will have to lift the pool out and refine the excavation to ensure that the bottom of the pool is completely and reliably supported.

Eventually, the pool is unstrapped from the crane, steadied by temporary bracing across its width, and connected to the recirculation system rough-in and above-ground equipment. As with vinyl-lined vessels, the pool is filled with water and backfilled at the same time to balance the pressure on both sides of the walls; in the case of fiberglass pools, the backfill is typically a wet (or "washed") sand that fills any and all voids between the exterior shell walls and the excavated hole. To provide stability and drainage for the coping and deck material surrounding an in-ground pool or spa, some contractors advocate a bed of ½" or ¾" crushed and washed rock for the top four inches or so of the backfill.

In-ground fiberglass pools can be slightly more expensive than comparably sized and standard-shaped concrete pools, simply because the bulk of the construction process occurs in a factory using more expensive materials than re-bar and gunite,

and also due to the costs of shipping the shell to your home.

However, above-ground fiberglass pools are more cost-competitive, primarily because there is no excavation required and, in the case of spas, the pump, filter, heater, and other system components are usually contained in the package from the factory.

As mentioned earlier, fiberglass is also used as a structural frame material for in- and above-ground, vinyl-lined pools, just as a gel-coat can be applied to a concrete pool or spa shell to achieve a smooth, easy-to-clean surface. Pools and spa construction methods that use more than one material (e.g., concrete and gel-coat) are often called hybrids.

What fiberglass pools lack in available shapes and sizes, they make up in convenience and durability. While a concrete pool might require a month or more to complete, a fiberglass pool or is ready to enjoy in a week's time or less, depending on any necessary excavation or surface preparation and balancing the water quality prior to use. They are also smaller than most in-ground pools, and therefore require less water and chemicals—and therefore less expense—to maintain properly.

Standard coping strategies like the tile shown here are still prevalent with fiberglass pools. Some manufacturers, however, are improving their ability to form coping into the actual vessel, further lowering the maintenance needed for a fiberglass pool.

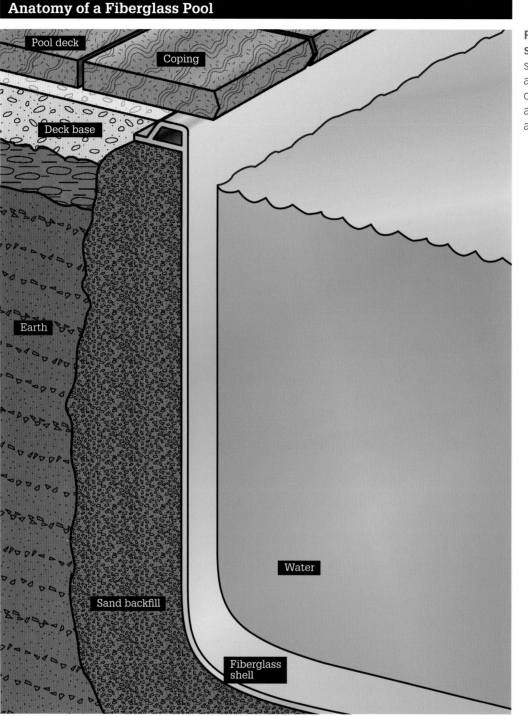

Pool deck

Coping

Deck base

Earth

Sand backfill

Water

Fiberglass shell

Fiberglass pool shells are simply set into the ground and wet sand is dumped in from above to backfill around the shell.

As with any pool or spa, fiberglass is not immune to wear and tear; like vinyl liners, the inside gel-coat surface can become brittle and crack from neglect and, eventually, wear and tear over time. Severe surface damage may even affect the fiberglass material behind the coating, requiring a patch that may necessitate re-excavation if it is serious enough to cause a leak.

Furthermore, the material cannot withstand a lot of weight on its edges; a pool deck or coping material, or perhaps landscape boulders, that rely on the shell for structural support may buckle the fiberglass. As an alternative, fiberglass pool manufacturers are broadening the design options for the integral coping (or top edge) molded and finished into their products.

Above-ground Pools

Long perceived as a cheap alternative to in-ground pools, those resting above ground have recently and dramatically been improved in appearance, durability, and performance to close the status gap. Resins are now the rule for exterior shell materials, providing one-piece finishes that not only open up design options in color and pattern, but last longer than their predecessors. Inside shells (usually liners), meanwhile, feature factory-applied patterns that replicate the tiled waterline borders of concrete pools, among other finishes. Manufacturers are also creating perimeter top edges that are 10" wide, providing enough surface area (and the perception of bulk) to meet demand from consumers who don't want or cannot accommodate a full deck around the pool

or spa. Responding to smaller backyard lots in today's new housing landscape, above-ground pool makers have re-engineered the structural system to eliminate buttresses (the supports projecting from the exterior walls, as backfilling does for an in-ground pool), saving six feet or so in the overall width and length of the pool. Similarly, the latest above-ground pools are 50" or more deep to more closely resemble in-ground pool depths. Automation and better equipment have also crept into the market, including provisions for automatic cleaners and chlorinators, not to mention more powerful pumps and filters. Aesthetically, fiber optic technology has enabled more options in underwater and decorative lighting above ground, while pool designers have applied their talents to adding fountains, rock formations, and other features to above-ground pools as well.

Inflatable & Temporary Pools

The last distinct category of pool construction is inflatable and temporary pools. These above-ground products are truly mobile, though often as big (if not as deep) as any other type of pool, and requiring just a flat, clean surface and a garden hose. More sophisticated models feature attachable pumps and filters to circulate and help clean the water, as well as covers, cleaning accessories, and repair kits that make it easier to maintain them during heavy seasonal and multi-year use.

As their name implies, inflatable pools feature sidewalls filled with air to create a vessel for water. Some sport inflatable top collars that pull the sidewalls up to their full height as the pool fills with water. Similarly, temporary pools feature flexible sidewalls held up and in place by strategically spaced structural members and filled with water, and offer a consistent depth, usually about 4 feet.

Made with tough, thick vinyl (the thickest layer forming the bottom), inflatable and temporary pools can be up and ready to enjoy in minutes,

and tear down just as quickly. If they are to remain standing or filled for multiple uses or certainly a season, they can (and should) be sanitized and chemically balanced as a permanent pool or spa to maintain their integrity and value.

Primarily, however, inflatable and soft-sided pools are an inexpensive and easy way to enjoy the water, and can be stored and moved simply, making them ideal for renters and budget-conscious homeowners. A 12 ft. × 30 ft. inflatable pool with a 1,353-gallon capacity (about twice that of a good-sized spa or hot tub), retails for less than $200, including a pump and filter set. For that kind of investment, a portable pool pays for itself, and can be replaced, after just a few years while allowing you to (literally) get your feel wet as a pool owner. Such pools are also not considered "real" or taxable property, as a more permanent pool or spa would be assessed, thus saving you a bit on your property taxes and homeowner insurance premiums.

Inflatable and temporary pools are being made in ever-larger sizes, dramatically increasing their appeal for backyard use. A recirculating pump with a small filter is the only equipment that accompanies most inflatable pools.

Jetted home spas may be set into the ground or into a deck, but often they are trimmed with decorative wood skirting to conceal the plumbing and the unappealing outer surface of the vessel. They are formed from fiberglass-reinforced resins with an interior gel-coat. It is common with above-ground spas for the equipment set (or at least part of it) to be housed inside a small, ventilated step.

Spas

All of the three main pool construction methods can be applied to spas, though with slight differences to accommodate their often more distinct purposes, such as relaxation, hydrotherapy, and exercise. Hot tubs, meanwhile, refer specifically to the deep, wood-built, above-ground barrels popularized in the early 1970s.

Like pools, spas can be built into the ground or set above ground. Increasingly, in-ground spas are integrated in their design and construction with an adjacent pool, allowing users to soak and cool down, perhaps several times, without necessarily getting out of the water. Typically, such combinations are built using the concrete method described for pools; in such cases, the pool and spa also typically share the equipment set and recirculation and filtering process, though pool experts often advise separate systems to accommodate the different chemical and sanitation needs of pools and spas. Like the pool itself, a concrete spa can be designed, built, and finished to just about any shape, size, depth, and appearance, and integrate features including spill-overs into the pool or waterfalls of recirculated water cascading into the spa from a rock formation.

For obvious reasons of time and cost efficiency, it makes sense to build an integral spa into a new concrete pool project, assuming a spa is on your wish list at all; for existing or inherited concrete pools, adding or integrating an in-ground concrete spa is certainly possible, but requires significant remodeling, a process akin to an entirely new project. For inherited-pool owners, a portable spa is a cost-effective alternative to an in-ground spa addition.

An in-ground vinyl-lined or fiberglass pool and spa combination, meanwhile, is rare given that both the pool and the spa requires separate excavations (and thus would not be truly integrated, as a concrete combination can); more likely, a portable, self-contained spa is installed to complement an in-ground vinyl-lined or fiberglass pool, perhaps excavated, if not backfilled, to bring its deck flush to that of the adjacent pool's.

That said, a fiberglass spa shell, designed, manufactured, and roughed-in for the multiple hydrojets and integral seating of a portable spa, can be set in-ground like a pool, and finished and landscaped on grade to replicate a concrete project.

The vast majority of home spas, however, are portable, above-ground fiberglass units with

Swim spas offer the exercise benefit of a swimming pool, but with a footprint that's closer to a spa in size.

self-contained equipment sets, or skids, concealed by the spa's a perimeter skirt. These units, ranging in capacity from about 100 to more than a thousand gallons, are available in a wide variety of molds to suit general and particular needs or tastes, from simple relaxation in hot, gently bubbling water to true clinical hydrotherapy or rigorous exercise.

Typically weighing no more than 500 pounds when empty and requiring a 120- or 240-volt, 20-amp dedicated circuit from your home's electrical service panel (or perhaps from a separate subpanel, depending on the main panel's capacity), portable spas are easy to install and remove. The average portable spa accommodates six adults, and the newer models can be equipped with CD/DVD players and television monitors to enhance the experience.

As such, portable spas serve as perfectly adequate complements to existing in-ground pools and often provide more functionality than an in-ground spa. The self-contained equipment set is easily accessible for maintenance and repair, and the acrylic interior surface is less cumbersome to clean than traditional plaster or a vinyl liner. Both portable spas and hot tubs can be set flush to or on top of a deck (with proper structural support) and placed in a gazebo, on a covered porch, or even inside. A portable spa's fiberglass mold and perimeter skirt often provides a wide enough deck to sit on and get in and out of the water safely.

Swim Spas

As residential building lots continue to shrink and the home exercise craze increasingly offers new and innovative methods and products to get or remain fit, swim spas have become a distinct category of the pool and spa industry.

Hiring a Pool Builder

Hiring a professional pool or spa builder (or remodeling contractor) is similar to that for any construction project. All in-ground and most above-ground projects (except truly portable units) require or should include a soils test and property survey, design services and working drawing submitted for building permits, excavation, construction, mechanical rough-in and finishes, and other basic carpentry skills. A professional pool builder, like a general contractor, can typically serve as the ringmaster of these various components, shepherding you through the process toward a finished project. To find and select a pool builder for your project, consider the following:

■ Ask friends, neighbors, and pool service technicians for recommendations of local pool design-build companies; also, search online directories for pool builders in your area and check out their web sites, if available, to narrow your list of candidates.

■ Determine a budget for the project based on what you can afford to spend and how you'll finance the project (e.g., though your normal income, savings, or a loan), and be prepared to share that information with your contractor candidates.

■ Contact the pool builders remaining on your list and ask them for a presentation in your home, making it clear that you are not prepared to sign a contract yet; prepare for the interview process with questions and request references.

■ Consult the references for those candidates that impressed you during the presentation/interview regarding the candidate's professionalism and the owners' satisfaction with his/her work.

■ Select one contractor from those remaining on your list and negotiate a contract for his/her services based on your stated budget for the project (as opposed to soliciting "competitive" bids from three contractors, which reduces their value simply to numbers rather than professionalism, customer service, and personality match).

Swim spas feature jet systems designed to deliver a constant, if adjustable, current from one end, providing enough resistance to "hold" a swimmer in place as he swims against the current. Initially, suppliers provided accessory swim jet packs that attached to one end of a small in-ground pool or large or elongated spa to deliver the proper resistance; more recently, portable spa manufacturers have come out with their own swim spa models that measure about 15 ft. long, 8 ft. wide (to the outside edges), and 4 ft. deep, with integral swim jets. That's certainly more space efficient than a non-jetted lap pool, which for a true lap-swimming experience requires dimensions of at least 75 meters long, 10 ft. wide, and a depth that enables flip-turns at each end.

As larger vessels, portable swim spas offer water capacity that's perhaps four times a standard portable spa, and are quite a bit heavier— perhaps a ton or more without water (or "dry weight") and more than 10 times that when full; as such, they require more thoughtful planning regarding their placement and structural support on a wood-framed deck or concrete slab.

Though focused on providing a cardiovascular workout or resistance training benefit for competition and recreational swimmers alike, the latest portable swim spas also incorporate more traditional relaxation and hydrotherapy features, among other amenities, in their molds.

The foot of the spa, for instance, might include one or more contoured seats and strategically placed jets for a hydro-therapeutic massage after a workout in the swim end of the spa (which can also be used for other water-aerobic activities, like jogging), or other seating and jets throughout the mold to provide a more relaxing soak. Some provide accessories and attachments that enable other resistance training, like rowing, from within the spa.

Portable swim spas are shipped with self-contained equipment, requiring only an electrical connection. For exercise purposes, the spa water can be kept cooler (about 78 degrees F.), then heated for less-strenuous activities. As with most modern spas, the jet system is completely adjustable in terms of strength and numbers to suit your tastes and needs.

Otherwise, swim spas require the same care and maintenance as a standard portable or in-ground spa; if used regularly for exercise, they might require more attention to their chemical balance and water quality, or perhaps more draining and refilling to keep the level of total dissolved solids (TDS) in check.

A custom spa that's integrated with the pool offers the ultimate in luxury and convenience. And with the right combination of styles, shapes and colors, it can be visually stunning as well.

Jet Lesson

Spas (and some hot tubs), especially portable units, are available with a variety of hydrojet designs and placements depending on your budget and needs. Most portable spas allow you to control the number of jets that operate at a given time, as well as the strength of their streams, to enable a relaxing soak or a true hydrotherapy experience or perhaps a powerful current (called a swim jet) for resistance exercise. Hydrotherapy, however, is more than just a powerful jet; effectively managing aches and pains requires the placement of multiple, high-pressure jets, in various sizes, in a contoured seat. That kind of power and volume requires a more powerful pump, which often adds a slight price premium to the spa, as well as a few more dollars on your monthly energy bill.

Costs to Consider

In addition to the up-front costs of a new or remodeled pool or spa, including engineering, design, and construction, owners must also consider the on-going costs of operating and maintaining that investment. As you contemplate a pool or spa project, check with various agencies and your own means to calculate on-going costs, including:

■ Property taxes: Most pools and some spas are considered real property, adding to the overall value of your home, and thus a reassessment of your tax burden.

■ Insurance: Pools and spas carry some risk for user safety, as well as replacement costs in a fire or flood. Consult with your mortgage and/or home insurance company to define coverages and calculate any increase in premiums.

■ Utilities: Pools and spas require water and the energy to heat them and operate their recirculation and filtration systems. Expect a bump in your utility bills, regardless of which energy source you choose for the project.

■ Maintenance: Whether you do it yourself or hire a service, the various chemicals, testing equipment, cleaning tools, and other gear and toys for a pool and spa are not only an up-front investment, but are usually on-going costs that need to be accommodated in your monthly household budget.

■ Safety: Proper pool and spa safety requires a comprehensive approach, including education, signage, a cover, and lifesaving equipment, among other gear.

Hot Tubs

Since their heyday in the 1970s, the deep, cylindrical wooden hot tub remains a cult favorite, a rustic alternative to the sleek, contoured, multi-jetted fiberglass spa. Built using the barrel-making craft of coopering, hot tubs remain the vessel of choice for relaxing soaks. Though they can be fitted or built with hydro-jets for a spa-like experience, purists need only an integral perimeter bench and a heater that can maintain 104 degree F water temperature.

Hot tubs employ sturdy softwood timber species that are naturally resistant to moisture decay and chemical damage; clear heart, vertical grain, kiln-dried redwood, cypress, cedar, and teak are common hot tub-building materials, used for every component of the tub's construction to ensure a reliable and consistent reaction to the water. Even so, even those woods eventually break down under constant moisture exposure (and certainly water-quality chemicals); given proper care, the expected life span of a new hot tub is about 15 years.

As wooden vessels, hot tubs require a slightly different measure of care and maintenance compared to modern spas. Simply, the wood staves (or vertical side slats) are designed and built to swell in the water, aligning and self-sealing against the metal hoops that contain them; if emptied and left dry longer than two days, the wood will shrink, perhaps never properly or entirely swelling again—and thus leaking—once the tub is refilled.

Preparing (or opening) a new hot tub also takes a bit more time and care than a modern fiberglass or concrete spa, as the wood naturally leaches tannins into the water and leaks or seeps as it swells to water-tightness. A hot tub may need to be filled, emptied, and refilled a half-dozen times, and scrubbed with a stiff brush and cleaned each time, before all of the tannins and their remnants are removed and the water can be chemically treated and sanitized.

As an organic, porous material, wood also accumulates bacteria and algae faster than other spa materials, meaning the tub may need to be emptied and refilled more often to get the water back in proper balance, especially under heavy bather loads. That's an important consideration in terms of water and chemical use and cost, as well as your available time to stay on top of regular maintenance chores.

Traditional wood-built hot tubs are exclusively above-ground vessels; at five feet or more deep, they are often accessed by a ladder or steps if set on top of a wood deck or patio; more conveniently, they are built into and flush with a deck (or at least partially surrounded by one), providing easier access and a place to cool off between soaks.

Though not self-contained like portable spa skid packs, modern hot tubs can be purchased and shipped with all of the recirculation, filtration, and heating components necessary to maintain the tub, if not contained within the tub's structure. Or, the equipment is can be purchased separately and installed near the tub's location.

Soft-sided Tubs and Spas

Blow-up, collapse-and-carry, and other soft-sided spas, with attached or integral jets and filtration systems, are a more affordable way to enjoy a relaxing spa experience.

Though smaller than most stay-in-place spas and hot tubs, these products can comfortably accommodate multiple adults, and typically require no extra structural support than what a new wood-framed deck or concrete patio slab provides.

The obvious benefit of such spas, like their pool counterparts, is their portability. Inflated by a motorized pump or raised up manually and self-supported, soft-sided tubs need only a flat stable surface, a GFCI-protected electrical outlet, and a garden hose to ready them for use.

They are easily and quickly emptied and refilled, but also can be treated with standard pool chemicals to maintain water quality and sanitation during sustained use. Manufacturers and retailers, however, will likely suggest (and sell) a particular mix of chemicals best suited for the vinyl structure and finishes of these spas. While some are equipped with heaters, others use an innovative system of recovering or capturing heat from the pump motor to boost the temperature of the spa water, which has several cost and operational benefits. Most manufacturers offer covers that help retain heat, keep debris out of the water, and maintain safety.

The pool and spa industry has always had its share of style and innovative design, but the bar is rising ever-faster and higher in recent years. Simply, consumers demand more variety and customization in their pools and spas to make them distinctive showpieces and comfortable retreats.

Soft-side and inflatable spas generally are intended for on-demand use and aren't designed to be set up on an ongoing basis. This makes them more economical in the long run, but also eliminates the possibility of an impulse soak whenever the motivation hits you.

Infinity edge pools depend on a bit of trickery, as the water that is apparently falling off the edge of the Earth from the main point of view is really washing down a short ledge into a catch basin to be recirculated.

Infinity Edges

One of the most popular, relatively new pool design techniques is the infinity edge. Always dramatic, and often set against a spectacular view, the infinity edge requires a bit more thought and planning to incorporate into a pool design and operation. But the "wow" factor of a disappearing edge pool cannot be understated.

Essentially, infinity or disappearing edge pools and spas feature a catch basin concealed behind an uncontained edge; the pool or spa is "flooded" to breach the edge, with the water falling into the basin and carried to the recirculation system. From the pool deck, however, the water's edge seems to curiously disappear into the horizon.

First designed and perfected in Europe, infinity-edge pools and spas are still in their infancy in the U.S., as designers and builders continually tweak both the aesthetics and the more complicated water circulation systems required to meet consumer demand and deliver reliable performance. By one estimate, only about one percent of all new pools or spas incorporate a disappearing edge design, in part a function of its cost premium, as well as the relatively tricky design and installation hurdles.

The main issue with infinity edge pools and spas is properly calculating the amount of water needed to flood the edge without overloading the recirculation system. The pool's pump, meanwhile, needs to be sized to keep the edge underwater (or the illusion of it being non-existent). In addition, overflow edge (or

Indoor pools or pools in three-season structures have many wonderful advantages and few major drawbacks, not the least of them being the scarcity of homeowners with adequate space in their house for a pool. A spa, however, is a common indoor appointment.

weir line) needs to be perfectly level so that that water flows evenly over it for the intended affect.

In addition, the water volume from an integral spa and/or aquascape (such as a waterfall) must be calculated into the catch basin design and pump size, allowing those features to be emptied for maintenance without having to drain the entire pool.

Though predominantly designed into concrete pools and spas, infinity edges have been featured in vinyl-lined and fiberglass vessels, and many of the leading packaged pool suppliers now offer it. They also can be part of a pool or spa remodeling project, albeit an extensive and expensive one. As more homeowners demand the dramatic look of a disappearing edge, expect the technology—and the training to apply it—to follow.

Indoor Pools and Spas

Though far less common than pools and spas located and built outdoors, indoor facilities allow people in extreme-climate areas to enjoy the same amenities.

The design, construction, and finishes of an indoor pool or spa itself are no different than those located outdoors; simply, they are enclosed to effectively keep out the weather and allow year-round enjoyment.

What is different, of course, is the design and function of the enclosure. Essentially, it must be designed and built to accommodate the humidity and potential condensation generated by the water and the indoor environment to maintain healthy air.

Managing the humidity (the amount of moisture in the air) also concerns the effect that moisture has on the structure and components of the enclosure; if not controlled adequately, high humidity can result in condensation (which occurs when the air is cooled to a point that it cannot contain moisture), which in turn can cause warping, rot, mold, rust, other latent defects to the structural components and finishes in the room, leading to myriad health and maintenance problems.

In the past, the conventional wisdom for controlling humidity in a pool enclosure was to simply vent the hot, moist air out of the structure, often using exhaust fans, and passively replace it with fresh, dry air from the outdoors. In cold-climate areas, that theory usually works because the outdoor air is typically drier and cooler than the moist air it is replacing, thus keeping the humidity level in check.

Even so, a relatively uncontrolled or passive system to maintain healthy humidity levels is inherently unreliable. And in warmer, more humid climates in which the owners might want a pool enclosure to ward off pests or create a milder environment for swimming or soaking during extreme heat, the out-door air might be more humid than the air in the pool room, thus adding to the problem.

More recently, mechanical engineers and pool builders involved with indoor pool or spa projects have switched to systems that provide a higher level of humidity and overall environmental control. Instead of venting and replacing the indoor air, a mechanical dehumidifier manages the task of removing moisture from the indoor air before reintroducing it into the room, similar to the pool's or spa's water recirculation and filtration system.

Such systems not only maintain proper levels of relative humidity (RH, which is best kept at 50 to 60 percent), but also significantly reduce the energy required to achieve that balance of air and moisture—in part because the flow of fresh air is not left to chance, but also because the system's operation can be leveraged to provide room heating, water heating, and air conditioning for the pool enclosure.

The pool deck should marry well with the other elements of the yard and the pool structure itself. The pavers and cast coping stones seen here blend beautifully with the tiles in the pool vessel.

It is critical, especially with a comprehensive mechanical system, to design, build, and operate the pool enclosure or room as a separate structure and environment in terms of temperature, humidity, ventilation, and other conditions, as well as with building materials and finishes that offer superior moisture resistance. Simply, the room needs to rely on products and systems dedicated to its use rather than sharing those installed for the rest of the house.

In addition, even though an indoor pool is "covered" from the outdoor elements, a pool or spa cover is still a smart investment. Used after each use of the pool or spa, a cover reduces evaporation and heat loss, which in turn lessens the burden on the dehumidification/air conditioning system and lowers the cost to operate it. A security-rated cover makes sure the pool or spa is safe when not in use or closed for the night.

The Pool Deck

The pool or spa deck has quickly evolved from a standard wood-framed structure and straight surface slats to intricate and impressive rock formations, integral climbing structures, slides, and fire pits. They also increasingly incorporate covered lounge areas with televisions and fireplaces, complete outdoor kitchens, wet bars, and dining areas, and full-service pool houses and equipment storage sheds.

The pool or spa deck (or just "deck") refers more to its design and function than any particular building material. While a "deck" in another construction context might more precisely define a wood-framed and finished structure protruding from the house, a pool or spa deck is any flat surface that serves as the approach and extended edges of the pool.

Traditionally, the deck surrounds the entire pool or spa, providing a safe and convenient surface to exit

Some pool decks are best appreciated from above, which is a perfectly legitimate design strategy if your pool or spa area is open and visible from higher vantage points in your house.

Natural flagstone decking can be worked into landscaping materials to frame a stunning view, as was done with the infinity edge pool seen here. Flagstone pool decks work better if they are mortared into place on a concrete subbase, not dry-laid into a sand base.

and enter the water and clean the pool or spa. Designed and built at least equal to the size of the pool, the deck also acts as a buffer between the water and any landscaped areas, helping keep dirt and debris out of the pool or spa.

More recently, especially with the growing popularity of "natural" pool designs, water features, and infinity edges, the deck might encompass only a fraction of the pool or spa's perimeter. The result is certainly more dramatic-looking pools and spas, but one that also is more difficult to access for cleaning chores.

In either case, the pool deck usually incorporates coping, or a perimeter edge material, that is slightly cantilevered over the water or set flush to the sides of the pool or spa. In addition to providing a safe handhold and non-skid surface for swimmers and soakers, the coping is usually sloped slightly away from the edge to help keep dirt and debris out of the water.

Conventional coping materials include precast concrete pavers molded and finished into a variety of shapes, sizes, styles, and colorfast colors to complement the overall décor of the pool or spa and surrounding architectural features. Solid stone materials are also used for coping, but must be honed down on the water side to provide a safe, smooth edge.

The coping is supported by (and conceals) the bond beam of a concrete pool and the structure of a vinyl-lined pool (the latter requiring concrete footings to support to coping or deck). In both cases, coping prevents water from getting behind and causing pressure on back side of the pool or spa shell. To mitigate that possibility even more, the back edge of the coping may also feature a flush-mounted drain between

The Pool House

When you have enough land to accommodate one, a pool house can offer a variety of practical benefits. A basic one can serve as a secure and covered storage shed for cleaning tools, chemicals and accessories. It can shelter the equipment set for a spa. More elaborate pool houses can include a changing room, a restroom, a shower, and even laundry facilities to keep dripping swimmers and soakers out of the house. But why stop there? A top-of-the-line pool house might include a mini- or full kitchen and/or wet bar setup.

Like any house, however, one built for a pool requires maintenance and upkeep of its finishes and systems. Depending on what it includes, the pool house may require the same kind of care as your main house, albeit on a smaller scale. Figure those costs, in terms of direct expenses and time, as you consider a pool house as part of your pool or spa project.

A pool house should be designed, built, and finished with maintenance in mind, often employing tiles or concrete floors with integral drain systems, and utilitarian or commercial-grade plumbing fixtures and passive ventilation, rather than an intricate mechanical system.

it and the rest of the deck to catch and shed water that is splashed out of the pool or spa during use. For in-ground fiberglass shells, a wide edge simulating a coping material is built into the mold.

As traditional pool and spa designs begin to wane, however, so does the use (or at least the look) of the coping and overall deck. Some deck materials are simply carried right to the edge, eliminating a separate coping material, while infinity edges, decorative rock formations, and other landscaping also replace customary deck designs and materials.

Coping or not, the deck can be made of any number of materials, from wood to poured concrete and stonework—the choice and design of which, like the pool or spa itself, depends on several factors, not the least of which is durability and maintenance. Solid-wood deck planks, for instance, must be treated at least once a year with a waterproof coating or sealant, while a flagstone deck needs to rest as flat and even as possible to minimize sharp edges.

Poured concrete, brick, or pavestone decks are arguably the easiest to maintain. Meanwhile, increasingly popular engineered or wood-resin composite wood decking materials eliminate the need for a

water sealant and promise years of reliable performance in even the wettest conditions, making them a viable alternative.

In addition to its functional purposes, the deck can be expanded or enhanced with covered areas for shade and relaxation, outdoor eating and cooking centers, planters, light fixtures, and perhaps an outdoor shower stall, fountain or water-spray garden, or a fire pit.

Landscaping

Landscaping that runs right up to the edge of the pool, or in some cases actually intrudes into the water, is becoming a popular design option. In addition to helping achieve styles that replicate natural settings, such as a woodland pond or desert oasis, trees and flowers set in planters built within the pool's shell are blurring the edges even further.

The problem with putting plants so close to the water, of course, is that it invites a greater measure of dirt and debris into the pool or spa, taxing your cleaning and maintenance chores, as well as the pool or spa's filtration system, even more than usual. Plants also require care, from watering to fertilization and

A touch of frivolity in the form of shooting streams of water transforms this swimming pool from the slightly cold and austere to fun and inviting.

pruning, which also can adversely impact pool or spa water quality and chemical balance.

For those pool owners wealthy enough to afford a pool cleaning and/or a landscaping or yard-care services, the result might be a relatively small price to pay from beauty and drama. But if neglected, the pool or spa system's performance and the cost to keep both the plants healthy and the water clean and balanced can be jeopardized, leading to costly repairs and replacement.

Water Features

Water features are quickly becoming popular upgrades in pool and spa design. Running the gamut from formal to informal waterfalls and fountains, sprays and mists, spill-overs and streams, and other "aquascapes," water features provide opportunities to create truly unique and personalized pools and spas.

The key to these features is to plan for them in the design phase of your pool or spa; they also can be accommodated in a remodeling project, though at a much greater cost. In the case of a new in-ground pool or spa, the pipes, wires, and other components for a water feature's operation and control are "roughed in" during construction and then finished

and connected to the pump, filter, and other equipment as the project nears completion. Adding these features to an existing pool or spa, especially if the goal is to share the equipment set, may require re-excavation and significant retrofitting of the pool or spa shell and/or liner, pool deck, coping, and/or other components, not to mention a necessary upgrade to the equipment.

That said, the cost of a remodel can be reduced when the pipes and water recirculation and filtration systems serving an aquascape are kept separate from the pool's. Even for a new pool or spa project, this arrangement might be the preferred option, akin to the benefits of a dedicated spa operation, as mentioned earlier in this chapter.

In the case of a shared recirculation and filtration system, it's important to precisely calculate the water volume and preferred operation of the water feature (such as the rate at which the water flows down a rockscape into the pool) and add it to the volume and recirculation needs of the main pool or spa to determine the proper sizing of the shared equipment. Those same calculations, minus that of the pool or spa's needs, will determine the size of the system equipment for a stand-alone or independently operated water feature.

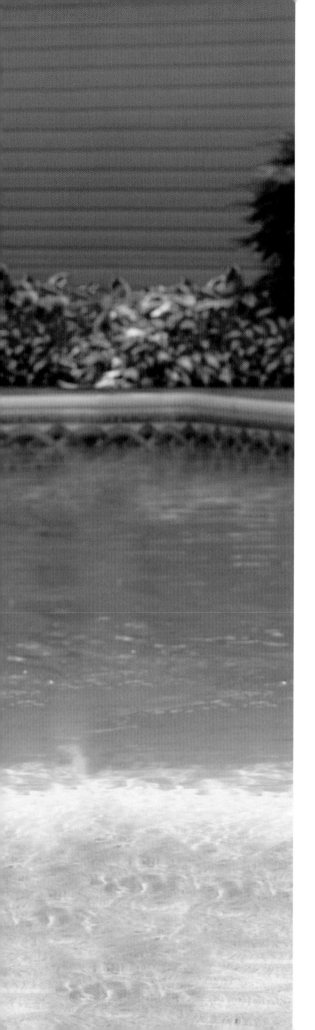

Cleaning and Maintenance

Cleaning and maintaining a pool or spa can be a lot work, but it doesn't have to be. You may spend an hour or more a day in the height of the swimming or soaking season making sure the water and filtration system are free of debris and working, or it may take just an hour or two a week. This is even more important after a pool party or a storm, and certainly if you own both a pool and a spa.

If you choose to tackle the cleaning and regular maintenance of your pool or spa, you'll no doubt come to appreciate the effort it takes, as well as gain invaluable insight into the inner workings of your investments. As with any task done on a regular basis, you'll soon develop proficiency and a personal routine to cleaning and maintaining your pool or spa that helps make the job go faster and better, while becoming an expert in everything from sweep-head cleaners to skimmer baskets and O-rings. You'll acquire a working knowledge and respect for pools and spas, enabling you to intelligently "talk the talk" with a retailer, technician, or contractor when seeking advice, services, or products.

That said, there's no shame in hiring out the job to a professional pool or spa cleaning service. Time is valuable, and there's little doubt that modern life is increasingly hectic. That's one reason people build and buy pools and spas: to get a break from the bustle of their lives and relax in a comfortable and carefree environment.

Contracting for cleaning and regular maintenance does not relieve you of the responsibility of becoming an educated pool or spa owner; playing ignorant is a risky game that often leads to miscommunication and costly mistakes and repairs.

This chapter gives you a roadmap to the cleaning and regular maintenance of a pool or spa so you can at least be well-informed, if not personally experienced, in these tasks. You'll get a crash course about the various tools and equipment—both manual and automatic—used to keep a pool or spa clean, as well as why, when, and how to use them.

This chapter includes detailed schedules for daily, weekly, monthly, and annual cleaning and maintenance chores, from scooping out leaves and debris to checking the pressure on your filter pump, vacuuming, and shocking, plus a

Fair Warning: Cleaning Pools Isn't for the Squeamish

A swimming pool skimmer is an effective gatherer of floating debris, but it does its job indiscriminately. That means that from time to time you'll find a surprise or two floating in the skimmer basket, or somewhere else in and around your pool. Drowned rodents, toads, frogs, birds, bats, insects and other small creatures are a fact of life for swimming pool owners. So if you are of a squeamish nature when it comes to nature, think about outsourcing the pool cleaning responsibilities.

few trade secrets make these and other jobs easier to remember and manage.

For pool and spa owners who are sensitive to the rising costs of energy (who isn't?), you'll also find helpful tips for reducing your electrical and water usage; in turn, maintaining an energy-efficient pool or spa lessens the volume and cost of chemicals to keep the water clean and balanced—which also saves the time it takes to conduct those chores.

Plenty of owners contract with professional service providers to clean and maintain their pool or spa, just as a fair number prefer to do those jobs themselves. Whichever path you take, become an educated owner so that you can make intelligent decisions and take ultimate responsibility for protecting and maintaining the value of your backyard retreat.

Like any job, cleaning and maintaining a pool or spa requires special tools. Gathering the proper equipment and using each component appropriately will enable you to stay ahead of larger cleaning chores, limit unintentional damage to surfaces, and keep your pool or spa equipment working at a high level—all of which reduces water quality chores and saves energy and water.

The construction of your pool or spa somewhat dictates the types of tools and equipment best suited for its care. A stiff brush for a plaster-finished concrete pool, for instance, may be too abrasive for a vinyl-lined or acrylic-fiberglass vessel; a long-poled broom or vacuum system might be unnecessary for a small spa.

That said, there are some basic tools and equipment that almost every owner needs to clean and maintain a pool or spa, including:

Telescoping pole. If you own a pool or deep spa, an adjustable-length, 16- to 20-ft. aluminum pole with a head that allows a variety of attachments is a must for a variety of cleaning chores. The adjustable length and universal head enables you to reach the length of the sidewalls and along the bottom of the pool or spa, as well as adjust for comfort and effectiveness and perform myriad tasks, including attaching a shepherd's hook for safety when people are in the pool. (Hint: You also can use the same pole for household cleaning chores, such as attaching a duster head for clearing out cobwebs along high ceilings).

Use a leaf skimmer attachment on a telescoping pole to net floating debris from the water before it gets into the filtration system.

Algae brush. For cementitious finishes, including plaster and pebble aggregate, as well as ceramic tile, the stainless steel bristles of an algae brush (or brush head, for attachment to a telescoping pole) provide enough friction to scrub away stubborn surface stains caused by algae growth.

Vacuum. Special vacuums for pools and spas connect to the intake or recirculation outlets in the pool, the skimmer, or an independent generator to suction and collect dirt and debris that has fallen and settled below the water surface. Other models use water pressure, perhaps simply from a garden hose, to push dirt and debris toward skimmers and the main drain. It's important to buy a vacuum head or apparatus for the type of pool or spa finishes you have so as not to damage the surfaces as you clean.

A wall and floor brush (left) and a vacuum head (right), are two of the most important pieces of swimming pool maintenance equipment.

Wall and floor brush. A wide, stiff, nylon-bristled brush or brush head is all you need to clean a vinyl-lined or acrylic-fiberglass pool or spa; it also serves adequately for routine cleaning of plaster, tile, or aggregate finishes. Get one with rounded ends to accommodate curved areas and corners, and/or with a spoiler to keep the bristle housing from rubbing or tearing the surface of the liner. A hand-held version works great for spas and hot tubs, while a combination squeegee-brush allows you to gently scrub and remove excess debris from surfaces with two sides of the same tool or head attachment.

Leaf skimmer. This nylon mesh basket or net attaches to a telescoping pole so that you can manually skim and collect leaves and other debris from the surface of the water.

Tile brush. This stiff-bristled, hand-held tool helps remove stubborn deposits, scaling, and stains from ceramic tile at the waterline.

Bucket. A non-metal, 3- to 5-gallon bucket is handy for diluting dry chemicals in water, manually bailing out spas and hot tubs, and containing non-abrasive cleanser mixtures for spot surface cleaning. Remember to thoroughly rinse out the bucket after each use, and consider multiple buckets for different chores.

Sponge. A large, soft sponge is essential for non-abrasive spot surface cleaning and also helps soak up excess water when manually draining a spa for cleaning. Consider one with a nylon scrubbing pad on one side for ceramic tile surfaces.

Lubricant. Available at pool and spa retailers, a liquid lubricant can be applied to gaskets within the filter and pump housings to keep them supple and effective against air and water leaks.

Pump lid wrench. Specially designed to gently but safely and effectively remove the lid of the pump for cleaning and maintenance, as opposed to using a standard wrench or other tool that might damage the housing.

Squirt bottle. Fitted with an adjustable spray nozzle, use this tool to precisely apply tile cleanser directly to the finished surface, or spray the soap down the center of the pool's water surface to create a chemical reaction that "pushes" surface dirt, debris, and oils to the sides, where it is more easily collected and cleaned out.

Replacement gaskets and O-rings. Keep a few new and packaged gaskets on hand of each type and size you need (for the pump, filter, and other gasketed components) so you can easily replace them during your normal maintenance routine.

Among all of these tools, arguably the most effective one for keeping dirt and debris put of the water is a pool or spa cover. In addition to protecting the water surface from leaves and other organic matter, a cover reduces evaporation and heat loss and serves (if properly designed and rated) as an important measure of safety when the pool or spa is closed or not in use.

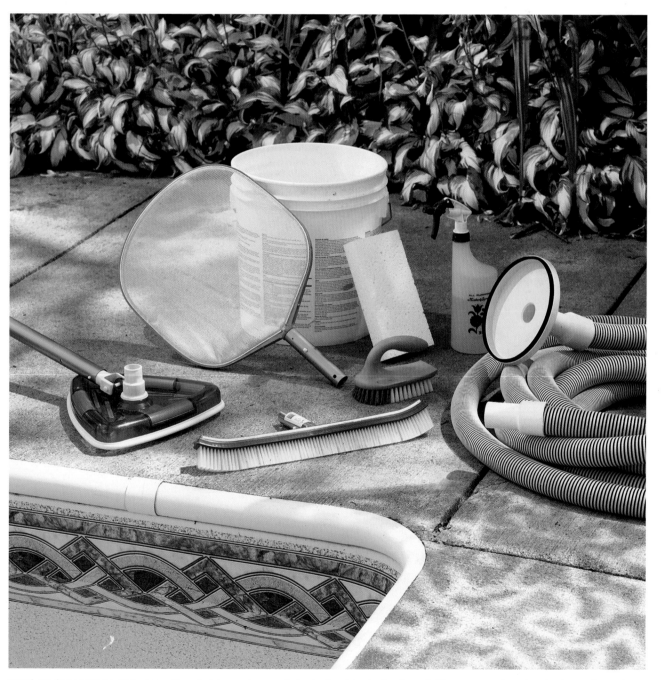

Pool maintenance requires the right equipment, including (clockwise from left): a vacuum head and telescoping pole; a leaf skimmer; a scrub bucket, sponge and stiff-bristle brush; a spray bottle; a vacuum hose that fits your skimmer port.

A variation of the skimmer vacuum, discussed later in this chapter, is the garden hose vacuum. Instead of hooking up to your skimmer and using the vacuum created by the pool pump motor, you simply hook a garden hose up to the cleaner head, turn on the water, and the water pressure blows through the scrubbing chamber, where it exits into a mesh collection bag, depositing loose debris in the bag.

Cleaning a pool or spa is essential if you expect to maintain healthy and balanced water quality, keep systems and equipment operating smoothly, and avoid a variety of serious structural and health problems down the road.

Under normal-use conditions, cleaning a pool or spa requires a regular, sometimes daily, routine. That schedule might be heightened for heavy-use instances, such as after a pool party or a storm, and is often lightened during the cooler off-season or times of light use. Regardless, you should plan on some measure of cleaning and maintenance every time someone uses the pool or spa.

Pools and spas require basically the same cleaning and maintenance regimen, but with some important differences, specifically how often they are drained for cleaning and slight variations of the tools and equipment required given their differences in size and surfaces. Cleaning a pool-spa combination made and finished with the same materials is almost identical; servicing an above-ground vinyl-lined pool and an adjacent portable spa is a more distinct prospect.

Cleaning a pool or spa can be done entirely by hand, or supplemented by various automatic or powered systems. Even when you employ automatic cleaners, there will always be some chore that needs to be done manually, such as scrubbing algae stains from the corners of the steps or cleaning out the skimmer's filter basket.

Helpful hints for cleaning a pool by hand using a variety of tools and equipment are covered in the maintenance schedule outlined later in this chapter. But before diving into that suggested routine, consider the benefits and circumstances that might inspire you to invest in automatic cleaning systems, and how they leverage your pool's or spa's normal recirculation and filtering schedule.

Automatic Cleaners. There are several automatic or powered pool cleaning tools and systems that are effective supplements to manual cleaning and maintenance chores.

While they certainly help make the job go faster—and often deliver superior results—an automated approach to pool and spa cleaning is more akin to cruise control than an autopilot, requiring a watchful eye and a good measure of manual work to keep the pool or

Tips for Cleaning and Maintenance

- Do the "little things" regularly and thoroughly.
- Budget enough time to do it properly.
- Know your pool's or spa's construction, finishes, and mechanical system.
- Develop a schedule or routine.
- Use the right tools and equipment.
- Consider energy-efficient products or upgrades.

spa truly healthy, safe, and operating efficiently. And don't forget, as mechanical products, these systems also require their own regular and periodic care and maintenance.

Automatic pool cleaners generally work one of two ways, either suctioning dirt and debris from the water surface and below (like a vacuum), or using pressurized air or water to agitate organic matter and push it toward the pool or spa's main drains, skimmer system, or other recirculation and filtering mechanism. Some cleaners do a bit of both.

Pools and spas fitted with automatic cleaners require a booster pump within the equipment set, a separate component from the standard pump that runs the recirculation and heating system. The booster pump attaches as the filtered water is going back out to the pool or spa, pressurizing it through flexible hoses attached to the outlets in the pool. The booster operates only during a cleaning cycle and/or when the recirculation system is operating, usually on a timed cycle; otherwise, it remains off, allowing the recycled water to enter the pool or spa normally.

The hoses, which remain attached to the outlets during normal- or heavy-use times, can be fitted with either a vacuum head or a sweep head. The vacuum attachment features a hose-like tail that not only propels the unit but also whips around under the power of the booster pump's pressurized water to stir up

Stubborn areas right around the water line are prone to staining and discoloration and should be hand-scrubbed with a stiff-bristle brush periodically.

How to Pressure-Wash a Pool

Swimming pools and outdoor spas collect dust, dirt, and debris that can clog the filtration system and compromise the quality of the water. Algae, the most common pool and spa contaminant, can carry bacteria and cause slipperiness in and around the water area. Adding pressure washing to your maintenance routine will help extend the life of your system equipment, providing you with added years of pool and spa enjoyment.

Pools and spas made from plaster, exposed aggregate, or concrete—typically troweled smooth and then painted or tiled—are ideal candidates for pressure washing. Vinyl-lined and fiberglass pools and spas should not be pressure washed, but instead should be cleaned with chemical treatments and non-abrasive cleaning methods.

Before you can clean your concrete pool or spa, the water must be drained. Check with your local EPA (Environmental Protection Agency) for proper wastewater treatment and disposal regulations. Vinyl-lined and fiberglass pools should not be drained after installation, as the weight of the refill water can cause the liner to buckle and separate from the frame. Always consult the manufacturer's specifications to determine if pressure washing is recommended. Never use an electric pressure washer around any pool area. Make sure there is adequate airflow to remove the carbon monoxide gas that emits from any gasoline engines.

Pressure washing is also ideal for maintaining the areas and structures around pools and spas, such as decking, cabanas, and patio furniture. When cleaning around a pool or spa, keep dirt and debris from being sprayed into the water. Do not pressure wash filter cartridges—the high-pressure spray will cause damage to the filter media surfaces.

Prestart Checklist:

Tools:

- ✓ Pressure Washer
- ✓ Multi-Purpose Cleaning Detergent Formulated for Pressure Washers
- ✓ Eye Protection
- ✓ Floor Brush
- ✓ Swimming Pool Algaecide
- ✓ Surface Cleaner
- ✓ Water Broom

Optional

Site Prep:

1. Drain water from swimming pool or spa.
2. Cover nearby electrical components.
3. Sweep away any loose debris.

Cleaning Performance:

Recommended Spray Pattern:

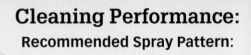

40° SPRAY PATTERN OR WHITE SPRAY TIP

Recommended Distance:

PSI Rating:	Nozzle Distance:
2000 or less	18 in. to 24 in.
2000 to 3000	24 in. to 36 in.
3000 or more	30 in. to 48 in.

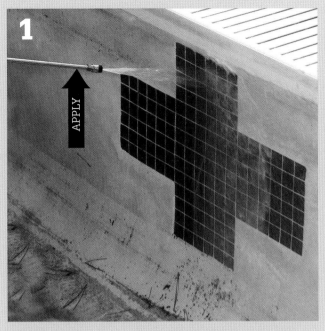

1 APPLY

After the water in a concrete pool has been properly drained, sweep up and dispose of any leaves and debris. Start pressure washing at pool walls, working in manageable sections. Always apply cleaning detergents starting at the bottom of the wall section and work upward.

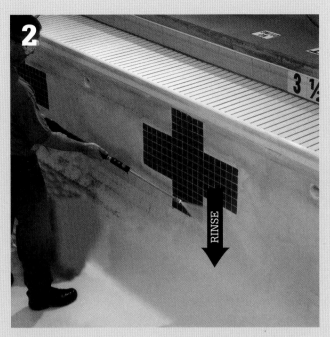

2 RINSE

As you rinse—working from top to bottom—direct the dirt and detergent residue away from the work area. When pressure washing the pool floor, start at the edges and work toward the drain, flushing dirt and residue away from you. For heavy buildup or stains, consider using a turbo nozzle.

3

If algae is a problem, it must be properly treated to prevent re-growth. The two most common types of algae, black and yellow (or mustard), both can be removed with a high-pressure rinse followed by a treatment of swimming pool algaecide or a mixture of 1 part bleach to 4 parts water applied by hand using a utility brush.

4

Allow the algaecide to soak for 10 minutes, then thoroughly rinse the area in high-pressure mode using plenty of clear water. Other stubborn stains—typically caused by leaves, metal objects, and mineral deposits—can be treated with a multi-purpose detergent.

Sweep pool decks frequently, taking care to brush debris away from the pool. Collect and dispose of the debris immediately to help maintain a clean pool area.

dirt and debris from the walls and floor, which the vacuum head collects into a catch bag; whatever the vacuum misses goes into the pool's recirculation and filtering system.

A sweep-head attachment, meanwhile, floats on the surface, with multiple smaller hoses trailing underwater that, also under the pressurized water from the booster pump, stir up debris on the pool's underwater surfaces so it can be taken up into the

skimmer and main drain. The pressurized water also propels the surface unit around the pool or spa to make sure the entire vessel is covered and cleaned.

A third, more sophisticated system is an in-floor automatic cleaner. Designed and built into concrete pools, the system employs multiple heads that pop up during the pool's timed recirculation process, spraying pressurized water across the floor and up the walls to agitate and loosen debris and dirt and drive it toward the main drain.

A Cleaning and Maintenance Schedule

The proper cleaning and routine maintenance of a pool or spa requires daily, weekly, monthly, as-needed, and annual tasks. Staying on top of the daily and weekly chores, and being mindful of ad-hoc needs, makes the larger, less-frequent jobs easier.

Use the following helpful cleaning and maintenance tips as a guide for managing your pool or spa care. If you need a template or starting point for developing your own routine (or a checklist for hiring a professional pool or spa cleaning service) see the maintenance schedules printed on pages 69 to 71. These schedules reflect the cleaning and maintenance chores you are most likely to encounter during normal, in-season pool and spa use.

Conserving Energy, Water, and Other Resources

It's no secret that natural resources, including water and those used to create or generate energy, are becoming less available and more expensive. The cost to heat, filter, and keep a pool or spa at a proper water level and quality is rising as fuel and water costs increase.

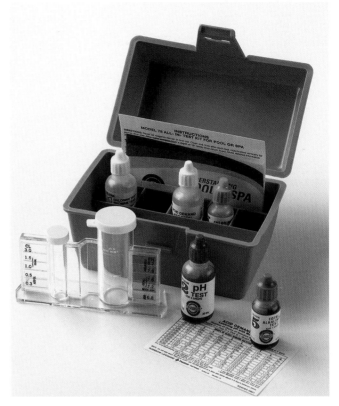

Water testing kits let you monitor how well your pool and spa filtering and sanitizing systems are working, which is an important part of the upkeep process.

After a Storm

Severe weather, especially rainstorms with high winds, can wreak havoc on your pool cleaning and regular maintenance routine. If you can't cover the water and protect it from the storm, chances are good you'll have a sizeable job on your hands once the skies clear, removing a large amount of debris, dirt, and other material from the water and running the filtration and automatic cleaners (if you have them) for a longer period of time to truly cleanse the pool or spa. If, however, you are able to place the cover before the storm hits, simply treat the post-tempest situation as you would after a normal use of the pool or spa; that is, thoroughly checking the condition of the water and equipment set and operation, and conducting any necessary or obvious cleaning or maintenance chores.

The Skimmer's Role

The weir is the one-way check valve that allows water into the skimmer. The minimum water level for the pool is known as the weir line. If the water level drops below the weir line, water cannot get into the recirculation system.

Though not an absolutely necessary component on every pool (and certainly not every spa), skimmers are often built in to a pool's construction and play a critical role in keeping it clean. Commonly set in multiple locations along the top of the walls of an in-ground pool, with a flapped opening (or weir) at the waterline, skimmers attract and contain a variety of debris from the water, trapping larger matter in a mesh filter basket while allowing smaller materials into the pool's recirculation and filtering system. (If they feature skimmers at all, above-ground pools use floating weirs or lily pad units that are positioned on the surface.) Because of their suction action, skimmers can be used to power manual and automatic pool vacuums. Simply, the vacuum hose attaches or is fitted to the skimmer opening; the skimmer can either serve as the collection basin for debris or supplement a separate canister attached to the vacuum (the latter of which is generally easier to clean out).

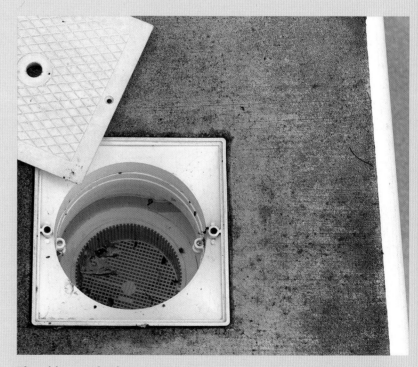

The skimmer body has a large opening that holds a basket for collecting debris as it's drawn into the water recirculation system for filtration and sanitizing. The skimmer cover usually has a finger hole so it can be removed easily. If small children will be using the pool, it's a good idea to screw the skimmer cover to the flange.

Skimmer baskets come in a wide range of sizes and shapes. If you need a replacement basket and are unsure of the make and model, bring the old basket to your pool and spa supplies store.

Hose out skimmer baskets from time to time to keep them from becoming coated with slime or algae.

Spas have a collection basket that fits into the water intake openings directly above the filter. Although not technically a skimmer, the set-up fulfills the same function as a pool skimmer.

How to Hook up a Skimmer Vacuum

The skimmer vacuum is the primary cleaning device in most residential pools. It consists of a long hose that connects at one end to the inlet port on a skimmer. The other end of the hose is connected to a vacuum head or brush. When the skimmer is operating, the pump motor will draw water in through the hose, taking with it any debris or grime that's loosened by the vacuum head. The debris collects in the skimmer baskets, while smaller particle and impurities are removed when the water passes through the pool filter.

(Left) To hook up a skimmer vacuum, begin by shutting off the valves that connect up to all but one skimmer (choose a skimmer that's centrally located if possible). Shutting off the other skimmers concentrates suction in the open skimmer line.

Submerge the water hose until it fills with pool water. This will prevent the pump/motor from drawing the air that's in the hose into the filtration system (this can damage the pump motor). If you are having difficulty getting all the air out of the hose, hold it in front of a return jet to force water in.

Making a conscious effort to reduce water and energy use for your pool or spa not only helps keep those expenses in check, but also reduces the amount of time and chemicals (and their cost) needed to properly clean and maintain a healthy pool or spa. From practical, manual means to replacing certain components with more efficient equipment, you can effect a significant amount of change in the resources your pool or spa requires.

Consider the following tips and techniques for lowering the burden on water and energy resources and your pocketbook.

Keep filters clean. A typical backwashing cycle for a pool-sized filter can use 100 to 150 gallons of water (50 GPM for two or three minutes); to reduce the times backwashing is needed (and related cost), regularly clean the other components of the filtration system, such as skimmer baskets.

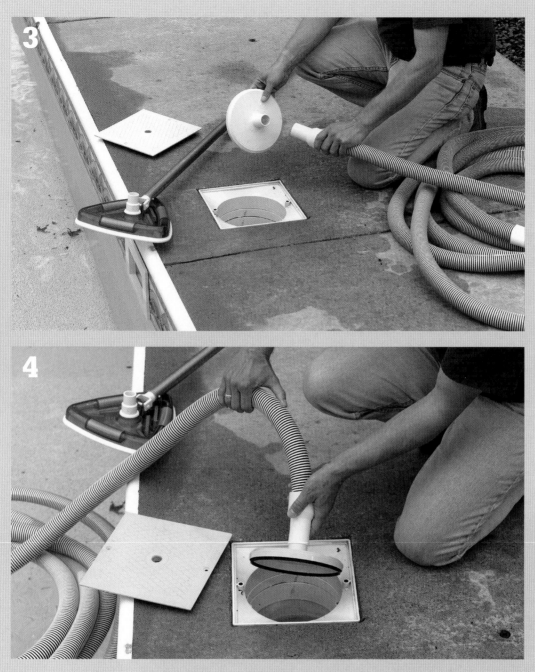

3

Connect one end of the water-filled hose to the hose attachment that covers the skimmer intake (these covers vary according to skimmer model, so if you're purchasing a set-up it helps to know the make and model of your skimmer.

4

Fit the skimmer cover attachment over the skimmer intake opening. There will be a brief period of gurgling as the systems restores the vacuum and suction flow. Once the vacuum is working you will feel water moving through the hose. Then simply attach the other end of the hose to a vacuum head on a telescoping pole and get to work.

Reduce the cycle time. Run the recirculation and filtration cycle as little as practically possible, perhaps just 6 hours a day depending on your pool's water volume, striking a balance between water and power use to run the pump and allowing the water to get out of balance, thus requiring more chemicals. If you employ an automatic cleaner, set it to run only 2 to 4 hours a day, during the recirculation cycle.

Control the cycle. Once you determine a balance between cycle time and water quality, use an automatic timer to set and control the recirculation and filtration cycle to maintain that schedule and lessen your own time commitment. Set it to run during off-peak hours, if possible, when utility rates are lower.

Lower the water temperature. If you heat your pool, keep the temperature at 78 degrees F (instead of the standard 82 degrees F) when it's in use, and

How to Vacuum Your Pool

Hook up your skimmer vacuum (see previous page) and begin scrubbing the pool walls. Do the wall first so any crud you scrub off that's not drawn into the filter system slide downward toward the floor. Once the walls are done, begin vacuuming at the shallow end of the pool. Move the vacuum head in slow, easy strokes to develop a rhythm. Avoid making sharp turns that can tug on the hose, possibly disconnecting it from the skimmer.

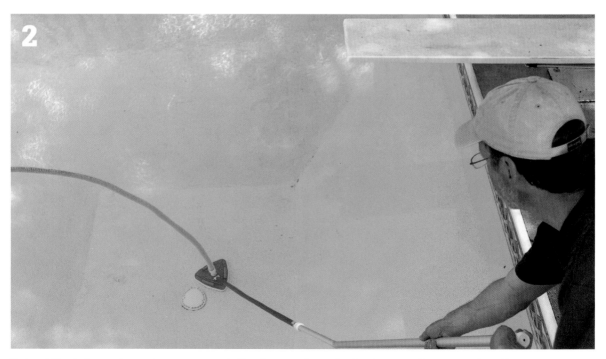

Extend the telescoping pole as you reach the deep end, continuing to move the vacuum head in an easy motion. Try to develop a pattern as you scrub, and avoid smashing too hard into the drain cover. After a while, you may find that vacuuming the pool is a very relaxing, almost meditative, job.

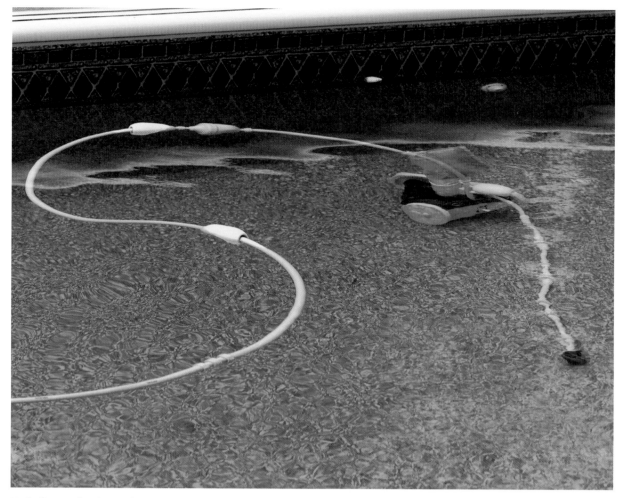

Variation: Robotic pool vacuums hook up to your pool skimmer and are driven automatically by the flow of the recirculating water. With a scrubbing brush mounted on their underside, these machines move in random patterns, relying on the law of averages to eventually clean the entire pool floor. They do not clean pool walls.

lower it to 70 degrees F when not in use, thereby reducing energy use by up to 40 percent and mitigating excessive evaporation. A cool pool is better in the summer, anyway (as the increased number of bathers will not only appreciate it, but warm up quickly from their in-pool activity), and is preferred for exercise.

For spas, either set a timer to automatically (and slowly) heat the pool to a desired temperature by a particular time of day or night, or manually adjust the heater an hour or so before you want to use it, keeping it in the high 80s or low 90s—or lower—during non-use times. Cooler water needs fewer chemicals to remain balanced and does not evaporate as quickly as heated water.

Replace or upgrade equipment. Newer pumps, filters, heaters, and automatic cleaners feature energy-efficient designs and technology. Look for tax breaks or incentives, as well as local utility rebates, for replacing outdated or less-efficient system components with more energy-efficient models to help offset the cost and/or price premium of newer equipment.

One such upgrade is a two-speed pump, which can be set at a higher speed or rate during times of heavy pool or spa use, and lowered during off-peak or non-use to run the recirculation, filtration, and other cleaning mechanisms at a slower, more efficient rate—which actually improves the effectiveness of those functions.

Similarly, replacing old sand or diatomaceous earth (DE) filtering systems with a modern filter cartridge eliminates the cost and time of backwashing.

Install a fence. Wind, even a cooling breeze across the surface of a pool or spa, can cause a startling amount of evaporation. A fence designed to block

Covers Are the Key to Keeping Clean

A cover placed over your pool or spa whenever it is not in use can reduce heating costs by up to 70 percent, as well as significantly stem the heat and water volume loss caused by evaporation. Whatever you sacrifice in passive heat gain (that is, what an uncovered pool or spa might collect from direct exposure to the sun) is easily balanced by the reduction in heating energy and replacement water costs of using a cover. A safety-rated cover also guards against accidental or uninvited use of the pool.

Spa covers are important as insulators and in preventing evaporation, but they also keep debris out of the water. This is perhaps even more important with spas because their smaller pipes and jets are susceptible to clogging.

A solar cover keeps debris out of the water, insulates the warmed water and even provides direct heat to the pool. Store the cover on a full-width roller near the shallow end for easy unrolling and uncovering.

Roll out the cover toward the deeper end of the pool. A helper greatly simplifies this task.

Cover the entire pool. This might mean piecing in over steps or other unusual shapes (yet another good reason to favor an ordinary rectangular pool if you're building a new one).

Emptying a Pool or Spa

A thorough method of cleaning is to empty a pool or spa completely, scrub and clean it thoroughly, refill it with potable water, and chemically balance it before using it again. Because of their much smaller water volume and higher bather load per gallon, spas and hot tubs often are emptied and refilled at least twice a year, and perhaps once a quarter, to flush out a variety of organic matter. Pools, meanwhile, are rarely drained—at least entirely—for cleaning or even small repairs, perhaps once every three years or much longer. In addition to the expense of refilling a 20,000-gallon vessel, you need a plan for where to drain that much water. Only in cases when a chemical imbalance cannot be rectified any other way, when a liner or surface material must be replaced or significantly repaired, or during a remodeling project that affects the structure, finishes, and mechanical system, should you drain a full-size pool; even closing (or winterizing) a pool or patching a small leak can be done with water in the pool, if perhaps with minimal drainage.

Pools and spas can be drained into your yard but only if the soil has good drainage (you don't want 15,000 gallons of water charging directly toward your basement). It is also important that you stop adding sanitizers and other chemicals to the water at least two weeks prior to draining the vessel into planted areas. You can use a small submersible pump (photo left) and a garden hose. For faster draining use a high capacity pump (next page).

and/or redirect the wind and installed at all open ends and sides or at least against the prevailing wind direction, will reduce evaporation and the cost to replenish the water volume to a healthy level, not to mention the chemicals needed to keep it in balance.

Reuse or recycle water. Whenever you know you're going to drain a spa or hot tub, allow it to sit, untended and open to the air, for a few days or apply other chemicals that neutralize the water. Then, direct the drainage to your lawn and garden for irrigation.

Fix cracks and leaks. Inspect all of the surfaces and components of your pool or spa, including the equipment set, for cracks and leaks. Small cracks are easily repaired without having to drain the pool or spa, at least not completely; if neglected, however, cracks can grow into leaks that not only lose water (and thus boost the cost to replace it), but also can involve severe structural or mechanical damage and significant repair and replacement costs.

Cleaning and maintaining a pool or spa requires a significant commitment in time and money, but it is a responsibility that most owners with even marginal skills and scant knowledge can quickly learn and gain

A high capacity pump such as the ½ HP, 7,000 gallon-per-hour (GPH) ejector pump with 2" hose above can empty a 6-person spa in 10 minutes. A smaller submersible pump, like the ⅛ HP, 1,300 GPH model on the previous page, will take close to two hours for the job. Be aware, though, that the smaller pump costs under $50, compared to $300 for the big model.

Clean swimming ladders and other metal accessories with metal polish at the start and conclusion of each swimming season.

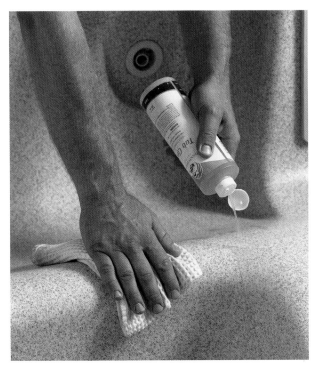

After draining the spa, scrub the surfaces with a soft bristle brush and mild detergent. Once the surface dries, apply a coat of acrylic surface treatment.

proficiency and expertise. Even if you decide to hire a pool cleaning and maintenance service, it's smart to know how, why, and when certain chores need to be conducted so that you can protect your investment and enjoy it for years.

Annual Maintenance

There are very few maintenance "chores" that need to be conducted annually. In fact, if you keep up with the daily, weekly, and monthly duties, the only real annual task is scheduling a professional check-up of your entire system, which, in turn, should reveal few (if any) surprises.

Even so, an independent evaluation of your water quality, various surface conditions (both above and below water), and recirculation, filtration, and automatic cleaning and cover system equipment and operation is an excellent way to assess and refine your skills as a pool or spa owner, learn about new chemicals and techniques, and consider upgrades or techniques that might save water, energy, or time.

A scrubbing glove might make you feel like an underwater Muppet, but these simple cleaning devices make scrubbing and scouring your spa or pool walls easy. You can buy them at most pool and spa retailers.

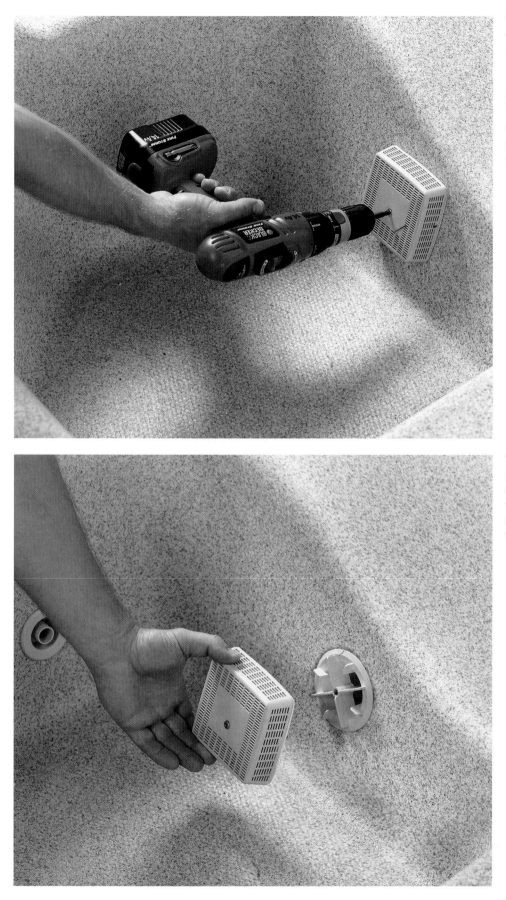

The intake port for the spa's water circulation system is usually at or near the bottom of the tub. A grate covers the intake port. When the tub is drained, remove the grate cover to clean it and to inspect the intake port.

The intake port shouldn't require extensive maintenance, but if you spot any blockages remove them with a bottle brush.

Cleaning Spa Covers

Rinse the cover once it is well cleaned and then treat it with cover cleaner and protectant. The protectant contains a UV inhibitor and is designed for spas that are located outdoors. It should be applied every two to three months.

Daily Maintenance

Every time someone uses the pool or spa, figure on at least a small amount of cleaning and maintenance. In the height of swimming or soaking season (sometimes at opposite ends of the calendar), the following chores are often required on a daily basis:

■ Remove leaves and debris from the surface of the water using a leaf skimmer (or shallow net) attached to a telescoping pole.

■ Check and clean out debris from the basket for each in-wall or lily pad skimmer, the latter just under the cover mounted flush to the deck behind each skimmer location.

■ Eyeball the water level of the pool or spa and refill to just above the weir line of the skimmer; during heavy or in-season use, expect more water loss from evaporation and splashing.

■ Test and adjust the water quality and chemical balance (if not daily, then at least every other day during regular use).

■ Run the recirculation and filtering system once every 24 hours to clean out dirt and debris and recycle the water.

Weekly Maintenance

■ Hose down or sweep the pool deck, aiming away from the water's edge to keep dirt and debris from getting into the pool or spa from the wind or on the feet of swimmers and soakers.

■ Gently scrub the sides and bottom of the pool or spa with a stiff-bristled brush attached to a telescoping pole, starting at the shallow end and moving from the tops of the walls with overlapping strokes and then along the bottom to direct the dirt toward the main drain in the deep end, and then into the filtration system.

■ Remove any lingering dirt or debris, once settled on surfaces, by vacuuming the pool using either a unit that attaches to the skimmer to suction dirt and debris into the filtration system, or one that attaches to a garden hose to force organic matter into a collection bag (hands-free robotic pool vacuums also are available).

■ Clean out the pump's strainer basket and check the condition of the pump's gasket or O-ring. Turn off power to the equipment set, lift the lid with a specially designed wrench (to avoid damage), and remove and rinse out the basket. Lubricate the gasket or, if it's already cracked or brittle, replace it with a new one.

■ Check the psi (pounds per square inch) reading of the filter's pressure gauge, a measure of how many gallons per minute are running through the filter during a recirculation cycle. If it reads 10 psi higher than normal (as determined when a new/clean filter is restarted), it's likely that the filter is clogged with dirt and needs to be replaced or cleaned. A psi reading that is lower than normal indicates a clog or blockage upstream from the filter, earlier in the recirculation system.

Monthly and Periodic Maintenance

■ Use a stiff, nylon-bristled tile brush and specially formulated tile soap (not household cleanser) to scrub ceramic tile at the waterline, removing scale, dirt, algae growth, and other build-up.

■ Shock or superchlorinate the pool water, using perhaps five times the normal amount of chlorine or sanitizer. Shocking the water kills off bacteria and algae, as well as ammonia and other chemicals and organic matter, that have accumulated as the "free" or available chlorine level has dropped. (For more details about clean water and superchlorination, see page 84).

■ Drain the spa completely (usually every 3-4 months) using a submersible pump or manually, with buckets, cups, and sponges. Refill the vessel to the level of the highest outlet or skimmer and run fresh water through the recirculation/filtration system to flush out any remaining dirt and debris from the pipes and outlets. Drain the water and use a non-abrasive cleanser (ideally the one recommended by the spa's manufacturer or builder) to thoroughly clean the inside surfaces. Rinse off any residue (to mitigate foaming) and clean or replace the filter. Refill the spa or hot tub (the latter within two days, ideally sooner, to avoid shrinkage) and test for and adjust for water quality before using the spa.

■ Use an appropriate cleanser and cleaning pad for all metal parts and accessories, including ladders, diving board frames, and handrails to mitigate corrosion.

■ Backwash the filter to flush out stubborn or excessive dirt and debris, which can accumulate in systems that direct surface dirt and debris into the pool or spa's recirculation and filtration system (as opposed to removing it independently). For more information about backwashing a filter, see pages 112 to 113.

Water Quality

There's no practical reason why you can't properly maintain the water quality of your pool or spa without hiring a professional service provider. Yes, it's a chore, but fundamentally it's not so different from other household tasks, like vacuuming or doing laundry: except, of course, that maintaining pool water requires a basic understanding of chemistry.

Even professional pool and spa service technicians would agree that, for the most part, homeowners are not only capable of maintaining the water quality of their backyard amenities on their own, but also are the best choice to do so. Simply, you live with your pool or spa every day, and therefore have the best access to it and ability to monitor and adjust, as necessary, the quality of the water.

At some point, perhaps on a regular schedule, you'll want or need to consult with a professional pool and spa expert to solve particularly troublesome problems, conduct a annual or seasonal checkup of the entire system, verify your water quality tests and chemical values, and become better educated about maintaining your pool or spa. In fact, that's how smart pool and spa owners protect the value of their investment and offer the safest, healthiest experience possible for family, friends, and neighbors.

In this chapter, you'll get the basics of water quality and how (and why) to maintain the proper balance of the various elements in your pool or spa that contribute to its quality, from pH to the sun's ultraviolet rays. You'll also gain knowledge about sanitation, arguably the most important aspect of pool and spa water quality. Though certainly not mutually exclusive from the water's level of acidity, hardness, or dissolved solids (all of which and more are explained in this chapter), a sanitizer such as chlorine is the critical element to maintaining healthy water for soaking or swimming.

There is a bit of chemistry-speak involved, but mostly about how assorted chemicals affect water quality, how to test for their presence and adjust them properly and in what order (yes, that matters), and the options that exist among them in terms of their performance, delivery into the water, and safe handling. There's also a troubleshooting guide that identifies common pool and spa water quality problems and offers advice about how to solve them.

Like umpires and referees in sports, the quality of your pool and spa water ideally should be virtually unnoticed by swimmers and soakers, allowing them to enjoy the experience without oily skin, bloodshot eyes, or distracting odors—or perhaps worse health hazards. Maintaining balanced, healthy water in your pool or spa is a chore, but one at which you can quickly become proficient and easily work into your normal household routine.

Ideal Water Quality

When it comes to the quality of the water in your pool or spa, look and feel go a long way—if not all the way—as reliable indicators. If you can see whether a quarter is lying heads or tails at the bottom of the deep end of a pool, chances are pretty good that the water is healthy and in proper balance; if after a soak or a swim your skin feels clean rather than filmy or with a slight burning sensation, the water quality is probably well maintained.

Even so, visual and sensual tests are inherently subjective and inexact. A pool or spa can appear clear for some time, for instance, while its chemical content gets increasingly out of whack, until one day the water is cloudy and discolored and you notice the pool's surfaces are stained or etched. A spa or hot tub might be seem to support a nightly routine of relaxation until its neglected and overburdened filtration system fails.

The lesson is that ideal water quality, in proper balance and with all of the elements within their respective recommended ranges, requires regular monitoring and adjustment even if everything looks okay from the deck or feels right in the water.

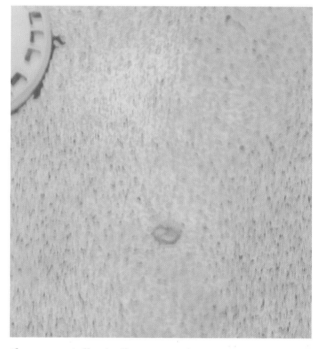

If you can tell whether a quarter is resting in a heads or tails position at the bottom of the deep end, your pool water is probably in good shape (and so is your eyesight).

Keys to Pool and Spa Water Quality:

- Maintain proper water filtration.
- Devise and follow a schedule to test for and balance chemical elements in the water.
- Clean the pool thoroughly after each use.

- Keep the pool or spa covered when not in use.
- Closely follow the directions of use for each chemical.
- Properly dispose of chemicals that have reached their expiration dates.

Cover your pool or spa whenever practical to minimize evaporation, preserving the water quality and the balance of sanitizing chemicals.

Ideal water quality is a balance among a variety of elements and chemicals, each of which impacts the other; boosting one to bring it into its recommended range can push another out of its suggested scale. Knowing those consequences, and tips for achieving balance, are discussed later in this chapter. For now, here's a primer of what contributes to the quality of your pool and spa water.

Sanitizers. Whether it's chlorine, bromine, or some other chemical or method, the purpose of any sanitizer is to kill bacteria and other waste materials in the water and to control algae growth. A sanitizer mixes

Leaves and other organic matter that pollute your pool or spa water begin to decompose and release chemicals almost immediately. Careful policing of the pool area and collecting debris supports healthy water.

Exposure to the elements is tough to avoid with an outdoor pool or spa, so it pays to learn how influences such as sun, wind, rainwater and organic matter affect water quality.

Clean, healthy water is essential to clean, healthy fun in a pool or spa.

with oxygen in the water to dissolve, or oxidize, bacteria and algae—in effect, both killing and removing organic matter. What's left over after the bacteria is eliminated is called the residual, the amount of which also needs to be monitored and kept within a recommended range to prevent new bacterial growth and help maintain sanitary water.

Stabilizers. To be effective over a longer period of time, chlorine sanitizers require a stabilizing agent. Cyanuric acid is a common stabilizer for chlorine, shielding it from the sun's ultraviolet (UV) rays and also slowing the water's rate of total dissolved solids (defined on page 77).

pH. The level of pH in the water indicates its acidity; the lower the pH reading, the higher the acid content. Extremely or chronically acidic water is corrosive, eating away at any metal components and most surfaces, including plaster, tile grout, and vinyl liners; it's also what causes your eyes to sting when you're swimming. Conversely, water that is allowed to remain too alkaline (or too low in acid content) leaves calcium deposits on pool and spa surfaces and inside the plumbing system and equipment components. In addition to these reasons, it is important to keep the pH level within the recommended range to help optimize the effectiveness of your sanitizer.

Recommended Ranges

Experts, including health officials, generally agree on the respective levels of various elements that render pool or spa water healthy, as indicated below.

Element	Recommended Level
pH	7.2 – 7.6
Total alkalinity	80 – 120 parts per million (ppm)
Cyanuric acid (chlorine stabilizer)	40 – 70 ppm
Chlorine residual (stabilized chlorine)	1.0 – 3.0 ppm
Calcium hardness	200 – 400 ppm
Total dissolved solids (TDS)	less than 2000 ppm
Chlorine (unstabilized)	0.3 – 1.0 ppm

Total alkalinity. While pH measures the relative acidity of the water, total alkalinity indicates the amount of alkaline material present. The proper amount of total alkaline helps resist sudden or extreme changes in the water's pH level by neutralizing or mitigating the effect of high levels of acid present in the water. Knowing your water's total alkalinity tells you exactly how much acid or alkaline to add to the water to achieve the recommended pH level.

Hardness. All water, even treated, potable drinking water, contains minerals, or alkalines. The amount of one such mineral—calcium—determines the hardness of the water. In plaster-lined pools, calcium slowly leeches from the plaster into the water, adding to its alkalinity, and thus its hardness. If the water is too hard, it can raise the pH level above the recommended range and form white, salty deposits on the pool's surface, usually at the waterline. Hard water can also be somewhat abrasive to your skin, while extremely soft water might leave a filmy substance.

Total dissolved solids (TDS). While hardness measures one mineral (calcium), the level of total dissolved solids in your pool or spa water accounts for the accumulation of all such content that has not been filtered out of the water. In addition to calcium, TDS includes chlorine, dirt and debris, exfoliation, cyanurate (a byproduct of cyanuric acid), perspiration, and other chemicals and elements present, in dissolved form, in the water; most TDS content, in fact, comes from the people using the pool or spa. In addition, the process of natural evaporation removes only pure water from a pool or spa, leaving dissolved solids behind and in relatively higher content due to the overall reduction in water volume. Total dissolved solids absorb the water quality chemicals you put into the water, rendering them less effective toward achieving proper balance and sanitation.

Climate. Factors including temperature (of both the outdoors and the water), relative humidity, sun exposure, wind, and rain all contribute to the quality and balance of pool or spa water. Sustained high temperature and sun exposure, for instance, promote algae growth in shallow areas of the pool; wind across the surface of the water not only speeds evaporation and deposits dirt, leaves, and other debris into the water (thus absorbing sanitizers and boosting total dissolved solid content), but also can carry and deposit algae spores. Rain into an open pool or spa quickly destabilizes your careful balancing act of all the elements.

Bather load. The contributions to total dissolved solids and other elements that can throw water quality out of balance and make it more difficult to achieve are most often the result of heavy pool or spa use. We humans carry with us, and unload, a lot of "baggage" when we swim or soak, including sweat, sunscreen, dead skin, hair, and other unseemly content. That's why it helps to install a shower on or near the pool deck and insist on its use before people use the pool or spa. Regardless, you'll need to calculate bather load (or use) to have any hope of achieving proper water quality and balance.

Chloramines. That smell coming off the pool water that most people associate with too much chlorine is, in fact, just the opposite. When a chloride sanitizer combines with naturally occurring ammonia and other nitrogen compounds in the water, it creates chloramines, rendering an often offensive, bleach-like odor. If that smells like your pool or spa, it may be time to shock, or "superchlorinate" the water, an extreme (but safe) balancing technique detailed later in this chapter.

New products that help maintain water balance include this capsule containing an odorless, tasteless oil that is distributed into the pool water through the skimmer. The oil floats on top of the water and forms a micro-thin skin that reduces evaporation and chemical loss.

Sanitizers

Among all of the elements that contribute to the quality of pool or spa water, sanitizers are the most critical. Your responsibility as a pool or spa owner is to offer a healthy and safe environment for relaxation, exercise, and enjoyment; unsanitary water is, simply, a health hazard with myriad ramifications and risks. Not only that, but you'll never get the other elements in balance if your water isn't clean.

Chlorine, in a variety of forms, is the most common sanitizer for pools and spas. It is available in three forms: gas, liquid, and dry granules or tablets, each with its own pros and cons regarding availability, affordability, safety, and ease of use.

In sanitation-speak, availability refers to what percentage of the chemical, in this case chlorine, is present in a given form to attack and kill bacteria and keep algae growth in check. A sanitizer's availability, then, helps determine how effective it will be and for how long. A sanitizer's availability is easily and quickly lowered when the chemical is exposed to the sun's UV rays, air, and light. Availability also deteriorates over time.

Shocking the system is done by adding larger than normal concentrations of sanitizer to the water to restore water that is badly out of balance. "Shock" is normally added when opening a pool for the season.

What is Algae?

Algae, the plural of the Latin word for seaweed (alga) refers to a species of plant life that ranges from microscopic to massive, fast-growing flora. In treated swimming pools and spas, it can grow even in well-balanced and sanitary water, typically in low spots and areas of low circulation, such as on and around steps. It feeds off the nutrients and minerals in the water, and its growth is promoted by exposure to the sun's light and UV rays. Over time, certain forms of algae may develop resistance to your regular sanitation efforts, requiring you to "shock" or superchlorinate the water periodically to get rid of the algae blooms. As with most water-quality problems, the best cure for algae is preventive action: keeping the water, filters, and surfaces clean, and maintaining proper chemical balance. It's also a good idea to wash swimwear with detergent and throw it in the clothes dryer after each use, rather than simply line- or air-dry it outside; doing so is not only cleaner for the water the next time you use the pool or spa, but also mitigates the chances of algae spores in the air and wind attach-ing themselves to your swimwear and being deposited into the water. Once it takes hold on the surfaces of your pool or spa, algae requires serious time and elbow grease to remediate.

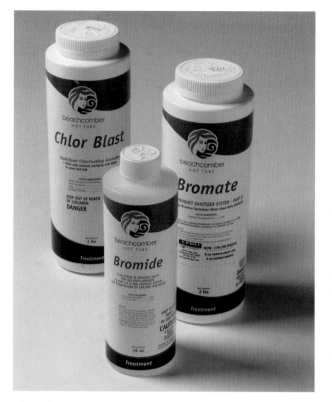

Chemical sanitizers are essential for clean, well balanced water. The two most common types are chlorinating granules (left), which are used mostly in pools, and bromide liquids, which are combined with bromate granules to sanitize water (usually in spas and hot tubs).

Chlorine gas, for instance, is pure chlorine and therefore 100 percent available when it is applied to the water. By far the most effective sanitizer, chlorine gas is also the least expensive chlorine option. But it's also lethal, requiring a sophisticated (and expensive) system of pressurized tanks, valves, wands, and injection devices to use it safely—far too costly and potentially risky for a private residential pool or spa.

On the other end of the scale, liquid chlorine is about 13 percent available in its plastic bottle, as it is already diluted in and by water (still, it's about four times stronger than liquid bleach at roughly the same price per gallon). Though it is simply poured (carefully) into the pool or spa water directly, and dissolves immediately, it carries a high pH level and also adds to the water's hardness.

Most commonly, private pool and spa owners use dry chlorine (or another form of sanitizer) to kill bacteria and control algae in the water. In granular or tablet form, this type of chlorine is available as a cyanurate (when the chlorine is mixed with cyanuric acid to help retain or extend its availability); lithium hypochlorite, an organic form of chlorine; or calcium hypochlorate, which contains no stabilizers, but offers higher (65 percent) availability. All three are easy to apply using floats or mechanical delivery systems within a pool's or spa's equipment set or skid.

Cyanurate and lithium are most often used as maintenance sanitizers, as they remain effective longer, if at a lower availability, than calcium hypochlorate. Cyanurate also emits fewer byproducts that can affect overall water balance and quality; it is offered as either dichlor or triclor formulations (indicating the level of stabilization), varying in chlorine availability, chemical byproducts, pH levels, and cost. Lithium usually comes in a powdered form that dissolves quickly in the water, making it ideal for vinyl-lined and dark-colored plaster pools and spas as it leaves less (or no) residue on surfaces.

Calcium hypochlorate is also a relatively inexpensive and convenient sanitation option, though it can raise the water's pH level. Its high availability also makes it a common method for superchlorination to "shock" the pool water to raise and restore the residual of the sanitizer to the recommended level, as well as to kill off any lingering algae bloom.

While chlorine, in all its forms, is the most popular pool and spa water-sanitizing agent, other sanitizers are available to kill and/or remove bacteria.

Bromine, for instance, is an increasingly common option for private pool and spa owners. Though it cannot be stabilized like chlorine, it is naturally more stable than chlorine at higher water temperatures, making it a popular choice to sanitize spas and hot tubs. Bromine also doesn't mix with ammonias in the

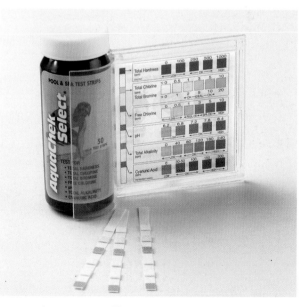

Test strips are an efficient diagnostic tool because they measure many water quality variables in one dip. The one above, for example, tests for total hardness, total chlorine, total bromine, free chlorine, pH, total alkalinity and cyanuric acid.

water that can emit odors. It is offered in granular or tablet form for manual floaters or mechanical distribution, though it requires a catalyst to work. Ironically, most often a small amount of chlorine is mixed in the formula. It's also more expensive than comparable chlorine treatments and loses its availability faster when exposed to UV light.

Another sanitizing option is iodine, an affordable, odorless, and taste- and irritant-free germicide that's equally easy to apply as dry chlorine or bromine. The problem is, it takes a significant amount of iodine to effectively oxidize bacteria—so much that it causes the water to turn green. Iodine also does nothing to kill algae, requiring a supplemental sanitizer or algaecide to do that job.

Potassium monopersulfate (PM) is another oxidizing agent that is most often used to shock pool and spa water without the use of chlorine. It also serves as a catalyst for bromine, contained within that chemical's granular mix to enable it to sanitize the water, and is rarely sold by itself.

Organic Sanitizers

The increasing popularity of natural or more environmentally sensitive alternatives to synthetic chemicals has given rise to organic means of sanitizing pool and spa water.

One such option is the sun's ultraviolet (or UV) light, an idea that initially seems counterintuitive given how UV rays reduce chlorine availability and promote algae growth. However, if harnessed as a beam of light through which filtered pool or spa water passes, UV light will kill bacteria if there is any

Ozonators are installed in the water lines to charge the water with oxygen immediately before it re-enters the pool or spa. They are designed to make sanitizers, such as chlorine, more effective, not to replace them.

in the water. UV neither creates nor leaves a residue to prevent bacteria growth in the pool or spa, and won't kill algae (which is not carried in water through the filtration system, anyway), making it a passive, reactive alternative to the preventive sanitation treatments of chlorine, bromine, and iodine. If used at all as a sanitizing method, UV must be supplemented by another, more active agent.

Another natural choice is ozone, which is simply turbo-charged oxygen delivered by an air circulation system (ozonator) attached at the tail end of the equipment set or spa skid, after the water has been filtered. The extra oxygen promotes more effective and faster oxidation, although it requires a chemical partner, like chlorine, to attach to it and kill and remove bacteria and algae growth. Think of it as a performance enhancement to chlorine or a similar chemical sanitizer.

Another nonchemical-based system uses the unique properties of copper and platinum, combined with oxygen, to sanitize water (see pages 88 to 89).

Testing and Balancing Your Water

For each of the elements listed in the recommended ranges chart (see page 76), there is a test to determine how your pool or spa water matches up and which chemicals, if any, need to be added to balance the water. In fact, there are several test methods from which to choose, again depending on your budget, comfort level, and convenience.

The most common water quality test methods for private residential pools and spas are test strips and liquid tests; in both cases, the results reveal colors that are compared to a chart to determine how closely the

various elements in your water match their respective recommended ranges for proper balance and quality.

You may also use electrometric testing, in which probes inserted into the water read the level of various elements simultaneously and provide a digital or analog readout for each of them, including total dissolved solids. While less subjective and more accurate than test strips or liquid tests, and the method used by most professional pool technicians, electrometric test kits must be kept calibrated and clean, and are historically too expensive for private pool and spa owners.

How to Collect a Water Sample

Dip a clean glass jar with a lid into the spa or pool, at least 12" deep. Avoid taking samples near water outlets or in the shallow end of a pool.

Tilt the jar so the air captured inside it escapes.

Cap the jar and remove it from the water. Take samples from at least three different locations.

Another test method is turbidity, also called the "cloudiness" test, in which the clarity of a given water sample determines the presence and relative value of cyanuric acid.

A comparative look at each test method—as well as tests for certain elements, such as total dissolved solids, that can only be conducted in a laboratory setting—reveals their ease of use, accuracy, and other qualities.

Test strips. These thin, narrow paper strips have one or more small absorbent pads along their length treated with a chemical catalyst called a reagent for a given element. You simply dip the strip into your pool or spa, swish it around for 30 seconds, and remove it. A single strip might be designed to test the level of chlorine residual, total and/or free chlorine, calcium hardness, total alkalinity, pH, and metals.

At once, or even while they are still in the water, the pad (or pads) begin to change color. You then compare those colors to a chart of the known values of each element, sometimes provided in the bottle or box of test strips, to determine the value of each element in your pool or spa water. A mustard-colored pad for total alkalinity, for instance, indicates a very low level in your pool or spa; a grayish color on the free chlorine (or chlorine residual) pad denotes an acceptable, if slightly low, level of that quality.

Test strips, especially those that test multiple elements on the same strip, are easy, convenient, and accurate, so long as you test three or four different locations in a pool and at least two places within a spa each time to reduce random values.

Liquid tests. Unlike test strips, liquid tests require you to gather small samples of your pool or spa water in clean vials, and then add drops of various reagents to determine the relative values of various elements. Also called a chlorametric test, this method is only slightly more complex than a test strip, and comparably accurate. It tests for pH level, chlorine residual, and both stable and unstabilized chlorine.

To collect a proper sample, plunge the vial into the water top-down to your elbow (about 12" deep), turn it right-side up and allow it to fill with water, and then cap it under water. Make sure to collect the sample (or samples) away from the return outlets and shallow areas of the pool or spa. Taking samples at this depth and in well-circulated areas, as opposed to at the surface or near a drain, mitigates the chance that dirt, debris, and other material will disproportionately affect the samples. (Also, never clean your sample vials with soap, which leaves a residue that can also affect the test; instead, rinse them thoroughly with your pool or spa water. And avoid touching the

Testing Spa Water

For the most part, spa and pool water can be similarly tested for the relative presence or level of various elements, commonly with test strips or liquid tests. But because a typical spa or hot tub experiences a much higher bather load compared to a pool with 10 or more times the water volume, and keeps that water at a higher temperature, spa water reacts faster to chemicals (read: uses them up more quickly) and suffers a higher rate of evaporation than a typical swimming pool, especially if it's left uncovered. In short, while you might test your pool water every few days during heavy use, it might serve well to test your spa water more frequently to keep the water clean and balanced. You may even want to drain and refill your spa or hot tub every two or three months, something you may only have to do with your pool, if properly maintained, every other year.

water sample or reagents with your fingers, which also might affect the readings.)

Pour or insert each water sample into the tester immediately, and then add the instructed amount of each reagent into its appropriate vial. The reagent will react with the water and turn color, which you then compare in a well-lit room, in bright, clear daylight, or (best) against a white background, with the corresponding color charts provided on the tester.

The liquid test for total alkalinity and calcium hardness is called titration, in which you add two reagents in measured amounts, often drop-by-drop, to each water sample until it reveals a change in color.

With all of these tests, it is critical to make sure the reagents are fresh. Properly stored in a cool, dry location and used on a regular basis (perhaps once every other day during times of heavy pool or spa

How to Use Test Strips

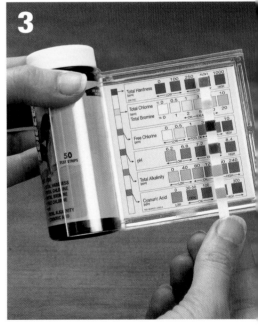

Test strips have absorbent pads that are coated with colored reagents. Each pad is sensitive to a distinct chemical or water quality standard. Dip the strip in pool or spa water and swish it around for 30 seconds or so.

Remove the test stick from the water sample.

Compare the colors of the reagent pads to the color guides printed on the reference chart that came with your test strips.

use), a bottle of 50 test strips should never reach its expiration date. Liquid reagents should also be replaced every few months, and entirely so rather than simply refilled or "topped off."

How often should you test your pool or spa water? In the summer, or in times of heavy (perhaps daily) use, consider testing the quality and balance of your pool's water every two or three days, and more often for spas used for nightly soaks. It's also a good idea to bring a sample of your water to a pool or spa retailer about once a month for testing, which most conduct for free using an electrometric tester in hopes that you'll leave with a boxful of chemical boosters and home test materials. As you dial down your pool's or spa's use in the off-season, you can test less frequently, maybe just once a month; if you winterize and close your pool, you need not test it at all until you re-open it.

Test strips and both chlorametric and titration tests are also useful after you've added chemicals to the pool to achieve healthy, balanced water quality. Depending on the delivery system of your chemical additives, it's best to wait several hours, or perhaps a day (without use of the pool or spa) before collecting samples and testing your efforts. In time, you'll become proficient enough to be accurate in this pursuit, though it always helps to check your work now and then.

Whether to determine how much (if any) chemicals you need to add to your pool or spa to bring the water into a healthy balance, or to make sure you've achieved that goal, always test every element you can before adding anything to the water. Once you have a comprehensive baseline, you can more accurately and reliably add what's needed to bring it into proper balance.

How to Use Liquid Test Kits

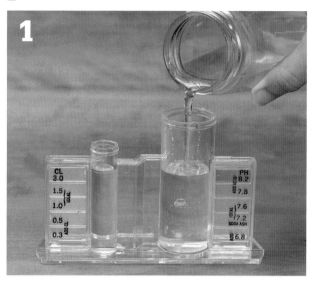

Collect samples of water and pour the water into individual testing vials (usually provided with the testing kit).

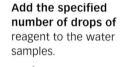

Add the specified number of drops of reagent to the water samples.

Compare the colors of the water samples to the charts or color gauges provided by the kit manufacturer and adjust the chemicals in your water accordingly.

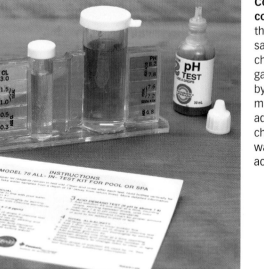

Delivery Systems

About the only thing that pool experts, service technicians, health officials, and experienced pool and spa owners agree on are the recommended levels of the various elements and chemicals in the water. Ask them how to achieve that balance, and you're likely to get a different answer from each of them.

In short, as you fiddle with various chemical boosters and additives, granules versus liquids, mechanical or manual means, partial draining and refilling, and other pool and spa cleaning and maintenance chores, you'll find your own method for balancing the water and keeping it properly sanitized.

There are, however, a few helpful (and generally accepted) tips to keep in mind.

The first is to rely on your regular home tests, assuming they are fresh and taken properly, as accurate indicators of what needs to be added and in what quantity. Remember, test for everything you can before adding anything to the water to get within a particular element's recommended range and reach an overall balance.

If you are using liquid chemicals, such as chlorine or muriatic acid (the latter to boost pH levels), pour it as close to the water surface as possible, and slowly, to reduce splashing that can irritate, stain, or damage your skin, clothes, shoes, and pool or spa surfaces. Liquid solutions should also be applied at multiple locations within the pool, and as far away as possible from drains, return outlets, and skimmers so that they thoroughly dissipate in the water before running through the pump and filter system.

Never mix chemicals and/or dump them into the pool simultaneously. A dramatic example: diluted dry or liquid muriatic acid mixed with chlorine creates chlorine gas that is potentially lethal if inhaled, even in small quantities.

Dry chemicals, in powdered, granular, or tablet form, can be delivered into your pool or spa water manually or by mechanical means. An easy manual system is to simply pour the powder or granules into the water, again close to the surface to avoid splashing and, in the case of a sanitizer, to maintain as much of its availability as possible.

The granules, however, may not dissolve before they reach the bottom of the pool, which means you'll have to stir them up with a cleaning brush; better still, consider dissolving each chemical separately in a clean bucket of clear water, then pouring them (also separately) into the pool. Remember, when mixing, always add a chemical to water, not the other way around.

Another, perhaps more reliable manual delivery system is a floating chemical dispenser, or "float" (see page 86).

Mechanical chemical distribution is similar, except that a large container (sometimes called a bed or feeder) is inserted into the equipment set or skid to treat water that's been filtered and is ready to be recirculated into the pool or spa. In so-called erosion systems, water pumped through the equipment runs through or over the chemical (again, typically a sanitizer), picking it up and carrying it on its way out. In less-common pump

A Shock to the System

Shocking, or superchlorinating, your pool or spa water is a common method for restoring your sanitation efforts and chlorine residual level to its recommended range. Simply, it involves adding 3 to 5 times the normal amount of chlorine or other chemical sanitizer to the water, by manual or mechanical means, to drive off unstable (or ineffective) chlorine residual and boost availability. Depending on bather load, you may have to superchlorinate once a month or even more often; water kept above 85 degrees, typically in spas and hot tubs, may need to be shocked twice a month.

Monitor the results of your home test methods to indicate if shocking is needed. Specifically, when both combined available chlorine (CAC) and free available chlorine (FAC) fall out of their recommended ranges, consider superchlorination. As with other sanitation efforts, shock your water after sundown to reduce the effect of the sun's UV rays on the chemical's availability, and make sure the water's pH level is within its recommended range so that the extra chlorine doesn't oxidize copper in your pool equipment's metal components, leaving black stains on surfaces.

Water Quality Problem Solver

Symptom:	Cause:	Remedy
Green and cloudy water; dark green spots on pool/spa wall	Algae growth	Brush and clean off algae from walls and surfaces; shock water
Odor; eye or skin irritation	Chloramines or improper pH level	Shock water; balance pH, chlorine residual, and total alkaline levels
Discolored/cloudy water	Algae or other organic matter; high pH level	Remove debris; shock and balance water; clean filters and circulate water at least 2 hours per day
Foaming water (spa)	Low calcium hardness and/or high level of total dissolved solids due to high bather load (specifically: lotions, oils, and cosmetics)	Add anti-foaming agent; shock water to boost hardness; drain and refill
Scale buildup	pH level out of range	Adjust/balance pH level; test for and adjust, as necessary, total alkalinity and calcium hardness

systems, the bed holds a liquid sanitizer that is added to the water after it has been filtered through the equipment set.

As with floats, a valve regulates the rate of distribution into the water. Unlike floats, the distribution of chlorine or other chemicals is more even and consistent. Mechanical feeders, however, are often out of plain sight with the rest of the pool equipment set (usually tucked behind a fence or contained in a shed or skirt), which requires you to remember to maintain an adequate amount of the chemical in the container to keep the water clean and/or balanced. It's

also critical to use chemicals that are designed specifically for mechanical feeders.

Even if your water quality is way out of balance, add chemicals in small quantities at multiple locations in the pool or spa until you reach the recommended range. As long as you're moving in the right direction, toward the proper levels, there's little benefit in dumping large quantities to play catch-up. Remember, these chemicals do not act exclusively; several impact one another, making it more difficult to achieve balance if one or more are added to your water in large volume.

How to Add Chemical Directly to the Water

Dissolve powder or granular chemicals (or liquids, too, if directed) into a bucket of water.

Lower the bucket close to the surface of the water and slowly dump in the contents, avoiding splashes.

Floating chemical dispensers

When using floating chemical dispensers, the dry chemical is placed into a tube topped with a wide, hollow head that floats on the surface of the water while the granules or tablets slowly dissolve underwater. This method is usually reserved for chlorine and comparable chemical sanitizers, especially those with lower availability that are used primarily to maintain proper residual levels rather than "shock" the system. Dry acids and alkaline materials can also be added this way. Some floats are equipped with control valves to regulate the chemical's release into the water.

Place the recommended number of chlorine tablets into the float.

Replace the cover and let the float set sail into your pool or spa. Add more tablets as needed.

When adjusting for pH and total alkalinity, bring the latter level up first before adding any muriatic acid (to lower pH) or soda ash or baking soda (to boost pH). Achieving a proper level of total alkalinity will adjust your pH level somewhat, meaning you have to add less acid or alkaline, if any, to bring your pH in line, as well.

Another rule of thumb is to chlorinate or sanitize in the early evening, soon after the pool closes for the night and so that the sun's UV light has less of an impact on the stability and availability of the chemical. Similarly, add acid in the morning, assuming no one's going to use the pool until the early afternoon. Staggering your chemical treatments also reduces the opportunity for them to react radically to each other.

Typically, only a pool or spa professional or a retailer with electrometric testing equipment can determine an accurate level of total dissolved solids in your pool or spa water; there is no home test strip or liquid test for that element. There's also no remedy, except to partially or fully drain the pool and refill it, if TDS levels reach 2,500 ppm or higher. That's why installing and insisting on rinse showers before swimming or soaking, laundering swimwear, and covering your pool or spa when it's not in use are smart preventive measures to reducing the rate of TDS.

Similarly, while you can test for calcium hardness with a home kit, and boost its value, into the recommended range if necessary, there is no way to reduce water hardness except to partially or fully drain the pool or spa and refill it.

An inline chlorinator for a swimming pool, sometimes called a mechanical feeder, dispenses measured amounts of sanitizing chemicals at a constant rate.

Safe Storage and Handling

The final chapter in this book discusses overall pool and spa safety, including a thorough explanation of the safe storage and handling of various pool and spa chemicals. Suffice to say here that it is important for the health of your family (including pets), as well as your pool and spa water, to always respect the hazards of any chemical in your house. That means storing them in a cool, dry place away from the pool or spa, ideally in a locked cabinet out of the reach of small children, and using the proper eye, mouth, and skin protection when handling them.

It also means keeping and using chemicals separately, in their own, clean containers or transfer mediums (like a bucket or scoop), following use directions to the letter, and replacing them if they are damaged or reach their respective expiration dates. It's also important to allow chemicals to completely dissolve and dissipate in the water before you allow swimmers and soakers to use it again.

Store chemicals in a secure (lockable), dry cabinet or dedicated shed or poolhouse.

A Chemical-free Option

If you are a pool owner you may have heard of some water treatment systems that do an effective job of sanitizing without adding any chemicals to the pool: no chlorine, no bromine and none of the smelly or eye-burning compounds they create when added to pool water. Known generically as pool ionizers, most of these systems are based on the specific properties of copper that affect water quality.

One system that advertises this approach is the ECOsmarte purifying system (see Resources, page 236). Instead of sanitizer chemicals, it relies on chemical reactions between ionic copper, platinum and oxygen. Housed in a clear chamber that's plumbed directly into the water recirculating line, the plates of pure copper are mounted opposite the platinum plates. When oxygen from a tank and the pool water flow through the chamber and mix with the metal, the cumulative effect of the elements is to neutralize organic contaminants in the water. The system, which runs on an as-needed basis, not continually, is controlled by a programmable sensor/control box.

A programmable control panel monitors the water balance and triggers the ionizing system to kick in as needed.

For those who'd rather not dump muriatic acid into their pool to reduce the pH level, a carbon dioxide (CO2) tank can be installed in line to the same effect. Inspect the clear tube coming out of the tank periodically and replace the tank or have it refilled when it is empty. This is not part of the ionizing system.

The mixing chamber is the heart of this ionizing system. Inside the chamber are a pair of copper plates and a pair of platinum plates that each require occasional cleaning and replacement. A drip tube adds trace amounts of bottled oxygen, which serves as a catalyst to the chemical reaction created when ions of the copper and platinum are shed and mixed in the pool water.

Systems and Repairs

It's easy to forget sometimes, but that large body of water in your back yard is a fairly complex machine, complete with a motor, a filter, and various other components that help keep it clean, healthy, and ready for your enjoyment.

Of course, like the water itself, those components need to be kept in top condition if you expect to sustain their value. And while there's no shame in hiring a professional technician to service the equipment and offer guidance about its care and condition, it's ultimately your responsibility as a pool or spa owner to know the basic parts of the system and their respective functions so that you can make intelligent decisions about their operation, maintenance, repair, and replacement.

Though each component of your pool's or spa's equipment set is interdependent, the heart of any such system is arguably the motor and pump, a one-piece device that pulls water from the pool or spa through the other components and back out into the vessel. It is essential that the pump and motor be properly sized to handle the water volume and the rate at which it needs to be refreshed completely (called the turnover rate), among other factors, as well as maintained regularly to keep the system working at peak performance.

From there, the rest of the system components fall into two basic categories: essential and auxiliary. Those that are necessary to maintain a clean, safe pool include: the main drain and/or skimmers (from which the water is pulled into the system); the pipes and valves that serve as the supply, return, and control conduits for the water; and the filter, which cleanses the water before it is pumped back into the pool or spa through a series of inlets. A time clock sets and controls the recirculation cycle, making sure the entire volume of water is turned over and filtered within a prescribed amount of time.

One component that is considered non-essential by some pool owners is the heater, although they're likely to get an argument about pool heater value from anyone who has enjoyed a late-evening swim, and a heater certainly is a requisite for a spa. However, a heater is not necessary to refresh the pool or spa water as it circulates through the system, and is therefore considered a "luxury" in that sense.

Other auxiliary devices include chemical feeders, flow and water level meters, temperature and operational controls (all of which are increasingly automated to further boost their convenience), and a variety of water and on-deck features, lighting, and landscaping features.

Pool and spa covers also are considered "non-essential," though, as with heaters, plenty of owners and industry experts will argue that the myriad merits of a cover are, in fact, essential to a pool or spa system's performance. The same might also be said for other supplemental components considering their added convenience in proper cleaning and maintenance.

This is a meaty subject, filled with technical terms and high-level maintenance and repair guidelines about a wide variety of devices and features that are typically left to professional pool technicians and other contractors to manage. But as with your house or car, being a knowledgeable pool and spa owner enables you to decide which parts of the system you want to tackle yourself in terms of maintenance and repair and which you prefer to hire out under your educated supervision to sustain your investment.

Before we dive into the details of each part of a pool or spa equipment set, it's important to get a bird's eye view of the components and how they all fit together, and in what order.

Every vessel, no matter the size or its intended function, includes some way for the water to be recirculated, or "turned over," in order to remain clean and healthy. A main pump, driven by a connected

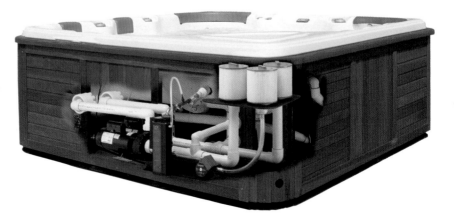

A glimpse inside a typical spa reveals an equipment set that packed together very efficiently. Some spas have an equipment set that's located outside of the vessel and surround, often inside a step for the spa.

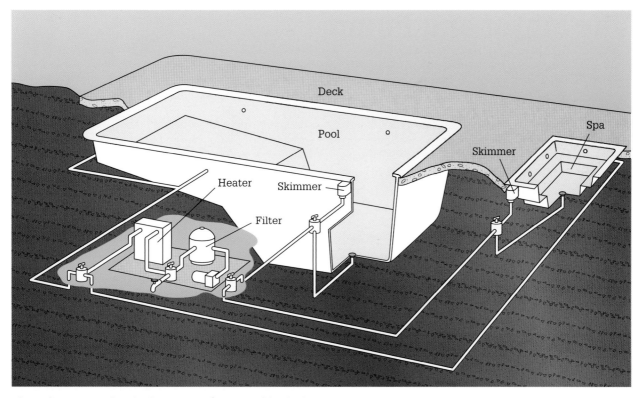

The primary mechanical systems for a pool include the filtration system, the pump and motor, the heater, the plumbing, and the pool vessel itself.

motor (usually electric-powered and integral to the pump device) pulls the water from the pool or spa through its drainage system, typically a combination of a main or multiple drains in the vessel's floor and one or more openings on the sidewalls at the waterline, called skimmers.

For in-ground pools and spas, the water is carried through underground supply pipes and "stubbed up" (or exposed above ground) at a remote location nearby to serve a variety of system components, including the pump, filter, heater, chemical feeders, and other parts—all of which, ideally, are shielded from view and the elements but are also easily accessible for service, maintenance, and repair.

The pump pulls the water through all of these devices, including itself, before disgorging the water back out into the pool or spa via the return pipes and inlets. Within a few hour's time or less, the entire water volume of most private, recreational swimming pools has been completely recirculated through the system (spas, with much less water volume than a full-sized pool, turn over faster); the cycle is repeated multiple times a day, at regular intervals, depending on the water volume and amount of activity (the "bather load"), among other factors.

Systems for above-ground pools work essentially the same way, though the skimmers might be hooked onto the sidewalls (as opposed to being built-in to the walls, as in an in-ground vessel), and the pipes often (but not always) are completely exposed between the pool and the nearby equipment set.

As self-contained units, portable spas come equipped with complete equipment packs—the same basic components as a pool's equipment set, but scaled down to a spa's needs and water volume. Spa equipment packs are designed into the spa's container rather than set off in a remote location. Concealed behind an access panel in the spa's skirting, the skid pack is easily exposed for service, adjustment (such as for water temperature), and repair, and enables the spa to be truly portable to any location with an adequate power source for the motor and pump.

Detailed illustrations of both a full-size pool equipment set and a portable spa skid pack reveal not only the components, but also how the water flows through each system to filter out impurities and particles, add chemicals, and perhaps get a boost in temperature before returning to the pool or spa. Because a pool or spa's equipment set is a looped system, with roughly the same water being recirculated through the pipes and other components, there's really no beginning and ending to the set. That said, there is one device that drives it all: the motor and pump.

The Motor and Pump

Usually installed as a single device, the motor and pump for a pool or spa are actually two distinct functions. The motor converts electricity from a dedicated circuit on your home's main service panel into mechanical energy that is used to power the pump; the energized pump then pressurizes the water in the pipes through centrifugal (or rotational) force, enabling the pump to pull water from the pool or spa to travel through itself and various equipment-set components before returning back into the vessel.

To perform properly, the pump side of the device is filled with water—or "primed"—and sealed off from air to maintain the water pressure it creates through the system. The motor side, meanwhile, is sealed in a moisture-resistant, corrosion-resistant housing separate from the pump so that it remains dry and its electrical parts isolated and insulated from moisture and for safety; the motor is vented, though, to exhaust the heat it creates when operating.

Most modern pool and spa pumps are self-priming, with the ability to fill with water and expel air upon start-up when newly installed or after a cleaning or service procedure. Some pumps also have an air release valve to vent any air trapped in the pump

The pump and motor appliance for a spa is relatively small, with most ranging between ½ HP and 2 HP. A canister on the pool side of the intake line contains a strainer basket to catch any debris that makes it past the skimmers. The pump and motor are sealed units, but the pump canister requires occasional lubrication.

after you seal it shut, or which might get in during operation (such as an air pocket caused by an obstruction in the pipes). Conscientious pool and spa owners and professional technicians, however, always make sure the pump is primed before leaving it to run the system. A dry pump, or one not primed with enough water, will overheat and damage both itself and the motor.

One easy way to make sure the pump remains primed is to maintain the water level of the pool or spa to just above the weir line of the vessel's in-wall skimmer (or multiple skimmers), enabling the pump to continually pull water from the pool or spa through the system. After each use and following a particularly hot and windy day that might accelerate evaporation, you may need to replenish or "top off" the water volume in the pool or spa to bring it back to an optimum level.

The motor and pump typically is the first system device in the set or skid pad to receive water from the pipes traveling from the skimmer(s) and drain(s) in the pool or spa; it therefore also features a strainer basket to filter out any large-scale debris (such as leaves or hair) that was not trapped by similar baskets in the skimmers or the owner's cleaning routine. This basket, as with all debris-catching devices (including the filter), must be cleaned out regularly to maintain optimum system performance.

Ideally, the motor and pump are placed at or slightly above the pool's water level and as close to the vessel as possible to reduce the length, number of turns, and minimum diameter of the pipes leading to and from the pumps; the shorter, straighter, and smaller the pipes through the system, the smaller (and less expensive) the motor and pump need to be. Smaller pumps also require less energy.

For a typical above-ground pool or a portable spa, the motor and pump is probably located below the water line, though often much closer to (and in the case of a portable spa, just underneath) the vessel, making for much shorter plumbing runs into and through the system.

Proper sizing of the motor and pump, typically expressed and rated for its horsepower and other

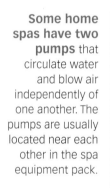

Some home spas have two pumps that circulate water and blow air independently of one another. The pumps are usually located near each other in the spa equipment pack.

Above-ground pools generally are serviced by smaller, low head pumps. The most inexpensive above-ground pools, including inflatable pools, very often are sold bundled with an undersized pump. If you are having difficulty maintaining your water quality in an above-ground pool, investigate replacing your small pump with one that moves more gallons of water per minute.

Minimum Pump Flow Rate

Pool Size Gallons(US)	Turnover Time*	Minimum Flow Rate
35,000	8 hours	73 GPM
35,000	10 hours	58 GPM
24,000	8 hours	50 GPM
24,000	10 hours	40 GPM
18,000	8 hours	38 GPM
18,000	10 hours	30 GPM

*Turnover time is the amount of time it takes the entire volume of pool water to pass once through the pool filter.

attributes as one device, is a critical consideration for the efficiency and effectiveness of the overall system. Most pool and spa motor-pumps are rated between one-half and 2 horsepower, but relying only on that measure is a mistake; in fact, a pump's horsepower is only a fraction of what must be calculated to determine the correct device for your pool or spa.

Accurately sizing a motor and pump is done by using a formula encompassing five key elements: water volume (expressed in gallons), pool volume (the size of the pool vessel, in cubic feet), the diameter and overall length of the plumbing pipes (including elbows and turns), turnover rate (the amount of time it takes to run all of the water through the system, usually about once every eight hours), and the total dynamic head of the system (a calculation of water resistance through the pipes and components of the equipment set of skid pad).

Each pipe, elbow, valve, device (including the motor-pump) and any other components of the equipment set are rated for their contribution to the total dynamic head (also called "head loss") calculation; in other words, how long it takes the water to flow through a 10-foot length of half-inch pipe, make its way around an elbow or through the filter, and expel itself through an inlet in the pool or spa wall all contribute to the head loss number used to help size the motor-pump.

It's important to note that adding components, such as a chemical feeder, to your equipment set, also adds to the head loss calculation; that may, in turn, require a larger motor and pump.

The higher the total dynamic head, the lower the water's flow rate through the system, expressed as gallons per minute (gpm). Most of a pool or spa's equipment set or skid pad components, specifically the pipes, heater, and filter, are rated to handle a maximum flow rate. A pump that is sized to achieve a higher flow rate than what those and other components can handle risks damaging them from the excessive force of the water's velocity.

Booster Pumps. Jetted spas, especially portable models, often include a two-speed motor-pump to boost the flow rate through one or more jets in the vessel. When the jets are engaged, the pump operates at a higher speed; when the jets are off, it dials back to a slower rate to recycle and filter the water through the skid pack or equipment set.

Some systems are designed with two pumps, one for standard recirculation and the other solely as a auxiliary booster for the jets; in this scenario, the booster pump is on a totally separate system, pulling water from the spa through a dedicated drain off of the main drain via a multi-port valve, and each motor-pump is sized to handle one-half of the jets' capacity.

Pools can also be outfitted with booster pumps, typically to accommodate or allow vacuum systems that help ease cleaning chores.

Booster pumps are auxiliary pumps that share the load by driving air through the jet system of a spa. Or, in the case of a pool, a booster pump like the one above may be installed to operate the pool vacuuming system.

High, Medium and Low Head Pumps

When you hear a term like "high head pump" you might assume that it refers to some physical property of the pump shape. In fact, pump manufacturers use the term "head" to describe the relative volume and speed of water moved by their appliances.

- **Low head pump:** Use for spas, above-ground pools, and in-ground pools with less than 10,000 gallons of water.

- **Medium head pump:** Use for in-ground pools containing between 10,000 gallons and 20,000 gallons of water.

- **High head pump:** Use for in-ground pools containing more than 20,000 gallons of water.

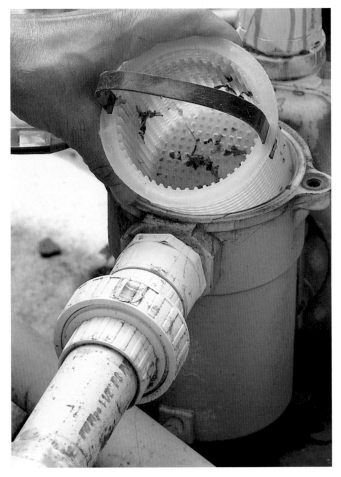

Pumps usually have a clear cover, so you can look in and see if the pump is operating or if the debris basket is full and needs emptying.

The pump basket in a pool equipment set captures leaves and other debris that makes it past the skimmers. The basket is located on the poolside of the pump to keep the debris from clogging the water circulation system.

Submersible Pumps. Another type of motor-pump is one that is submerged in the water to recirculate it through a fountain or other feature within the pool. Encased in a waterproof and corrosion-resistant housing and electrical conduit stubbed up above-ground and plugged into a nearby outlet, submersible pumps are best suited for small, low water-volume features and are designed simply to move water, through a tube, from the base to the head of the feature. More commonly, the water circulation needs of today's sophisticated integral features, including waterfalls, sprays, spillovers, and catch basins for vanishing edges, are factored into the size of the pool's main pump rather than relying on a separate, submersible device.

Air Blowers. Air blowers are an additional device for spas that simply forces air through small inlets in the vessel's floor and sides to create bubbles for a tingling sensation. Like a motor-pump, they operate on

eletricity (either on a dedicated circuit or a grounded outlet), but operate independently from the rest of the skid pack components that circulate and filter water, not air, through the system. Air blowers, however, can be designed to work in tandem with a standard motor-pump and/or booster to deliver an air-water combination through the spa's jets for a hydrotherapy effect that is stronger than standard water-jet action.

Motor-pump Maintenance

Except for submersible pumps, which are designed to get wet, standard pool or spa motor-pump and booster pump devices should be kept cool and dry. If sheltered from the elements along with the other parts of the equipment set, the motor needs enough clearance (about three feet square) to exhaust the heat it generates during operation and provide enough space for maintenance, service, and/or repair access.

In addition, the pump cover and gaskets that create an airtight seal need to be kept clean and lubricated. When you clean the strainer basket of the pump (having already drained it and the entire system of water to do so), also check the condition of the seals and gaskets (or O-rings) around the lid, and replace them if they are cracked or showing any wear.

Speaking of the strainer basket, it's worth the investment to have a second one on hand in addition to the basket already in the pump. That way, instead of waiting for the debris caught in the basket to dry out (and therefore become easier to remove), you can save time by simply swapping in the second (clean) basket, closing the lid and re-priming the pump, then cleaning out the first strainer basket later so that it's ready for the next maintenance rotation. That scheme also comes in handy when you find a damaged strainer basket, usually by wear over time, enabling you to get the system up and running again quickly instead of waiting until you can buy a new basket to replace it.

Other than that, keep an ear out for any sounds of the pump and/or motor laboring to operate, which may indicate damaged components or a blockage in the pump or elsewhere in the system. Turn the power off immediately and investigate the problem. If the pump and/or motor is damaged, it may not be worth repairing; instead, it's likely better to invest in a new motor-pump, though it's critical to find what caused the damage so that the new pump won't be similarly affected.

How to Replace a Spa Pump

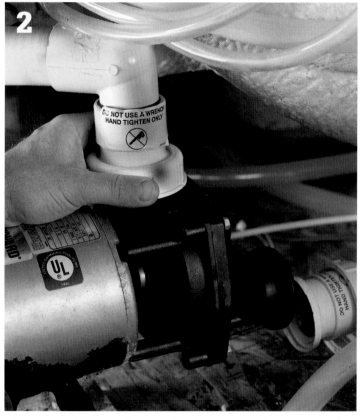

With the access panel removed, unplug the pump at the spa control box. Before proceeding further, look for shutoff valves in the outlet line directly after the pump and between the pump and the heater. Not all spas have these pump shutoffs. If yours does, close the valves. If not, you'll need to drain the spa completely before you proceed further.

Disconnect the water lines leading into and out of the pump. You may want to wrap an old towel around the base of the pump, as there is likely to be some residual water in the lines and pump. Remove the lines until you have clear access to the pump.

(Continued next page)

3

Disconnect the copper bonding wire at the top of the pump (the bonding wire is a ground wire to protect against ground faults).

Unscrew the nuts attaching the pump base to the mounting bolts in the floor of the spa pack. The bolt spacing is standard from pump to pump, so you should be able to reuse the mounting bolts for the new pump without making any adjustments.

Set the new pump into the pump area, aligning the slots in the pump base over the mounting bolts. Make sure the new pump is oriented in the same direction as the old one, with the wet end attaching to the same line fitting. Secure the pump base to the mounting bolts with locknuts.

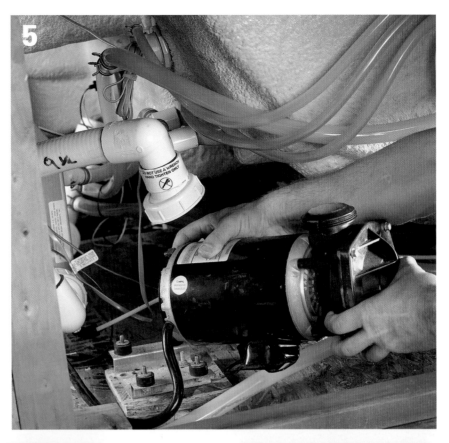

Attach the pipe fittings to the pump, insert the bonding wire into the bonding terminal and tighten the set screw. Fill the tub with water to the recommended level. To make sure water has reached the wet end of the pump (since you're relying on gravity alone to fill the lines), loosen the union between the pump and the heater a quarter turn. Listen for trapped air escaping. Once water starts to dribble out of the union, tighten it completely (hand tighten only). Now the pump may be plugged into the spa control box and safely turned on.

Filtration Systems

Another essential component of a pool or spa's equipment set or skid pack is the filter. Most often a filter is a simple device with few moving parts (unlike the motor-pump), but it performs the crucial function of eliminating impurities and microscopic particles in the water before it is returned to the vessel, thus reducing the cost and time to balance and clean the water with chemicals and sanitizers.

There are three basic types of filters for pools and spas—diatomaceous earth (DE), sand, and cartridge—but each of them performs roughly the same function: water from the pump flows into the filter, where it is strained through a material (called the filter media) to remove impurities and debris particles before the cleansed or filtered water goes on its way out into the system, eventually returning to the pool or spa.

The primary difference between the three types is their respective filter media. Each has its pros and cons, from maintenance and replacement chores to water waste, effectiveness, and design life. The good news is that, for the most part, filter devices are interchangeable in an equipment set; if the one you have for an existing or new pool isn't to your liking, you can swap it out for one of the other two types, especially if you plan to upgrade the entire system at some point to take advantage of new technology and better energy efficiency. Remember, though, that any new or replaced component, including the filter, may

Fresh diatomaceous earth (DE) is poured into the skimmer to be drawn up into a DE filter, where it adheres to a fabric grid to become your pool's filter media.

Common Filter Types

A sand filter draws water in through the top of the filter container, which is filled with sand. The water is pulled downward through the sand, trapping particulates on top of the sand layer. The filtered water is pumped out through the bottom of the tank.

Large filter cartridges for pools are most common with smaller pools, typically of the above-ground variety. They are becoming increasingly popular even for larger pools, however.

change the system's total dynamic head calculation, and therefore perhaps the size of the motor-pump.

Regardless of which filter type you choose or inherit for your pool, the tank's placement in the equipment set is always just after the motor-pump, also on a level surface above ground, anchored down, and easily accessible for service, repair, regular cleaning, and maintenance with enough clearance around it to allow adequate air circulation. It should be placed as close to the motor-pump as possible to minimize resistance (or head loss).

The required size of the filter tank, like that of the motor-pump, depends on several factors, including the filter media chosen; the filter's size and media, in turn, contribute to the system's total dynamic head calculation. Generally, a larger filter tank, regardless of the media used, increases resistance and head loss. When sizing the filter, select a capacity—expressed in terms of square footage—that meets the system's highest estimated turnover and flow rate.

DE (diatomaceous earth) filters. Traditionally considered the king of pool filters, DE units employ a series of fabric grids coated with diatomaceous earth, a naturally occurring, non-toxic, white-powdery substance derived from the dried skeletons of the diatom, a small water plant. This material is able to strain out the smallest impurities among the three filter types. DE filters use the grids to maintain their form and effectiveness in the filter tank, while preventing the formation of a thick, wet cake when exposed to water, which could potentially block water flow.

There are two types of DE filters: by far the most prevalent are vertical grid models, which are designed so that the water enters at the bottom of the filter tank, is pushed through the grid assembly and filter media (the DE material) by water pressure, and is expelled out the top. Spin models, long outdated and no longer made, sit horizontally and require a hand crank to spin the grids inside

A spa filter normally is located in the water intake port in the spa. The filter cartridge sizes vary widely. The cartridges can be cleaned and reused many times.

A DE filter is similar to a sand filter, but instead of sand it employs a sticky, white mineral (diatomaceous earth) that collects on a fabric grid inside the filter container. The coated fabric grids can catch and remove much finer particles than sand.

the tank as the water flows through them from one end to the other.

When the DE material (similar in consistency to talcum powder) is fresh, the filter can capture particles as small as 7 microns; that's nearly three times smaller than the other two filter types are capable of sifting out of the water. As any filter media, including DE, ages and goes through several usage cycles, however, its capabilities wane and the water cleansing process becomes increasingly ineffective, requiring the filter media to be cleaned or replaced.

There are several ways to clean a DE filter to restore its effectiveness. The most common is called backwashing, a process in which the pressurized water flow is reversed through the filter tank and flushed, with the particulates and some DE material, into a separate chamber for disposal (see pages 107 to 111).

Most DE filters are equipped with a backwash valve that enables this process; newer models also feature a separation tank with a canvas strainer that

contains the flushed DE material and allows the backwash water to flow into a sewer or storm drain, which keeps the cakey substance from clogging the municipal water system, enabling the pool owner to disposed of it properly—an extra step that an increasing number of city codes require.

Backwashing, which is also conducted for sand filters, is only somewhat effective in restoring the filter's capacity to cleanse the water. It may take hundreds of gallons of pool water running backwards through the system and flushed out into the street or nearby swale to get most—but certainly not all—of the waste particles out of the DE material. With that water, whatever DE material is expelled during the backwash process must be replaced on the grids, which is difficult to estimate.

For that reason, as well as more stringent regulations for disposing of used DE during backwashing and the increasing cost of water needed to refill the pool, professionals recommend the process only during a thorough, in-season pool cleaning—

Most of the important information about your sand filter is printed on the label, including the types of sand media that you may use and the amount of sand required (this filter takes 200 pounds, or four 50-pound bags).

perhaps once or twice within a six-month period—with a complete clean-out and filter media replacement following (and perhaps just prior to) heavy seasonal use.

A complete DE filter cleaning is laborious and must be conducted carefully, but it is the only true way to restore the filter to its optimum capabilities and effectiveness. With the system turned off and the tank drained as much as possible, open the tank and remove the grid system. Hose down and scrub out both the grids and the inside of the tank (using water only, as soap or cleansers will leave a residue). Collect as much of the DE material as possible in a bag, which you can simply toss in your regular trash can. Replace the clean, uncoated grid system back into the tank, check the seals on the lid (and replace, if necessary) and close the tank tightly.

To recoat the grids with DE material, turn on the pump and allow it and the rest of the system to prime, then slowly add the dry, powdery substance at the main skimmer opening—perhaps closing off any others to facilitate maximum suction—until you've reached the stated capacity of DE for your filter. Take care not to add too much of the powdered DE at one time to avoid having it clog up in the system before it reaches the filter and attaches itself to the grids.

To know when to backwash or clean out a DE filter, look for telltale signs such as cloudy or dirty pool water that can't be rectified by normal chemical additives and water balancing, and keep a close eye on the pressure gauge and/or flow meter attached to the filter tank; some filter tanks have twin gauges—one monitoring the water coming in (the influent line), the other for the water going out (the effluent line)—to provide an even greater measure of diagnostics.

The pressure, stated in terms of pounds per square inch (psi) indicated on one or both gauges will increase as the filter—DE, sand, or cartridge—gets dirtier with captured waste and debris particles. An increase of 10 psi from the tank's normal amount of pressure indicates either a blockage upstream or, more likely, that it's time to clean or backwash the filter.

Sand Filters. Like DE filters, those that employ sand rely on a naturally occurring material (or media) to

How To Clean a DE Filter Grid

1

Unfasten the spring bolt that secures the steel band tightened around the middle of the DE tank. Remove the band, disconnect the plumbing outlet and lift off the top.

2

Remove the DE media grid from the tank by lifting up on the handles.

(Continued next page)

cleanse the pool or spa water as its flows through the tank. Typically, a sand filter uses a combination of special, pool-grade gravel and sand; as the water works its way through the media, the size of the granules, beginning with fine sand, increases to a progressively coarser mix of gravel before the water is expelled and moves on in the equipment set.

There are two types of sand filters. The first is called a rapid or high-rate sand filter, in which water is pressurized by both the pool's or spa's plumbing system and by the filter itself through the media to optimize filtration. The size and type of tank varies; once made of corrosion-resistant metal (such as stainless steel), newer models are constructed of fiberglass or plastic, making them lightweight and, in some cases, smaller and less obtrusive in the equipment set.

Unlike DE filters, the water in a sand filter enters from the top and is drawn through about 18" to 24"

of fine media and another 4" or so of increasingly rough-edged gravel and into a manifold at the bottom of the tank. It is then pushed up through a center pipe (isolated from the sand and gravel), and expelled—clean—back into the system and eventually the pool or spa. A pipe and valve at the bottom allows you to drain the system for cleaning and backwashing chores.

Operating at peak efficiency, a rapid sand filter is able to capture particles as small as about 42 microns; though that's much larger than what a DE filter can catch, sand filters are more easily and effectively backwashed compared to DE units to restore optimum filtration. Though like a DE filter it takes hundreds of gallons of water to backwash a sand filter, there are fewer laws prohibiting the relatively slight amount of sand and gravel that might escape into the storm drain during the process. (Remember, though, that backwashing lowers the water volume of

3

DE material will not pass through the holes in the filter fabric. Instead, it clings to the outside of the grid. It can look like quite a mess. It is recommended that the DE filter grid be removed and cleaned at least twice a year.

4

Place the filter grid onto a tarp and spray it with a hose and spray nozzle to dislodge as much of the material as you can. After the material is removed, inspect each filter for tears or other damage that would allow new DE material to pass through. If you find damage, replace the filter grid. If not, continue cleaning.

the pool, thus requiring you to replenish it to the midline of the skimmer opening to keep the system running smoothly.)

In addition, the sand media itself is more easily replaced—and less often—than DE material; simply, after a complete clean-out every two or three years, a new mix of pool-grade sand and gravel is poured directly into the tank, thus restoring the rough surface areas of the media that clean the water and capture the debris it contains.

Although this specially-graded media is designed to last at least a few years (perhaps several) before requiring a complete replacement, it should be inspected annually and cleaned, when necessary (such as when the pressure gauge reads more than

10 psi of normal), with sodium biosulfate or a comparable cleaning solution added to the mix and allowed to filter through the media during a normal recirculation cycle. In addition, pool and spa professionals recommend replacing the top 6 inches of the sand layer every year.

The second type of sand filter is called a free-flow, sand-and-gravel filter. Rather than a separate, above-ground tank, the filter is located underwater above the main drain. As water is pulled into the system through the drain, it passes through the gravel and sand media, delivering filtered water into the system. Far less effective than traditional, pressurized filtration, a free-flow filter is typically used to help maintain ponds and other "natural" water

5

To clean grease, grime and certain mineral deposits from the filter, soak it in a filter cleaning bath. A 30 gallon trash can makes a good vessel for soaking the filter grid. Fill the trash can with water and mix in granulated filter cleaner according to the manufacturer's directions.

6

Submerge the filter and let it soak overnight.

(Continued next page)

features in a garden rather than for recreational swimming pools and spas.

Routine maintenance of a sand filter is similar to that for any type of pool or spa filter: keep an eye on the pressure gauge (and flow meter, if one is installed; see below), listen for sounds of laboring or rough action, watch for sand in the pool or spa water, and periodically check the backwash and/or drain lines for any clogs or remnants of filter media.

Cartridge Filters. The third and most recently developed type of pool or spa filter is a cartridge unit. In cross-section, a cartridge filter appears similar to a DE device, with multiple layers or grids of fabric-coated material. In this case, however, the fabric—

typically a tightly woven, pleated polyester mesh—serves as the filter media.

A new or recently cleaned cartridge media can filter particles as small as 20 microns, making it about three times more effective than a sand filter. A cylindrical cartridge filter tank also is shorter and thinner than that of a DE or sand filter, measuring about 4 ft. high and 18" in diameter. Its smaller size helps lower the total dynamic head of the system, perhaps downsizing the motor-pump or at least allowing it work more efficiently.

Because there is neither DE nor sand and gravel involved in the filtration process, cartridge filters are easier and faster to keep clean and restore to near-

7

Clean the gasket that fits between the two halves of the tank, using warm water. Also clean the rim of the tank cover thoroughly. Replace the gasket around the tank top.

8

Remove the tank drain plug and hose out the filter tank and plumbing connection. Scrub any stubborn material with a stiff bristle scrub brush.

optimum performance. They also don't require backwashing, which saves a significant amount of water.

Instead, to clean a cartridge filter (as determined by a higher-than-normal pressure reading), you simply pop the tank cover, remove the filter media, and use a pressurized nozzle on a garden hose to spray off the debris. Use your fingers to separate the media grids to get the water deep into the pleats, toward the center of the filter cartridge.

Once the large, visible debris is removed, fill a clean, dark-colored trash bin with a mixture of cool water, trisodium phosphate, and muriatic acid (each at one cup per five gallons, added to the water

separately) and let the filter cartridge soak for an hour in a shaded or cool location to loosen debris particles and oils set deep in the pleats. Then, remove and hose down the filter media thoroughly, replace it in the tank, check the lid's gaskets (and replace if brittle, cracked, or damaged), and secure the lid tightly to maintain the water pressure in the system.

As with the motor-pump and skimmer strainer basket, it might be worth the investment to purchase a second filter for the tank so that you can replace the dirty one with a clean media and get the system back online rather than spending 90 minutes properly cleaning the filter before restarting the system.

9

Replace the clean filter inside the DE tank making sure the water tube sleeve in the filter grid fits cleanly over the vertical water tube in the tank bottom.

10

Tighten the band that secures the two halves of the filter. Rap the band lightly with a rubber mallet as you tighten to make sure it is not kinking and is making a clean connection with the filter housing.

That way, you can allow the filter cartridge to dry out and leach oils and other debris, making it easier to clean and be made ready for the next cleaning cycle.

The primary downside to cartridge filters is that a second or replacement filter cartridge is more expensive than a bag of DE or pool-rated sand and gravel. Cartridge filters also get dirtier faster, requiring more cleaning cycles than the other two filter types—a process itself that taxes the media's effectiveness. After about 4 or 5 cleanings, the media might be exhausted and require replacement with a new cartridge. Obviously poor filtration (as evidenced by either cloudy water or the use of more chemicals to

keep it clean and balanced) without a significant increase in pressure indicates that water is simply passing freely through the filter media without capturing most, if any, debris particles and therefore needs to be replaced, not just cleaned.

Because of their smaller size, filtration effectiveness, and relatively simple cleaning process, cartridge filters are the principal system in portable spas; for the same reasons, and because there is no backwashed waste to manage or dispose of properly, slightly larger and more complex cartridge grids are becoming increasingly popular for full-sized pools, as well.

How to Backwash a Filter

The backwash process is used for periodic cleaning of sand and DE filters. In essence, it reverses the normal flow of water through the filter, effectively rinsing out the medium and discharging the waste water away from the pump, often through a flexible discharge tube. Backwash your system at regular intervals (once a month is a common timeframe). If you notice that the water flow rate is slowed, it's likely that your filter has clogged somewhat. Try back-washing as your first remedy. If the flow rate does not improve, you either have a clog or blockage in the waterlines (you'll probably need to call a pool service techni-cian) or your pump/motor may need replacing.

1

Start by making sure at least one valve that regulates pipes leading to and from the filter is open. Shut off power to the pump, either by shutting off the circuit breaker that controls the pump or by flipping a power switch.

2

Turn the handle on the backwash valve (a multiport valve) from the "filter" setting to the "backwash" setting.

3

Let the water discharge. You may want to attach a piece of piping or a flexible tube to the discharge outlet to direct water away from the equipment set area. Restore power to the pump. Let the pump run for about 90 seconds. Shut off power to the pump and change the valve setting to "rinse." Restore power to the pump and run at "rinse" for 10 to 15 seconds. Shut off power, set valve back to "filter" and restore power to resume normal operation. The process normally results in the loss of up to 100 gallons of pool water, so it may be necessary to add water to the pool.

How to Clean a Sand Filter

1

Open the air release valve at the top of the filter to depressurize the sand tank so it can be drained. Note: Always open valves on the inflow and outflow lines before you turn on the filter pump. Closed valves can cause dangerous pressure buildup in the tank.

2

A small cap at the top of the sand tank can be unscrewed so you can inspect the sand and remove small amounts of debris without unbolting the the two halves of the tank.

To get the water from the pool or spa through the various equipment set components and back to the vessel requires a reliable conduit or channel, specifically the pipes, fittings, and valves of the system.

Multiport valves. A multiport or three-port valve redirects water from one pipe into two or more pipes, allowing it to be shared or redirected within a complex plumbing system. Typically employing a gasketed (or positive seal) ball valve mechanism to completely block water flow when engaged, the device may also allow water in only one direction, shutting off the flow to the other pipe (or pipes) connected to it.

Multiport valves are necessary when a pool and a spa share equipment. They can be controlled, either manually or automatically, to supply or receive water to one or both vessels. Manual devices are controlled by a handle that extends from the top of the valve, while automatic versions feature a small motor that performs that operation based on a timed schedule or remote control, especially convenient when the equipment set is secluded or difficult to access. The remote control (usually a poolside keypad or touch screen) often manages several components, including the heater, lights, spa jets, and water features.

Multiport valves are also used in pools and spas to control or facilitate backwashing cycles for DE and sand filters (directing waste water

Unscrew the bolts securing the two halves of the filter. A nut driver mounted in a cordless drill/driver makes efficient work of this job. Place the nuts and bolts into a container to avoid losing any of them.

Bail out the old sand from the filter and dispose of it properly. Take care to avoid damaging the internal filter parts.

(Continued next page)

to a spigot and hose while blocking it from returning to the system). Other uses include draining water from individual components in the equipment set or skid pad in need of maintenance without having to drain the entire plumbing system, and bypassing ancillary devices, such as those serving water features, when they need repair, cleaning, or are simply not in operation.

Maintaining a multiport or three-port valve is, like most pool and spa chores, a practice of prevention. The most common problem with such devices is leaks, which are usually attributed to a loose or improperly gasketed cover, corroded lid fasteners, or faulty fittings connecting the valve to the pipes it serves.

Multiport valve gaskets, specifically, need to be kept lubricated with pure silicone (an oil-based lubricant will dissolve and dry out) at least twice a year, or as needed if the ball mechanism operation becomes stiff and the handle (and shaft it controls) is difficult to turn. The screws holding the cover in place also need to be replaced if they show any signs of rust or corrosion, ideally with stainless steel fasteners that resist such effects of water and moisture exposure.

On automatic units, the motor also requires care. Water or moisture in the motor housing creates an electrolysis that eventually disintegrates the motor shaft that turns the ball valve mechanism, thus rendering the entire device ineffective; another possible cause of a burned out motor is a stuck (or improperly

5

Before replacing the filter lid, clean the round gasket and the channels it fits into with warm water. Replace the gasket.

6

It isn't critical to remove every grain of old sand, but you can use a wet-and-dry shop vacuum to remove most of the sand from around the fingers at the bottom of the filter tank. While they're exposed, inspect each finger to make sure none of the slots is blocked with algae or debris.

or un-lubricated) valve mechanism. In either case, and even if there is an active electrical current to the device, the motor is best replaced rather than repaired. No electrical current, meanwhile, indicates a problem with the power supply, which may be its connection to the device, a short in the line, or an issue at the service box or subpanel.

Reverse-flow valves. These are valves that enable the water flow to run backwards through the system, or at least sections and certain devices within it, such as to backwash a filter (see also "Backwash Valves," below). Reverse-flow valves have also been installed to run heated water through system and out the main drain and/or floor outlets in the pool bottom or lower

sections of the pool wall to more uniformly heat the water in the entire vessel, rather than just through the supply inlets located within the top two or three feet of the water line.

Reverse flow valves are somewhat controversial, however, and some pool experts question their value and consider them problematic—one more device to maintain or cause problems, especially if it's motorized to operate automatically or by remote control. As mentioned earlier, backwashing a sand or DE filter has become environmentally sensitive, both from a waste and water-use perspective, thus fueling the debate further regarding the worth of reverse-flow

7

If you find that sand is mysteriously appearing in your pool (and your house is miles from the nearest beach), chances are that one of the fingers in your sand filter's finger hub is damaged. The fingers have slots that are small enough that sand will not fit through them, but still allow water to be drawn in. If the area around a slot breaks, the sand grains may be able to pass through and will migrate out into your pool along with the filtered water. Fingers can be removed either by unscrewing or with a twist fitting.

8

Replenish the sand in the filter, making sure to use sand that has been sieved to the correct size for sand filters. The required amount of sand is printed on your filter nameplate. Reattach the cover.

mechanisms in favor of alternative filter types and cleaning methods.

Existing pools or spas equipped with reverse-flow valves can be turned off or even disassembled or removed from the plumbing system to allow a traditional water flow through the equipment set or skid pad. It's critical to shut off all power and water flow through the system when maintaining, cleaning, and certainly removing any component; in the case of the latter, you'll likely be required to replace the device with a section of new pipe or perhaps install an entirely new length between devices on either end of the valve's location.

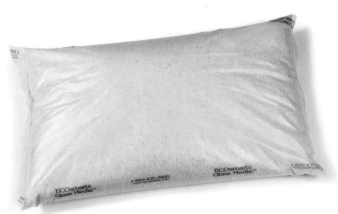

Alternative (nonsand) media is now available at some pool materials suppliers. The grains are sized to work in a sand filter, but it is a more effective filtering agent.

The typical sand filter has a two-part, egg-shaped reservoir. Unfiltered water from the pool enters the reservoir and sprays out of the inflow tube and up against the top of the tank. From there, the water rains down onto the sand filtering medium and is drawn to the bottom of the tank and back into the pool via the slotted fingers at the bottom of the reservoir.

Backwash valves. Like reverse-flow valves, these devices enable water to flow in the opposite direction, in this particular case through a sand or DE filter to facilitate a backwash procedure. The valve, in fact, is an integral component of such filters (not

Pool filters have a pressure gauge located near the backwash valve so you can monitor how well the system is functioning.

added on later or elsewhere in the equipment set), unlike remotely located reverse flow valves.

There are two types of backwash valves. Piston-driven units feature a handle (usually located on top of the filter) that controls a pair of two rolled pins within the filter. The pins serve as stops to direct water in either a normal or reverse flow through the device. In a backwash mode, water driven and pressurized by the motor-pump upstream in the system enters the filter from its outlet opening (in normal position, where filtered water would flow out of the device), through the filter media, and exit the inlet opening into a waste repository or separate plumbing line that is directed and carried to a storm drain or swale away from the pool or spa, typically by a length of garden hose connected to the waste line during backwashing.

▶ Troubleshooting Tip

If you have a rapid-sand filter and notice sand in your pool or spa, check the backwash valve on the filter to make sure it is in the proper (normal) position to allow the water to flow through the filter rather than in reverse (as it would for a backwash cycle). If that's not the problem, it may be that some of the sand has eroded to the point that it is small enough to get into the tank's manifold and be expelled with the filtered water, signaling that the media needs to be replaced.

Above-ground Cartridge Filters

Cartridge-style filters for swimming pools are maintained in much the same manner as smaller spa filters (see pages 122 to 123), except the larger filter housing unit should also be cleaned during maintenance.

Remove the drain plug and rinse out the tank bottom. Also rinse and clean the inside of the tank top.

Large filter cartridges for pools can be backwashed in the same manner as sand and DE filters (see pages 112 to 113). It is still necessary to remove and clean the filter cartridge from time to time.

Clean the filter cartridge with a hose and sprayer. Occasionally you should refresh the filter by soaking it in a filter bath overnight (see page 109).

How to Remove a Spa Filter

The debris tray and filter cartridge are accessed through the trap. The tray collects floating debris that's drawn in by the pump. It should be cleaned after every use.

The filter cartridge should be inspected regularly and cleaned at least once a month during normal spa usage.

Backwash Valves

The backwash valve is a type of multiport valve that directs the flow of water through your filtration system. It is used primarily during filter maintenance to allow you to backwash the filter (see pages 112 to 113)

A filter-cleaning nozzle directs water from a hose into the filter pleats for a more thorough cleaning that will not damage the filter material.

The second type of backwash valve is a rotary device. Exclusive to vertical DE filters, rotary backwash valves employ a gasketed ball mechanism (similar to what's used for multi-port valves) to redirect the water flow through the filter depending on the mode, normal or reverse. This type of backwash valve is mounted to the bottom of the filter tank and controlled by a handle; newer models, however, may be available in automatic or remote-controlled versions for added convenience. Like a piston valve, the waste water and filter media material (sand or DE) is directed to a waste line or container and, more recently, separated for disposal.

In addition, some sand filters are equipped with multiport backwash valves, which allow a "rinse" cycle of clean water through the backwashed filter media to wash out the integral openings and valves in the filter before engaging a normal filtration mode and water flow.

Whether your sand or DE filter features a piston or rotary backwash valve, it's important to know that these valves can only be engaged (or disengaged) when the motor-pump is not running, such as between scheduled recirculation and filtration cycles. In other words, if the pump is running, you can't turn the backwash valve handle to initiate a different flow through the device.

To maintain a backwash valve, make sure the O-rings or seals gasketing the valve from air and water leakage are supple and free of cracks or other signs of wear, and replace them as soon as they show such signs (a small drip or leak from the backwash line is a good indicator in addition to a visual inspection). A neglected backwash valve seal can, over time, allow water to drain out of the filter and flow back into the pool, resulting in unbalanced water quality and perhaps even affecting the pump's ability to remain properly primed, and thus run dry, overheat, and become damaged.

Hydrostatic valves. This structure in an in-ground pool or spa can receive a significant amount of stress from moisture build-up in the backfill behind the walls and floor of the vessel. A hydrostatic valve (also called an equalizer line), part of a pool or spa skimmer or main drain assembly (see below), helps relieve that pressure to preserve the integrity of the structure and ward off costly leaks and cracks in the concrete, fiberglass, or liner.

Essentially, a hydrostatic valve is a check valve, allowing the usually small amount of water that might collect along the walls of an in-ground pool or spa to flow into the skimmer from below but block the pool or spa water from flowing back through and into the backfill. Groundwater is drawn up through a length of perforated, PVC pipe extending along the pool wall under each skimmer to a float that blocks large debris particles (mainly dirt) but enables the water to flow into the skimmer opening and through the equipment set.

Pressure gauges and air release valves. Pressure gauges are essential and integral to the proper maintenance of the filter, indicating blockages upstream or down or, more commonly, the need to backwash or clean the filter to restore its effectiveness. But such devices are also handy, for the similar reasons, when attached to other components in the equipment set because they enable you to more easily pinpoint and isolate obstructions, leaks, or other problems in the system.

How to Clean a Spa Filter

1

The filter should be chemically cleaned every two months or so to remove oil, dirt and scale residue. Add powdered filter cleaner and water to a cleaning canister and mix thoroughly according to directions on the container.

2

Insert the dirty filter into the canister, attach the canister cover and let the filter soak overnight.

Pressure gauges installed on pool or spa equipment components typically provide a reading between 0 and 60 psi (pounds per square inch). Normal operating psi—indicating a clean, open flow of water through the system or a particular device pressurized by the motor-pump and other factors—varies slightly each time you clean the system, install a new or repair an existing component (especially the filter), or make some other adjustment to the equipment. Once the system has been restarted and primed, the pressure gauge will read "normal," whatever that is, and generally remain at that pressure reading during each recirculation cycle.

Each time you restart the system after a thorough cleaning or repair/replacement job, it's important to note what each pressure gauge reads as "normal," and, if possible, mark that reading right on the gauge's glass with a permanent felt pen as a handy reference (you can also write it down in your maintenance log or other record-keeping method). That way, when you check each gauge during your normal cleaning or maintenance routine, you can know if the pressure is running higher or lower than "normal."

If a pressure gauge is reading lower than normal, it indicates a clog or perhaps a leak somewhere upstream, or prior to, the device

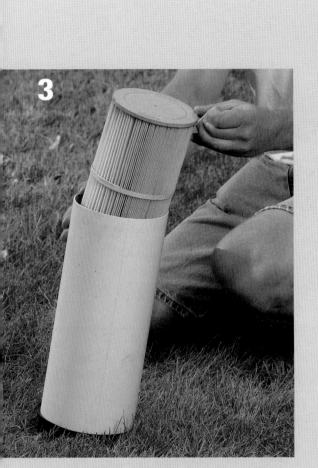

Remove the filter and rinse clean with a hose and filter nozzle attachment (See page 121). Pleated filters should last for several years. But once the filter material begins to visibly degrade, replace the cartridge and filter.

and able to fill (or prime) the pump and the system.

On pool and spa filters, especially, an air release valve may supplement the pressure gauge. Though it provides no readout, it does enable you to let excess air escape the filter and help restore proper water pressure through the device. Often a simple, threaded plug, an air release valve is typically installed on one end of a T-fitting connected to the filter, with a pressure gauge attached to other end of the fitting. Your only chore to maintain it is to make sure it is secured tightly to the fitting (and that the fitting is tight to the filter or other device) so it doesn't leak air uncontrolled, and to replace it if it shows wear or damage.

Sight glasses. Though not technically a valve, sight glasses are a helpful (if ancillary) component of a pool or spa plumbing system. Essentially, a sight glass is a section of pipe with a portion of its length cut out and replaced with a water- and air-tight metal frame and glass or clear plastic section that allows you to see the water flowing through the pipe.

Sight glasses are especially helpful during the backwash cycle of a DE or sand filter (see above). Set between the filter and a separate waste chamber, the sight glass allows you or a technician to monitor the quality of the water as the filter is cleaned; once the water appears clear, the backwash cycle is complete.

Like pressure gauges and air release valves, sight glasses can come in handy when installed at other points along the equipment set as a way to more easily diagnose or locate a leak or other problem; however, each sight glass section requires fittings on both ends to connect securely to another section of pipe or a device, increasing the head loss of the overall system and thus impacting the sizing of the motor-pump, and perhaps the filter.

Sight glasses are set permanently into a pool or spa plumbing system to maintain the set's water pressure and mitigate leaks, so they are not easily removed. However, if the glass becomes too cloudy, dirty, or certainly cracked or broken, the entire section needs to be replaced, usually by cutting it out and replacing that section with a longer length of pipe securely connected at each end to the rest of the system.

being monitored by the gauge; simply, there's not enough water getting into the device to provide enough pressure for it to operate properly.

Conversely, if the gauge reads 15 psi higher than normal, there's likely some sort of obstruction downstream from the device, or perhaps in the component itself (such as a clogged or dirty filter), which also requires some detection and maintenance to restore peak operating efficiency. If the gauge reading fluctuates, it probably indicates a low water level in the pool or spa and/or an obstruction in the skimmer, requiring you to fill the vessel until the water level is above the skimmer's weir line

Heaters and Electrical Systems

Pool owners and industry experts argue over the necessity of a heater in an equipment set; surely, one is not required to facilitate proper filtration. Adding this extra component also increases the heat loss calculation for the overall system, making the motor-pump work harder and resulting in higher energy use and costs. It's also one more device to maintain within an already complex set. A heater is, of course, requisite for a spa or hot tub, which is discussed in more detail later in this chapter.

But if you want to get the most use out of a swimming pool, a heating system is essential. Even in predominantly warm climates, such as in the Southwest and Gulf Coast, where pools are most prevalent and normally used year-round, heaters enable owners and their families and friends to enjoy the water any time of the day or night, as well as across multiple seasons. At last count, about 60 percent of all new pools are equipped with a heater—a rate that is rising steadily.

Heaters for pools and spas are designed differently than a typical water heater for your home. Primarily, there is no tank containing hot water, unless you consider the pool or spa to be that reservoir. Like other components of the equipment set, the heater is sized according to the pool's capacity or volume of water, estimated heat loss caused by evaporation, sun and shade exposure, and even altitude (the higher up, the larger the heater). The typical temperature differential is also a factor: that is, the difference between the desired maximum temperature and the average

Swimming pool heaters are fueled by natural gas or propane in most cases, although electric heaters are more common in some places. Removable access panels conceal and protect the heater and circuitry.

ambient temperature for the pool's location. Each pool heater also is rated for its flow rate (maximum gallons per minute) and BTU output, the latter a reflection of how much heat energy it is able to create. A BTU (British Thermal Unit) raises one pound of water one degree F.

A properly sized heater can warm the water volume of a full-size, residential swimming pool about 25 degrees F, at the most—a process that takes about 24 hours to complete. If the heater is too small, the unit won't heat the water fast enough or be able to reach the desired temperature setting; too large, and it's a waste of energy.

Unheated and uncovered, a pool's water temperature will typically settle as an average of a given day's high and low ambient temperature; on hot, summer days, it may not need to be heated at all, at least during the afternoon and early evening hours, but may require a boost during milder spells, seasons, and times of the day to reach a comfortable level, usually about 80 to 85 degrees F for recreational swimming and pool play.

How pool heaters work. Pool heaters heat the water as it flows from the filter through a series of hollow-tube coils, also called heat exchangers. Modern units transfer about 90 percent of the heat from the coils to the water, making them very efficient in that regard (the U.S. Department of Energy requires at least a 78 percent efficiency rating on all new units). Overall, however, pool heaters can require a significant amount of energy to operate, but there are ways to lower energy consumption (see "Energy Saving Tips," below).

The heat exchanger tubes are warmed by radiant heat from a burner tray below the coils. The burner tray creates heat from an energy source, typically electricity, natural gas, or propane (heating oil, while a possible source, is uncommon in residential-sized pool heaters). Systems with a pilot light also require a dedicated electrical circuit to ignite the flame when the heater is engaged. That energy dynamic, plus the fact that the water itself is pressurized within the overall plumbing system (and thus through the heating unit), makes a heater one of the most potentially hazardous components of a pool or spa operation.

As water passes through each tube or coil, it is warmed from 6 to 9 degrees F; the tubes themselves are typically made of copper, which conducts heat very effectively, but also can corrode if the pool or spa water is chronically out of balance. In addition to a thermostat (similar to what's in your home to determine and set the temperature), the heater employs an integral flow-control valve that regulates the heat in the coils to prevent them from overheating, which can cause condensation to form if there is too great a disparity between the temperature of the cool water coming into the heater and the heated water going out to the pool.

Most heaters for residential pools are fueled by natural gas or propane, primarily because that energy source is the most available, cost-effective, and

Energy Saving Tips

In addition to recent improvements in traditional gas and electric pool heaters that, by design, help reduce their energy use and cost, pool and spa owners can lessen that burden even more with a few simple energy-efficient practices, such as:

- Except in the heat of the day (when the ambient temperature is above the pool's unheated temperature), use a cover to mitigate evaporation and heat loss into the outside air; a security cover is an especially effective thermal retardant.
- Heat the pool only for peak-use times, such as over a weekend, rather than on a constant, daily schedule.
- Once the pool is heated to the desired temperature, program the thermostat during low-use times to maintain a slightly lower temperature instead of turning off the heater entirely and allowing the water to cool to its average ambient level. That way, it requires less time and energy to raise it back up.
- Build a fence to block prevailing breezes over the water surface and mitigate evaporation and heat loss.
- Keep a floating or underwater thermometer in the water to get an accurate reading of its temperature and to gauge your comfort level. You may find that you can stand it a little cooler, and adjust to it faster, especially if you are using the pool for exercise (which generates body heat).

Solar swimming pool covers are not to be confused with solar-powered pool heaters, which are installed in line as part of the equipment set. But solar covers do serve the double role of preventing evaporation while transmitting heat from the sun to the pool water.

efficient for most homeowners. Electric heaters, meanwhile, have a higher operating cost, heat the water at a slower rate, and require a high number of amperes (or amps) from a dedicated circuit at the electrical service box when used for a full-sized pool. For spas and hot tubs, however, they are compact and efficient enough to serve the lower water volume (if higher temperature differential) of that vessel.

Alternative pool and spa heating systems have emerged as well, to address the energy use and cost issues associated with gas and electric-fueled units. Consider the following options given appropriate circumstances, such as the cost and availability of more traditional energy sources, climate conditions, pool use, and personal preferences.

Solar-powered systems. Modern solar-powered pool heating systems are much more reliable and efficient than those that emerged in the mid-1970s. Like traditional heaters, they feature hollow tubes through which the water flows and is heated via thermal exchange; the difference is that, instead of using natural gas or electricity to heat the tubs, a solar system uses the sun's heat by absorbing it directly into the tubes and also by reflecting it off a glass-surfaced (or "glazed") plastic or metal frame, called panels or flat-plate collectors. The panels are insulated on the back (non-glazed) side to retard heat loss.

The glazed panels and the tubes are oriented to capture the most solar heat possible, and are therefore typically located on a roof or in an open area as near as possible to the pool's equipment set. The placement should, if possible, protect the panels from prevailing winds, which might reduce the temperature or, if strong enough, damage the components. If it's far enough away from the rest of the equipment, the system may require a booster pump to keep the water properly pressurized and moving at the desired and designed flow rate.

Most solar pool heaters have an "open loop" configuration in which the water flows through and is heated by the coils. Closed-loop systems, which are more common in desert climates that experience extremely hot daytime temperatures but near-freezing overnight lows, keep the water out of the tubes; instead, a separate pump circulates and heats antifreeze through the panels and coils, and then

Solar heaters require about three-quarters of the total surface area of the pool to be the sole heating plant for your pool. And even then they are dependent on changing weather conditions. For this reason solar heaters are usually supplementary to traditional fuel-based heaters. But they can still save a lot of money on energy costs.

uses a separate heat exchanger to transfer the heat to the water. In addition to protecting the coil and panels from potential freeze-thaw damage, a closed-loop design also mitigates potential corrosion from the chemicals contained in the water from causing scale buildup, cracks, and leaks.

In a climate in which there are a significant number of sunny days, and presuming an ideal orientation for solar heat collection, a solar pool heater can generate perhaps 2,800 BTUs per collector. The number or size of the collectors (or panels) depends somewhat on the size of the pool; generally, the square footage of all of the panels should be about 75 percent of the vessel's square footage. An 800-sq.-ft. pool, for instance, would need 600 sq. ft. of collectors, or about nineteen 4×8 ft. solar collector panels.

While solar collector design has certainly evolved from the obtrusive and ugly metal-framed units of the technology's early days, mounting 19 panels on your roof or finding an open place for them in the yard might be problematic. For that reason, as well as the fact that the sun is not always shining brightly overhead and is therefore an unreliable source of heat, solar heaters for pools are often used to supplement traditional heating systems.

Above-ground pools are popular for installation of solar heaters, largely because the water volume tends to be lower and the space next to the raised poolside provides a perfect location for solar collectors.

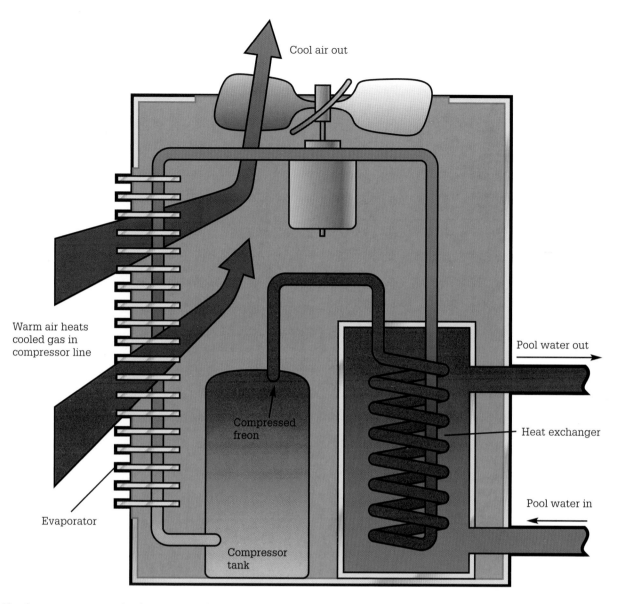

Cool air out

Warm air heats
cooled gas in
compressor line

Evaporator

Compressed
freon

Compressor
tank

Pool water out

Heat exchanger

Pool water in

Heat pumps are growing in popularity for heating pools in warmer climates. Functioning like reverse air conditioners, heat pumps use compression to raise the temperature of a gas (usually freon or Xenon) in a closed tube system. The heated gas warms pool water in a heat exchanger, cooling the gas in the process. The cooled gas circulates through an evaporator, where it is warmed by the ambient air before it is recompressed and the cycle starts anew.

In a supplemental heater scenario, the water is first heated by the solar tubes and panels and then run through the standard heater. That way, the traditional unit doesn't have to work as hard, as long, or as often (or use as much energy) to raise the temperature to the desired level. To avoid unnecessary energy consumption by the motor-pump serving the entire system, thermostat sensors indicate whether the panels are warm enough to heat the water. If not, the system automatically engages a valve to bypass the solar coils and panels and send the water directly to the main heater.

Solar panels can also be used to simply collect the sun's heat and convert it to electricity, rather than specifically or exclusively to heat water. In that case, the electricity is either stored in batteries or, more likely, used instead of the electricity supplied by the local utility. Though not directly heating the pool water, such systems reduce the overall utility-supplied electricity consumption of the house, including what's used by the pool heater.

Maintaining solar heaters. Unlike traditional pool heating systems, open-loop solar schemes have few moving arts and no electricity and/or combustion fuel to worry about, making them safer and easier to maintain. Owners should, however, check the tubes periodically for leaks and ream them out, as necessary, to get rid of scale build-up from the water's chemicals.

Heater Capacity Requirements

HEATER INPUT: (BTU/HR) SPA VOLUME (GAL)	125,000	175,000	250,000	325,000	400,000
	MINUTES REQUIRED FOR EACH 30-DEGREE TEMPERATURE RISE				
200	30	21	15	12	9
300	45	32	23	17	14
400	60	43	30	23	19
500	75	54	38	29	23
600	90	64	45	35	28
700	105	75	53	40	33
800	120	86	60	46	37
900	135	96	68	52	42
1000	150	107	75	58	47

When dirt and other debris collects on the panel surfaces it reduces the panel's heat absorption capabilities, so clean them with soap and water periodically. Every few years, the panels may need to be recoated or reglazed to restore them to peak efficiency.

Heat pumps. Another alternative heating system is a heat pump. Though it still requires natural gas, propane, or electricity, the system primarily employs the outside air to heat the water. For that reason, as with solar heating, a heat pump is generally best in hot, year-round swimming climates, where ambient temperatures remain above 45 degrees F; otherwise, there's probably not enough heat in the air to allow the unit to be effective.

A heat pump works similarly to other heating systems, in that the heat is exchanged or transferred to the water. In particular, the unit removes the warmth from the air by compressing a gas (typically Freon) and using the energy generated to heat the coils or tubes in the exchanger.

Heat pumps are generally more energy-efficient than gas or electric-powered pool heaters, and often last longer, but they're also more expensive than conventional heating systems. They are generally inappropriate for spas, as well, because they take much longer to heat the water. For a pool, however, a heat pump is able to maintain a desired temperature longer than a gas-powered unit.

Radiant heaters. Like the sun will heat the inside of your car, even on a cold day, radiant heating systems for pools employ copper tubes set just behind the walls and floor of an in-ground concrete pool. Water from a separate source heated by a boiler flows through the tubes and transfers its heat through the thermal mass of the concrete and plaster, ideally creating an even heat throughout the water. The ground (or backfill) helps insulate the system to mitigate heat loss and retain the heat generated and exchanged.

Obviously, a radiant heating system is complex and requires careful thought and planning during a pool's construction, but can be an effective alternative if no other energy sources or systems are available or practical.

Spa heaters. Though not for filtration, heaters are necessary for spas and hot tubs, assuming you own one to enjoy a relaxing hot soak. Specially sized and designed for spa skid packs and custom equipment sets (including within a system shared with a pool), these heating units are capable of raising the temperature of the water to more than 100 degrees F and in a relatively short amount of time compared to a full-size swimming pool.

Like full-sized pools, though, spa heaters are sized for the vessel's water volume and bather load. Portable spa skid packs include right-sized heaters, but an in-ground or custom-built spa or hot tub requires careful calculation and considerations regarding how often you'll use the spa. A 400-gallon spa with a temperature differential of 25 degrees F and a heat-up time of 30 minutes, for instance, requires a heating unit with a 250,000 BTU capacity.

If the spa shares equipment with a pool, it's likely you'll need a separate heating system for each vessel, as the heating requirements and temperature differences between ambient and heater water are vastly different between a pool and a spa.

Pool Heater Maintenance & Repair

Any type of pool heater, just like any component within the pool's equipment set or portable spa skid pack, requires regular maintenance. Modern heating units, however, are self-cleaning; unlike a heater or a pump, they do not need to be disassembled to keep their parts in good working order.

- The copper coils and the valves and connections between the heater and the rest of the pool's or spa's plumbing system can become corroded, loose, or leak over time. The insides of the tubes, for instance, might develop high levels of calcium scale buildup from the sanitizers and other chemicals present in the water as it passes through the heater.

- When a heater seems to be on the fritz, it's smart to consider other components of the overall system before rushing into a repair job or replacement unit. In fact, you might discover that a problem with the heater can be traced to a dirty filter or another obstruction in the system that is hampering water flow, and therefore the ability to heat enough water to raise the pool water's temperature.

- Start by making sure the pump is fully or adequately primed and operating properly and, with that, the water in the pool or spa is at a correct level and the skimmer and main drain(s) are clean of debris to enable a good flow of water through the system. Check other system devices, namely the pump, for any obstructions or air or water leaks, and clean and re-lubricate them, as necessary. If the problem persists, check the systems serving the heater directly, such as electrical and, if appropriate, natural gas or propane connections and valves. For instance, make sure the propane tank is full (or have it filled) and—with a pocket mirror—look to see that the pilot light is not only on when the heater is engaged, but that the flame is a healthy blue and measures 2" to 4". If you find a damaged connection or valve, replace it (or have it replaced), then retest the system.

- Make sure the thermostat is set at the desired temperature and that the switch or control mechanism is on or programmed to the heating schedule you desire. Even if it checks out, you may want to restart and/or reset the thermostat, time clock, or automatic controls to make sure.

- If everything up to that point checks out, you've likely narrowed the problem to the heater itself. Check the tubes for blockage caused by scale buildup and ream them out, if necessary. Then, check all of the connections and fittings, valves, and other exposed parts of the unit and replace any that are damaged or showing wear. Relubricate seals and gaskets and make sure the unit is closed tightly against air and moisture infiltration. If the problem persists, it's likely that a new heater is in order. Rarely is it practical to repair a pool or spa heater or any of its parts; rather, it's probably less expensive and more reliable to simply replace the entire unit. Because of the plumbing and electrical work involved, it's advisable to hire a professional pool technician to perform the work, as well as properly size the new unit and suggest some energy-saving alternatives, though high-level do-it-yourselfers can certainly tackle the job by following basic plumbing and electrical directions, as well as those for installing the new heater.

The multimeter is an electrical diagnostic tool that is a very valuable tool to own, whether or not you also own a spa or pool. With it you can test receptacle and other devices to measure the amount of current (if any) they contain. In this project we'll use the multimeter to check fuses in the control panel for continuity (that is, to find out if they're blown).

Troubleshooting Spa Heaters

Electric spa heaters contain automotive-style fuses and circuit boards of varying complexity that are located in the central control box, which resides in the spa equipment pack. Fuse failure is fairly common with home spas, so if your heater ceases to function, check the fuse first, using a multimeter (also check the circuit breaker in your home electrical service panel). If the fuse is blown you can probably find a new one at your pool and spa service store. Otherwise, bring the old fuse to an automotive parts store and there is a good chance they'll have a replacement part.

If your fuse is fine and the breaker is working, the heating element on your heater likely needs replacement. If you've ever changed an element on a water heater or electric oven, the process is very similar and not as difficult as it might sound.

Spa Control Boxes

The circuitry inside the control box that is the brains of the spa is protected by at least one 20 amp or 30 amp fuse. From time to time, the power source can surge or experience other conditions that cause the fuse to become blown.

How to Diagnose and Repair a Spa Heater

To inspect the fuses and heating element, first locate the spa control unit and remove the cover.

(Continued next page)

2

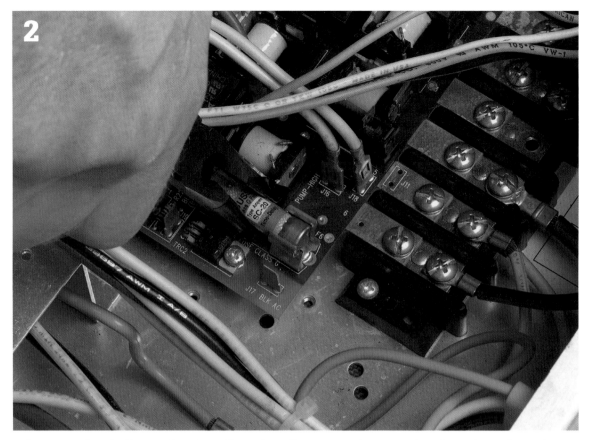

Before removing, testing or changing a fuse, shut off power to the spa at the subpanel or main service panel. To remove a fuse, use a fuse puller or wrap the jaws of a needlenose pliers in electrical tape. Then, grasp the fuse with the pliers and withdraw it from the housing.

Test the fuse for continuity using a multimeter. Continuity is tested by setting the multimeter to read ohms (usually indicated by an omega sign). With the multimeter switched on, touch one probe to each end of the fuse. If the fuse is good (the circuit has continuity), the readout will be 0.00. If the fuse is blown, the readout (usually "1") will not change when the ends are touched with the probes. Replacement fuses may be purchased at most pool and spa stores.

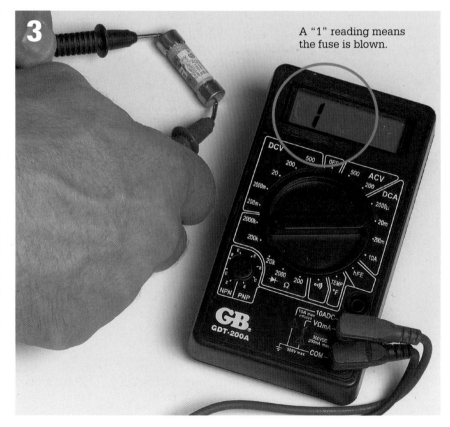

3

A "1" reading means the fuse is blown.

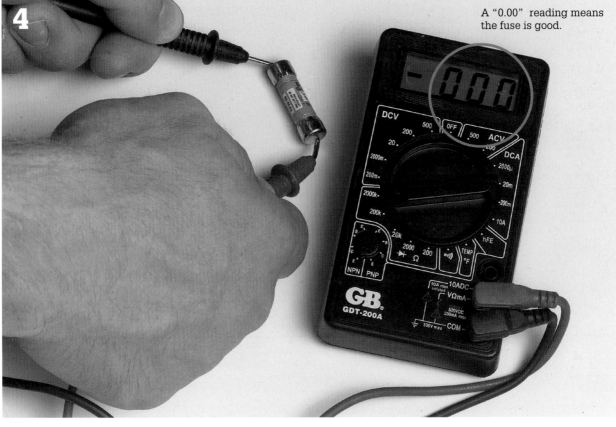

4

A "0.00" reading means the fuse is good.

A **reading of 0.00** means the fuse has continuity and is therefore functioning. The next most likely problem is that your heater element has burned out.

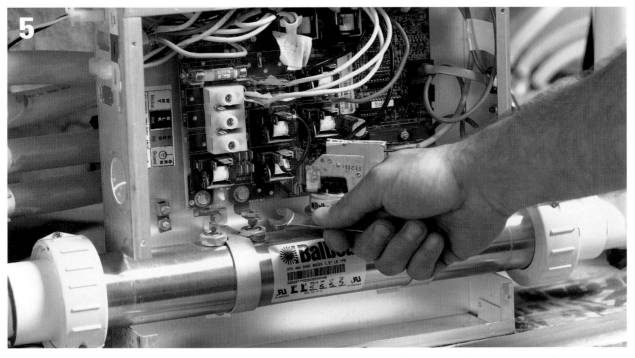

5

To inspect the element, you need to remove it from the cylindrical housing. Locate the copper straps that are bonded to the contact terminals for the heater element inside the cylindrical heater element housing. Remove the lock nuts that secure the straps and bend the straps upward and clear of the terminal contacts.

(Continued next page)

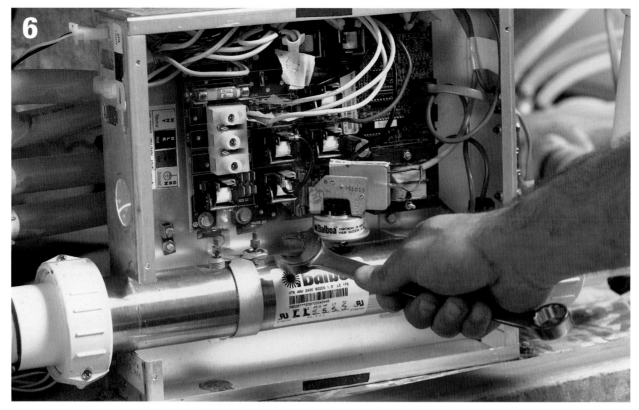

6

With an open-end wrench, loosen and remove the mounting nuts that secure the element contacts to the cylindrical housing.

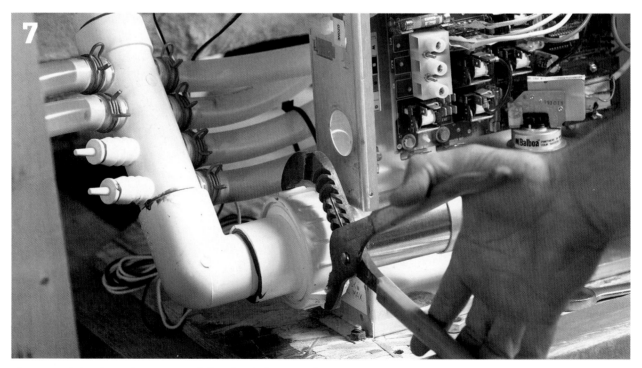

7

The water inlet from the pump and the circulating manifold are connected to the cylindrical housing with split-nut unions. Remove the unions, using a large channel lock pliers if necessary to loosen them. Note: These unions are common trouble spots for leaks to develop, particularly if a freeze causes them to crack. If your split nut union develops a leak, unscrew the set screw that holds the union together and fit the new split union over the flared end of the cylinder before joining the two union halves together.

Press the terminal contacts down through the holes in the cylindrical housing until they clear the top of the housing. Insert a pair of pliers into the open end of the housing and pull the heating element to loosen it. Pull it out of the housing and discard it.

Insert the replacement element into the housing with the contact terminals oriented upward. Slide it in until the contacts align with the holes and pop up. Reassemble the plumbing and attach the terminals in reverse step order from the removal of the old element.

Time Clocks

A time clock sets the schedule for the pool's or spa's recirculation and filtration process within its prescribed turnover rate. Most are designed to enable basic on and off settings within a 24-hour or perhaps a weeklong time frame. Like the motor-pump, time clocks work on electricity and, for reliability, are hardwired to a circuit at the service box (either shared or dedicated) rather than running on batteries or being plugged into an outlet.

The face of a typical time clock features a round face with the hours of the day, which rotates to a hand (or pointer) to indicate the time of day it is when you set it. Trippers (or "dogs" in pool and spa lingo) are then set to the desired on and off time, the length of which is determined by the turnover rate; the device usually provides more than one set of trippers so the water can be recirculated multiple times during the day during peak-use seasons.

Traditionally, time clocks are set manually, and replace even more simple on-off switches (which are easily neglected, wasting energy) to engage the pool or spa system. On the other end of the spectrum, electronic programmable time clocks offer touch- or menu-driven screens and keypad controls to set the circulation schedule, as well as the operation of water features, the heating system, lighting, in-wall cleaners, and perhaps even the cover. Some even

Timers are found most often on spas, where they control how long the spa runs.

operate on a low-voltage current (albeit still hardwired), allowing them to be located near the water for the ultimate in convenience and precision.

Though time clocks, especially twist models, are relatively simple machines, they can wear out or become damaged from corrosion, insect infestation, and a burned-out motor from neglected lubrication of the gears. If that happens, simply replace the entire unit rather than trying to fix or replace its parts.

Lighting

In addition to its obvious and important safety benefits, pool lighting is another design feature that adds to the overall pool and spa experience. Whether in the water, set on or around the deck, placed within the surrounding landscape, or hung from a nearby structure, lighting is used to highlight special features, draw the eye to the water, and extend your enjoyment well past daylight hours.

Traditionally, underwater or in-pool lighting often meant a single incandescent fixture set into the pool wall at the deep end, anywhere from 18 inches to four feet below the water surface. Either flush to the wall or with a slightly domed, waterproof cover, such fixtures are like a bare bulb in the basement: handy, but hardly impressive.

Then along came fiber-optic technology, and the realm of underwater lighting took off in myriad directions and designs. No longer shackled by the

limits of high-voltage connections and built-in niches within the pool or spa's structure, designers were able to place lights just about anywhere to create dramatic, custom effects.

Simply, fiber optics carry light, not electricity, to the lamp (or lamps), which is projected through a lens. As a result, the system is much safer and easier to troubleshoot than a standard, 120- or 240-volt fixture.

Another electrical evolution that opened more doors for pool and spa lighting is the advent of low-voltage circuits. Simply, a transformer converts (or drops) a 120- or 240-volt circuit to 24 volts, making it safer for use near the water. The downside of low-voltage is that the dim light it is able to produce has little, if any, value with regard to safety; that said, its low light is often perfect for setting a mood, both in and out of the water. The installation, repair, and

Multicolor LED spa lights

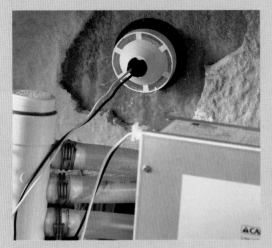

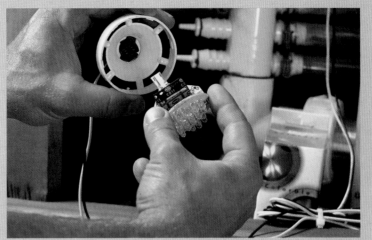

Underwater spa lights must be accessed through the skirt area if they require a new bulb. To remove the old bulb, twist the housing counterclockwise and pull out.

Consider replacing your old single-color bulb with a multicolor bulb. Controlled by an integral microprocessor, multicolor bulbs pulse in a variety of colors and patterns and at sporadic intervals, to very romantic effect. By punching the ON/OFF button in a specific sequence, you can freeze your favorite color or pattern.

troubleshooting of a low-voltage fixture is exactly the same as for a high- (or standard) voltage unit.

Another relatively new lighting alternative is solar, in which the top of each fixture housing is equipped with a small solar panel that collects the solar energy that powers the lamp. Requiring no cables or electrical input, solar-powered lights can be placed anywhere and in any arrangement so long as each fixture can gather enough energy to light its lamp. Even then, like low voltage lights, the result is typically a soft illumination that's best used to supplement other lighting schemes.

Despite these advancements, standard, high-voltage lighting still plays a significant role in pool and spa lighting. Mounted in watertight niches built into the structure of an in-ground concrete pool or spa during construction, or provided in the mold of a portable spa, these units are hard-wired to an electrical circuit on a nearby, above-ground junction box that is, in turn, wired to thesubpanel or main service panel.

Underwater lights like the one shown here can be placed in pools that are in a natural setting to add some drama.

Plumbing Systems

The prevailing pipe material for pools and spas is polyvinyl chloride (PVC), a tough plastic that is rated by "schedule," a term referring to the pipe's strength. The higher the schedule, the heavier and stronger the pipe. Most pools employ schedule 40 PVC pipes for their recirculation systems, in which the inside diameter of the pipe measures 1½" to 2". By contrast, PVC pipes that supply gas lines are schedule 80, twice the strength of what typically is installed for residential pool systems.

Spas, meanwhile, are typically outfitted with chlorinated polyvinyl chloride (CPVC) pipes, also in a schedule 40, which are designed to carry water heated to 100 degrees F or more without failure. In fact, the section of pipe from your pool's heater to the vessel may be CPVC instead of the standard PVC used for the rest of the system, to accommodate heated (if not 100-plus degrees F) water, simply as a precaution.

Both PVC and CPVC pipes are engineered to be installed below ground and remain impervious to chemicals in the water as its flows through the system. If exposed to the elements, especially ultraviolet rays, both types of pipe can become brittle and crack. This is why you may see the stubbed-up and exposed sections to and within the equipment set painted or coated with carbon black or a similar chemical inhibitor applied to outside surface of the pipes.

Available in both rigid and flexible versions, PVC and CPVC pipe is easily installed in tight spaces and around obstructions, either underground or within the equipment set or skid pack. As plastic pipes, they do not require solder to secure a joint fitting or other connector; rather, the various connectors, valves, and other system components either screw on to a threaded section of pipe or are cemented to or between the pipes using an epoxy.

The plumbing system for a spa
is mostly self-contained between the spa walls
and the skirting (for outdoor spas). It is a relatively simple set-up, compared to other types of
plumbing systems. But getting at the pipes can be tricky (see next page).

Before the relatively recent advent of PVC and CPVC pipe and fittings, pools and spas were equipped with copper pipes and connectors. A staple of indoor plumbing systems, copper proved to be problematic when used outdoors and particularly underground, as it is susceptible to corrosion and especially so when exposed to harsh chemicals, such as those used to balance pool and spa water. Also, fitting the pipe runs together typically require soldering, though the mandated use of lead-free solder and the option of threaded pipes and fittings, respectively precluded the environmental hazards and time and skill associated with its installation.

Galvanized pipes and fittings are the third type of system that has been installed for pools and spas. Made from heavy iron coated with zinc and other non-corrosive alloys, and designed with relatively simple-to-connect threaded components, galvanized is especially effective in carrying hot water (similar to CPVC). Its bulk, however, makes it a cumbersome system to install, while the rough interior surfaces of the pipes tend to trap debris and cause calcium build-up that could clog the works. For that reason, galvanized pipes and fittings, if used at all for a pool's equipment set, might be installed only from the heater to the vessel (after filtration has occurred), allowing PVC to serve the rest of the system.

Though it's best to limit the number of connectors between sections of pipe to lower the system's total dynamic head, and thus perhaps the size of and/or energy required for the motor-pump, it is impossible to avoid at least some along the way. In plumbing

Main Drains: Pools vs. Spas

Most full-size residential swimming pools feature one main drain at the deep end of the vessel's floor and a series of waterline skimmers. Spas, especially molded portable units, often feature multiple underwater drains, or ports, each supplying one or more pumps or booster pumps to feed the hydrotherapy jets in the spa. (In fact, spas may not employ skimmers at all because of greater water level fluctuations caused by bather load and evaporation of the super-heated water.) While most pool drains are covered by a simple grate (given their far-removed proximity to swimmers), spa ports are often protected by domed, antivortex covers to protect soakers from getting their fingers, hair, or other objects caught in the suction of the drains, which in a spa are all in close proximity to the spa's users.

The Access Issue

Access to pipes, jets and other parts of a spa's or pool's plumbing system can be a true impediment if you need to find and fix a leak or perform any other service on them.

In the case of spas, the plumbing is often encased in high density, blown-on urethane insulation. To get at the pipes you must remove the foam. An insulation knife is a good tool for cutting the foam, but whichever tool you use you must be extremely careful to avoid cutting into the pipes or damaging any part of the tub itself.

In the case of swimming pools, pipes are buried deep in the ground. The main drain line is located underneath the pool bottom, and the rest of the pipes are typically below the pool deck. Gaining access to them is a major job involving lots of digging.

lingo, these connectors are called fittings and are available in a wide variety of shapes and sizes to accommodate just about any circumstance.

The primary types of fittings are couplings (which bridge two straight sections of pipe of the same dimension), elbows (which enable 90-degree turns), and T-fittings (which spilt one pipe run into two directions of flow, and is often fitted with a valve to open one, both, or neither, see below). Other fittings include: plugs and caps; those that enable 45-degree angles; transition fittings that go from one pipe size to another (called reducers); and fittings that connect one type of pipe material to another (such as PVC to copper).

A union is connector installed between the end of a pipe and a device, such as the filter or heater. Instead of connecting a length of pipe directly to the device, the union enables you or a pool or spa technician to remove the component for service or seasonal storage without cutting or damaging (and thus having to replace) the entire length of pipe serving it. It may be that the union is damaged when the device is disconnected, but it is much less expensive and time consuming to replace compared to an entire length of pipe.

All of these and other fittings are designed to be the same, standardized dimensions and are available in the same material—PVC/CPVC, copper, and galvanized—as the various pipes they connect. In addition, fittings are designed to accommodate one of several connectivity options, including threaded, compression, slip, and soldered. These days, threaded connections between pipes and to various pool equipment devices prevails, although slip fittings (in which the components slide into each other and are connected with an epoxy) can be found in some areas.

Given the standardization of pipe and fitting sizes and connectivity options, it is possible to interchange materials, such as threaded PVC fittings connecting threaded galvanized pipes of the same diameter. However, plumbing contractors and pool and spa professionals overwhelmingly advocate using the same materials for the entire system (or within isolated sections) to better ensure its integrity. This is chiefly because each material is rated differently in its ability to carry water and might vary slighting in its standardized interior dimension, perhaps causing unsecure or unreliable connections.

In addition, to prevent system failure building codes limit the flow rate that each type of material is

Schedule 40 PVC pipe

Schedule 40 CPVC pipe

Copper supply pipe

Galvanized supply pipe (threaded)

Ball valves are very important components of a spa or pool plumbing system. They are easy to operate and they integrate well with PVC pipes.

Supply pipes for spas and pools traditionally were made from galvanized steel pipe or copper pipe. But these materials have been replaced by plastic pipes (PVC and CPVC). In turn, Schedule 40 PVC is being replaced by more flexible plastics, including crosslinked polyethylene and flexible PVC products.

allowed to carry. For instance, water flow through copper pipe can be no more than 8 feet per second, while PVC/CPVC pipes are allowed to carry water at 10 feet per second.

The diameter of the pipe serving your pool's equipment set are (or should be) somewhat determined by the capacity and efficiency of the motor-pump, as well as by what the other system components can accommodate. In general, the larger the diameter of the pipe, the less stress on the system. It's also okay to use a slightly larger pipe dimension than what some devices can handle (for instance, a 2" diameter pipe connected to the filter's 1½" influent line using a reducer fitting). The reverse, however (a smaller pipe leading into a larger opening), is not

recommended because the device will not receive sufficient volume of water to operate properly.

Other considerations regarding the size of the pipe and fittings include the system's estimated or calculated flow rate, the length of the plumbing runs (mostly underground from the vessel to the remotely located equipment set), the number of angles and connections, and the needs and sizes of the components within the equipment set—all of which underscores the complexity of estimating a right-sized system.

Valves. While pipes and fittings enable the flow of water through a pool or spa system, valves are the means by which that flow is controlled and directed. Simply, valves are installed into the plumbing system at strategic locations between pipe to regulate water flow, either by blocking the water at that point, allowing it to flow freely through that section, redirecting it, or reducing it somewhat.

There are four main types of valves, each able to deliver one or more control functions. A ball valve, for instance, can be employed to perform a variety of tasks; essentially, it employs a ball that measures the precise interior dimension of the pipe (hence the value of standardizing interior pipe and plumbing component dimensions) and features a hole through its center. Controlled by a handle, the ball can be set in any position. When the hole aligns with the two sections of pipe separated by the valve, for instance, the water flows unabated; when the hole is turned away from the pipes, the flow is stopped completely.

Another type of valve design is the slide, which resembles a guillotine. In a closed or down position, the "blade" stops the flow of water through the valve between two pipes; when the slide is open, or up, the water flows freely. The slide can be set in any position between open and closed to partially restrict water flow, if necessary. A gate valve, meanwhile, swings or swivels in the valve housing and, like a ball or slide mechanism, can be fully or partially open or completely closed.

All three of these valves can be used in a variety of ways, including reverse-flow circumstances (such as for filter backwashing). A check valve, however, only opens to allow flow in one direction; as such, it is used almost exclusively to keep water from passively drifting or flowing back on itself or intruding on components that must be kept dry.

There are two types of check valves: flapper and spring-loaded. The former is manually or automatically controlled to be either in the open or closed position; the latter opens and closed based on the water pressure against either side.

Union fittings function like manifolds, redirecting the water flow from multiple sources at one junction point. Tees, wyes and elbows are typical shapes.

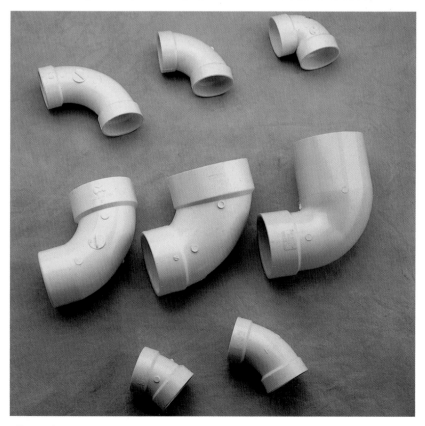

Elbow fittings connect straight runs of pipe to follow a directional line. Most have a 90 degree or a 45 degree curve.

A **multiport valve** like this backwash valve can be set to several different openings to direct the water where you want it to go.

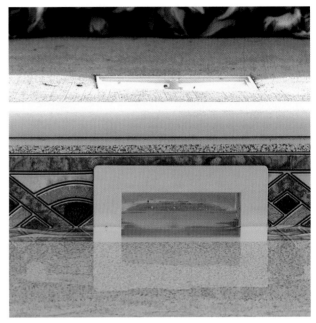

A **check valve, such as this skimmer weir,** allows water to flow through in only one direction.

A good example of a spring-loaded check valve is the weir of a pool's in-wall skimmer device (see complete explanation below). As water is pulled by the pump from the pool into the skimmer, the weir folds or lays down to allow the flow, then pops back up to block water and debris from flowing back into the vessel. In other words, the force of water on one side opens the valve, while the force from the other side closes it, thus effectively shutting off any backflow of water through the system.

Check valves are commonly installed at the intake line of connection to the heater, so that heated water does not flow back through the filter, and in spa blowers to keep water out of the pressurized air environment. They also help maintain the proper flow through chlorinators and other chemical feeders installed in the equipment set or skid pad, and sometimes are installed between the main drain and the pump to keep water from gravitating back into the vessel when the motor-pump is not running. In that case, the valve automatically engages when the pump is off, rather that requiring the owner to open or close it manually.

Not only do valves differ in their operation, such as by a swinging gate or a turning ball, there are special valve devices and designs for specific functions within a pool's equipment set or portable spa's skid pack.

The last essential components of a pool's equipment set or the skid pad of a portable spa are the skimmers and drains. Either one or the other, or both working together, serve as the "supply" conduits for the water to enter the filtration system.

When the motor-pump is operating, it creates a pressurized environment that pulls, or suctions, water from the pool or spa through the drain and/or skimmer into the system; larger vessels typically include both, and often a pair of drains in the floor and multiple skimmer openings at the water line, either built into the walls of an in-ground concrete or vinyl-lined pool or hung from the top of the walls of an above-ground unit.

Though the name may spark images of a device that floats on and moves along the surface of the water, a skimmer is a stationary component. Once custom-built out of several pieces and parts during an in-ground pool or spa's construction, modern skimmers are now one-piece, molded plastic units that are set into the top of and flush to the inside of the pool walls, just below the coping, at strategic locations and equal distance from one another. Some newer models also feature automatic chlorinators that deliver a scheduled dose of sanitizer into the water.

A skimmer typically features a rectangular opening into the pool vessel about a foot wide and half as high, with a floating weir (or one-way, spring-loaded check valve) set just below the water line. The weir is

Detecting a Leak

Leaks are the bane of every plumbing system, especially when there are portions of that system buried underground. Suffice to say that leaks—no matter where they occur in a system—are usually difficult to detect and repair, though certainly those you can see within an above-ground equipment set or skid pad are easier to diagnose. If you are refilling your pool's or spa's water level with increasing frequency and/or water volume, or notice unusually low pressure gauge readings on one or more pieces of equipment, it's likely there's a leak somewhere in the system. If you can't see a leak within the above-ground components and piping, look for wet spots and/or depressions in the ground along the underground plumbing runs between the pool/spa and the equipment set, which often indicate an excessive amount of water resulting from a leak in a pipe or fitting. Another leak detection method is to plug or block the inlet valves into the pool or spa (where the filtered water returns to the vessel) and the skimmers and drain (where the water exits the vessel); if the water level remains steady after a few hours, you likely have a leak in the plumbing system. If you're still losing water, however, unplug the inlets; if there are air bubbles in the return line from the filter, it's likely there's a leak in the skimmer, drain, or other intakes serving the system. If that's not it, open the skimmer/drain lines and plug each inlet line or fitting one at a time; when the bubbles stop (indicating a flow into the vessel), you've at least found the line with the leak, which will need to be repaired or replaced before you can restart the system and resume enjoying your pool or spa.

designed so that is lays down to allow water from the pool or spa to be sucked into the skimmer (and therefore the entire plumbing and filtration system) when the system is running, but closes or stands up to any passive reverse flow or backwash from the skimmer when the motor-pump is offline, thereby blocking water (and debris) from flowing back into the vessel.

It is critical to maintain the water level of a pool or spa to just above the weir line, or the top of the flap, so that the entire plumbing system is properly and constantly primed with water. A low water level—from use, evaporation, or a leak—can cause the system to run dry or at least at a lower pressure, perhaps damaging some of its components and reducing the effectiveness of the filtration process.

A skimmer for an in-ground pool or spa also is accessed from above by a cover that is set flush to the pool deck. When the cover is removed, the opening provides easy access to the skimmer's strainer basket (to catch debris) and the end of the pipe that carries water to the equipment set, to which you can connect a vacuum system for cleaning chores. For obvious reasons, the skimmer attached to the walls of an above-ground vessel is much easier to access, maintain, and service or repair compared to those set into the ground.

In addition to making sure the water level of the pool or spa remains just above the weir line, it's also prudent to clean out each skimmer's strainer basket after each use, and especially so following a windy day or a pool party. Like the basket installed in the pump, a skimmer basket is easily removed via the opening below the pool deck cover and the debris cleaned out.

Skimmer baskets vary by brand as to their basket mesh designs, but the tighter the mesh, the more debris the basket will catch, and the more often it will need to be cleaned out. For the most part, skimmer baskets are designed to capture large pieces of debris, from leaves and twigs to hair and other floating objects, leaving finer particles for the pool or spa's filtration system.

Large, private residential pools typically feature multiple skimmers (usually one every 500 square feet of pool surface area) in combination with at least one main drain, which is installed on the pool bottom, usually at the deep end. Like the skimmers, the main drain serves as a supply line to the equipment set; when the motor-pump is running, it pulls water through the drain and into the pool or spa's plumbing system for filtration.

How to Solvent-weld PVC Pipe

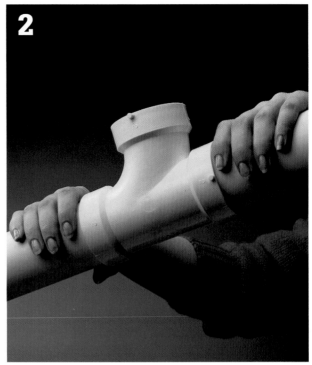

Clean up the edges of the cut pipes by trimming them neatly with a utility knife (this process is called deburring).

Test fit all of the pipes and fittings. All pipes should fit flush against the bottoms of the sockets in the connectors and unions.

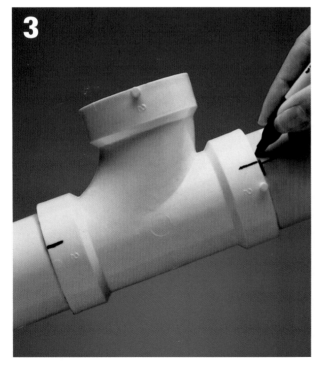

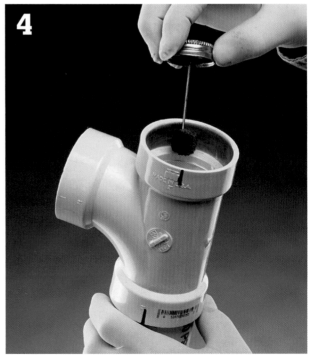

Draw reference lines at all joints with a permanent marker. The lines should indicate how deeply the pipes fit into the fittings. Also draw pairs of alignment marks on mating pieces.

Apply plastic pipe primer to the ends of the pipes and to the insides of the fitting sockets. Primer dulls glossy surfaces and ensures a good bond. It colors the pipes purple so plumbing inspectors know it has been used.

5

Solvent-glue each joint by applying a thick coat of solvent glue to the end of the pipe. Apply a thin coat of solvent glue to the inside surface of the fitting sockets. Work quickly: solvent glue has a working time of only 30 seconds.

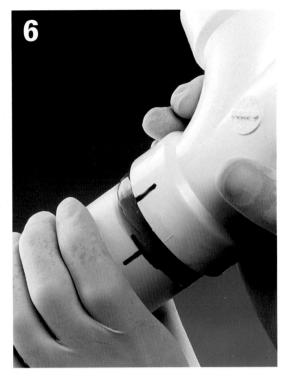

6

Quickly position the pipe and fitting so that alignment marks are offset by about 2". Force the pipe into the fitting until the end seats flush against the bottom of the socket.

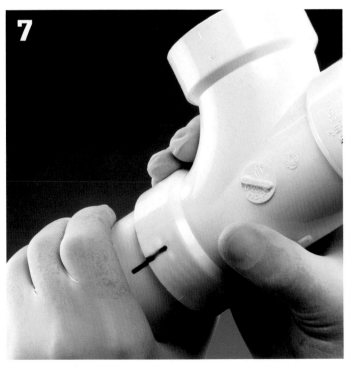

7

Spread solvent by twisting the pipe until the reference marks are aligned. Hold the pipe in place for about 20 seconds to prevent the joint from slipping.

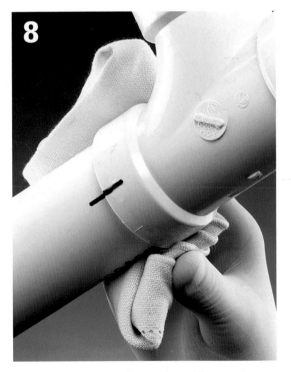

8

Wipe away excess solvent glue with a rag. Do not disturb the joint for 30 minutes after gluing.

How to Repair a Leak In a Flexible Supply Line

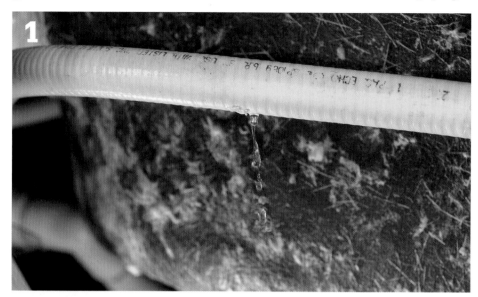

Most failures in waterlines are caused by freezing. Ice in a line, even a flex line like the one seen here, can cause the line to rupture. The best solution is to cut the line and attach a repair coupling.

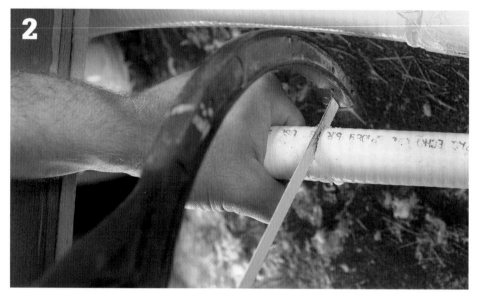

Cut through the line at the damaged area using a hack saw or a reciprocating saw with a metal-cutting blade. Trim off another ¼" or so from the line.

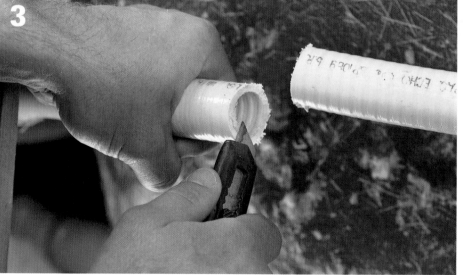

Clean up the edges of the cuts by trimming them neatly with a utility knife (this process is called deburring).

Wearing protective rubber or latex gloves, apply primer to the ends of the cut lines all the way from the end past the area where the repair coupling will be. Let the primer dry (normally just takes a few minutes).

Apply glue to the primed mating ends and the inside of the union. Be sure to use glue that is compatible with the type of line. Here, glue that is rated for PVC or PVC flex is being used.

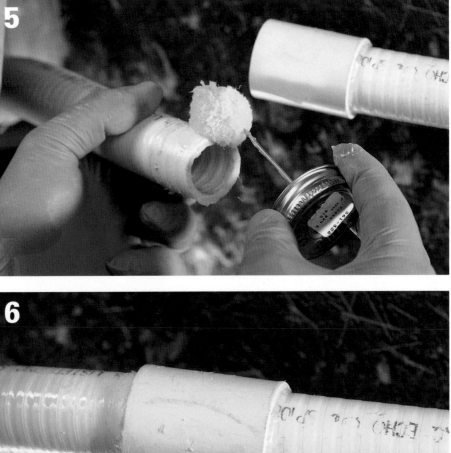

Before the glue sets, insert one of the cut lines into the coupling and twist it from side to side to ensure even coverage. Then, insert the other cut line into the open coupling end, twist and let the repair dry.

How To Repair a Leaking Jet Body

Jets are installed at the factory. The jet body is secured against the wall of the spa with a mounting flange and a locknut, or with a threaded bulkhead that is mounted on the wet side of the tub wall and fits into the jet body to draw the two together as the threaded escutcheon is tightened. A gasket is slipped between the flange and nut to create a seal. Once the jet body is installed, the fittings are solvent welded to it so it can be plumbed into the water line. If you leave water in the plumbing and it freezes, the jet body may crack. If this happens, you'll need to remove and replace the body and the fittings.

Disconnect the water supply lines from the jet body by cutting the lines or taking apart fittings. If cutting, use a hack saw or a reciprocating saw fitted with a metal cutting blade. The goal is to keep the cuts as clean as possible.

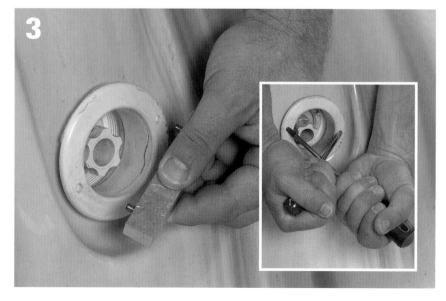

Unscrew the threaded bulkhead on the tub side. These parts (you may need to remove a decorative chrome escutcheon to gain access to the bulkhead) usually have a pair of holes on opposite sides of the flange that are designed to fit a bulkhead wrench. (The hole configurations vary among manufacturers, so make sure you get a bulkhead wrench that's made for your tub brand).

Inset: If you can't locate a bulkhead wrench (or don't even want to try) you can usually spin the bulkhead free by inserting a phillips-head screwdriver into each hole in the bulkhead and twisting counterclockwise.

Unscrew the nozzle insert from the jet body and inspect it for damage and wear. If it is in poor shape, order a new part when you order the new jet body. Otherwise, just clean it up and re-use it with the new jet.

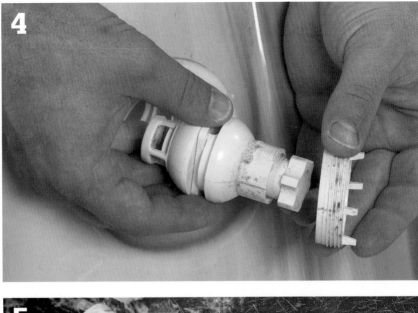

Twist the jet body and remove it from the opening in the tub wall.

Remove the rest of the jet body assembly from the spa (the remaining portion is called the bulkhead). If the piece does not come out easily, cut the seal around it with a utility knife and then drive it through the hole with a rubber mallet. Clean any sealant residue from around the opening.

(Continued next page)

Bring the old jet body to your local pool and spa retailer to purchase (or order) a replacement. These parts differ quite a bit according to age and manufacturer. But most are two-part assemblies, with a male threaded bulkhead that fits through the opening on the tub side and is screwed into a female threaded body. A gasket normally fits between the bulkhead and the finished tub surface. Make note of the labels on the jet body ports: one normally says air and the other says water.

Apply a bead of silicone caulk to the flange that fits against the non-tub, or dry, side of the tub wall.

Make sure the gasket is in position on the male-threaded bulkhead and insert the threaded end through the hole. Twist the female threaded jet body onto the bulkhead, holding it steady from the tub side. Tighten the bulkhead.

If the jet you are replacing is the first jet in line (like the one shown here), you'll need to connect it to the air intake port in the tub rim. Connect a small length of tubing or flex tube to the air intake port on the jet body. Solvent-glue a T-fitting to the open end, with the stem of the T pointing up toward the air intake port at the top of the tub. Connect the T to the air intake with a length of tubing and a repair coupling.

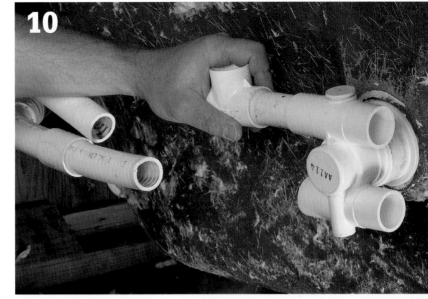

Connect the air line that feeds the circulating air system and connect the water line using solvent glue rated for flex tubing.

If the jet is at the beginning or end of the jet circuit, glue a short length of tubing into each open port and then glue a cap fitting onto the tubing.

Nonmechanical Repairs

Despite your best routine cleaning, maintenance, and winterizing efforts, and often due to factors out of your control (like an extreme freeze-thaw cycle or simple wear and tear over time), your pool or spa may develop cracks and possible leaks that need to be repaired to maintain the structural integrity of the shell and the efficiency of the support systems.

Surface problems are relatively easy to fix, whether they occur in a plaster-finished or vinyl-lined pool or spa (fiberglass damage is practically impossible for a homeowner to fix); of course, each finish material has its own patching materials and methods, but the prognosis for effectively patching the surface is quite good.

Similarly, cracked or damaged waterline tiles and coping materials can be easily replaced (assuming you can find matching pieces), requiring careful removal so as not to damage surrounding pieces and a few days of "cure" or drying time for both the mortar and the grout before they can be exposed to water.

Deeper and larger cracks, and certainly leaks, are a more expensive prospect to repair, although they are certainly not a death knell for your pool or spa. However, such occurrences usually require extensive resurfacing jobs, which means draining the pool or spa, finding and fixing the problem, and sometimes removing and replacing finish materials, including the deck and coping.

For obvious reasons, a leak in a below-ground pool or spa is typically more difficult and expensive to detect and repair, if only because the backfilled area around the leak will have to be excavated to expose the problem, and then refilled and refinished with coping and decking material once the leak is patched or fixed.

Patching a crack (See pages 164 to 167). Plaster-finished concrete pools and spas occasionally develop cracks due to shifts in the soil backfill, improper soil drainage that causes pressure on the outside of the shell, dramatic changes in water temperature, impact from a sharp or bulk object, seismic activity, or at a weak or thin spot in the shell or finish.

Plaster finishes may also show spalling, in which the finish flakes or chips off in spots, usually caused by long-term exposure to chemicals but also perhaps by a poor plaster mix or bond with the concrete shell.

In both cases, assuming a small, localized problem, a crack or spall can be patched using a plaster or epoxy compound available at a pool or spa retailer. Shut off the recirculation system and lower the waterline to a few inches below the affected area and allow it to dry. Then clean out all loose debris or flaking from the crack or spall using the sharp end of a can opener, a putty knife, and a stiff brush.

Prepare the patching compound per the directions on the package (only what you need for the crack, plus a little more) and wet the area with clean water using a paint brush. Apply the patching compound with a dry trowel or putty knife, pressing it firmly into the crack and floating or feathering it a few inches on all sides until it is flush with the surface.

While the patch is still damp, etch the surface of the affected area with muriatic acid (mixed one part to two parts water) with a small pool brush, and then allow the patch to dry (or cure) at least 24 hours. Rinse the pool brush thoroughly as soon as you are finished etching the patch.

Obviously, the patch will not match the color of the original plaster finish. If possible, take a sample of your pool's finish color to a pool or spa retailer to see if it can be matched with a paint coating formulated for plaster pool and spa finishes (typically rubber- or epoxy-based); if not, do your best to find a color that comes close, and apply it in three coats to the patched area and a bit beyond, feathering it out from the affected area. Let it dry for another day, then refill the pool. If the difference in color is too obvious or undesirable, consider repainting or resurfacing the entire pool in the future.

Patching a tear (See pages 162 to 163). Like plaster finishes on a concrete pool or spa shell, vinyl liners can also suffer surface damage. Small tears in the material, usually caused by a sharp object (such as a pool toy or cleaning tool) or from long-term exposure to chemicals and the sun's ultraviolet (UV) rays, can be repaired with a dry or underwater patch or liquid sealer.

As with a concrete repair job, a dry patch or liquid sealer requires you to expose and clean up the tear beforehand; lowering the water level to a few inches below the tear lessens the stress on the affected area, allowing you to work it more easily.

That said, a liner that is allowed to dry also shrinks, so schedule your repair work on a cool, cloudy day and limit the work to that day (allowing it to dry overnight) so you can refill the pool or spa and avoid other problems and potential damage to the liner.

Once the tear is exposed and allowed to dry, use small scissors or a sharp utility knife to clean up the edges and cut small circles at both ends, which will help mitigate any further tearing. Clean the liner with rubbing alcohol and rough up the surface of the tear and a few inches around it with a fine-grit sandpaper. Apply the patch per the directions in the package, working out any air bubbles from the center to the edges of the patch.

Like any patch job, regardless of the pool's or spa's construction or finish material, it's unlikely you'll be able to match the color of the original liner. A clear patch or liquid sealer might be your best bet in that regard, but even then you're likely to be able to see the patch in the pool.

Natural wood skirting is a beautiful addition to a spa or hot tub, but it gets a fair amount of abuse and will need refreshing with deck stain periodically to stay looking its best.

To refresh the skirting stain, first scrub the wood with a commercial deck stripping chemical, following the usage instructions on the label.

Coat the wood with semi-transparent deck stain once the stripper has been rinsed off and the wood is dry.

Other liner problems. In addition to tears in the material, vinyl liners can become discolored or fade over time, usually from prolonged exposure to chemicals and UV rays, as well as algae and improperly diluted chlorination. If the pool bottom becomes discolored, it might indicate fungal growth in the sand base underneath. Bulges in the sidewalls of the vessel signal problems with the structural system, often caused by shifting or a poorly draining backfill.

Extensive liner problems usually indicate a replacement job, allowing you to not only refresh the look of your pool or spa, but also upgrade to the latest liner technology in terms of material performance and wear resistance. A new liner can be made, just like the original liner, to precisely match your pool or spa's shape and features.

Extensive repairs and replacements. If your pool finish, liner, or structural shell show extensive damage or wear it's probably time to consider a complete overhaul.

Replacing or resurfacing a pool or spa is inevitable; no vessel is immune to the effects of time and the pressure of water, chemicals, and heavy use, among other factors. If you've taken proper care of your pool or spa, especially if you built it rather than inherited one or both (and thus the legacy of a previous owner's habits), the surface should last a decade or more. But eventually, it will wear out and need to be replaced.

Assuming there are no structural problems with the shell, a plaster resurfacing or liner replacement job is fairly straightforward. If you can wait, it might be cost-effective to schedule the work at the end of the swim or soak season to allow the new finish to adjust without the rigors or everyday use, cleaning, and frequent chemical balancing.

As mentioned earlier, a new vinyl liner can be fashioned to fit the shape and features of your existing pool, ideally by the same manufacturer. Regardless of the supplier, the liner is likely to be of better quality than the original, and with more color or other finish options from which to choose.

A new liner also affords you the opportunity to check the condition of the pool's or spa's structural components, make any minor adjustments or small repairs, and level the sand base (perhaps treating it with a fungicide, if necessary) before installing the new liner.

Applying a new plaster or specialty finish to a concrete shell is similarly simple, if certainly a more extensive and expensive prospect than a patching or repainting job. As noted above, one option is to sandblast the original plaster and expose the concrete shell, then apply a new plaster or specialty finish, such as aggregate pebbles or mosaic tiles, to the surface.

Some pool experts and builders recommend "hybrid" solutions, in which a vinyl liner or acrylic gelcoat is installed or applied, respectively, over the old plastered concrete shell; in the case of the liner installation, the membrane is stretched over and attached behind the shell walls, then concealed by a new coping or deck material.

For most replacement jobs, especially those involving a vinyl liner, the coping material and perhaps some (or maybe all) of the pool deck will need to be removed and replaced, as well, adding to the time and expense of the job. Still, such a project may inspire—and allow—you to make a more significant change to the look and function of your pool or spa.

To Catch a Leak

Evaporation and heavy pool or spa use are common causes of lower water levels, which must be kept just above the skimmer's weir line to maintain the filtration system. But if you suspect that your pool's or spa's reduction in water volume is caused by a leak, conduct this simple test to confirm your suspicions: Fill a plastic bucket three-quarters full with your pool's or spa's water and indicate the waterline on the inside surface with a waterproof marker; at the same time, mark the waterline in the pool or spa on the wall. Set the bucket in the shallow end or where only the top 2-3 inches of the bucket is exposed above water. After 24 hours, check to see if the distance between the current water level and your waterline marks are the same between the bucket and your pool or spa; if they are, there's no leak. But a significant difference between the two indicates a leak in the pool shell or recirculation system, requiring further investigation and repair.

Use enamel paint to coat and protect the metal parts of a diving board. You'll need to clean off any rust first by scouring with steel wool.

Diving Boards

Though relatively few newly built residential swimming pools feature diving boards these days, for various reasons concerning available space and alternative water activities, pool owners who inherit them face fairly simple maintenance tasks but a much more serious safety concern.

Most diving boards (also called dive or jump boards, the latter of which are slightly shorter) are constructed of a wood core with a fiberglass coating and a rough, non-skid surface. The board is typically 6 ft. to 12 ft. long and about 18" wide, and is set on a deck-mounted stand that may or may not feature a heavy spring to help launch swimmers into the water. If not, the stand acts as a simple fulcrum to enable the board to bend slightly or remain stationary (called a platform) as users fling themselves into the pool.

The use, dimensions, and placement of a diving board are all subject to local health and safety codes. Essentially, there must be enough room in front of and on either side of the board, as well as adequate water depth, for safe usage, assuming divers leap off the front of the board instead of the sides (some-

thing a responsible, safety-minded pool owner will have to communicate and regulate during each use). A diving board (as well as a slide) can also raise your homeowner's liability insurance premium.

Despite a seemingly watertight fiberglass shell, a diving board can crack under heavy use and over time with constant exposure to the sun's ultraviolet light, and especially if the board is left unprotected in severe weather, such as over the winter. Signs of age and potential breakage include a noticeably warped surface, visible surface cracks, delamination of the fiberglass and wood core, and a cracking or creaking sound during use.

The only element of an old diving board worth trying to replace is the non-skid surface, which can wear away from years of use and is easily resurfaced with a spray-applied, adhesive-sand mix or other similar solution or product. The board itself, as well as the stand and its connection to the deck, should be replaced immediately if damaged, or simply removed and discarded. New dive boards cost about $400 wholesale, and maybe twice that at a retailer. Most are sold as kits, including the base, though it's certainly possible to replace only one or the other of those components.

How to Repair Vinyl Liner

Vinyl liners will tear from time to time. Fortunately, they're easy to fix (as long as you have some spare liner material for a patch). With some products, you can even glue on a patch underwater. But if the tear is near the top of the pool (most are), you're better off draining the pool slightly before you start.

Tears and gouges are not unusual with vinyl liner pools. One very common cause is having the cleaning head fall off of a pole while you're scrubbing your pool walls. Repairing the damage is easy if you have the right vinyl adhesive.

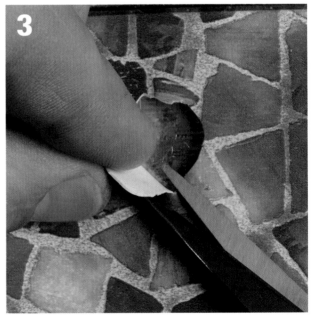

Trim around the damaged area to eliminate rough edges. Cut a patch from extra vinyl liner (if you don't have any extra, inquire at your pool and spa retailer – most will have a few scraps laying around that they'll be happy to let you have). The patch should be round or oval with no straight edges or corners.

Dab the area around the damage with a paper towel that has a very small amount of PVC primer/cleaner. This will remove the printed pattern from the pool liner, exposing clean, white vinyl that forms a more solid bond with the glue. Be careful not to expose the liner outside of the repair area to the PVC primer/cleaner (for fairly obvious reasons).

Apply a thin coat of vinyl adhesive product to the back side of the patch and to the repair area.

Press the patch in place over the damage and rub it lightly to make sure it is making good contact. Don't overwork it.

A good repair job doesn't have to be invisible. Especially on patterned liners, it is unlikely that anyone will ever notice it.

How to Repair a Crack in a Concrete Pool

Cracks in concrete are dealt with differently depending on how large and deep they are. Tiny hairline cracks may not require any maintenance at all, while larger, deeper cracks could suggest that you have a structural problem around the pool, probably caused by earth settling. Any crack that's large enough to admit water should be sealed as soon as possible and monitored to make sure it is not live. If it continues to widen, contact a professional pool service technician or a construction engineer.

Most concrete cracks you're likely to encounter around your home can be patched with inexpensive concrete repair products. In some cases, you may be able to get by with a product that comes premixed in a cartridge and is delivered with a caulk gun. Or, you may purchase a dry mix that contains additives designed to facilitate patching.

Cracks in concrete pool walls and floor surfaces generally are repaired with hydraulic cement: a patching agent that actually gets stronger as it gets wet. It is possible to plug leaks in concrete temporarily, but if you want to effect a long-lasting repair you'll need to drain the pool past the damaged area.

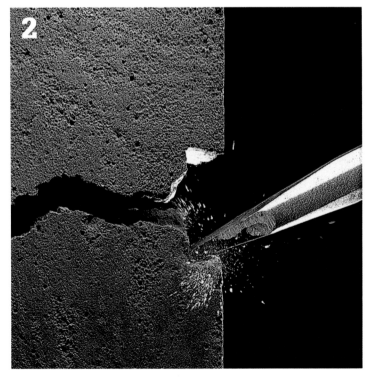

Cracks in concrete typically must be made worse before they are made better. By chiseling the top of the crack so the walls slope down and away from the crack, you create a bell shape that will hold the repair material in place. You can fill cracks up to about ½" in. wide × ½" deep with a liquid polymer crack filler available at lumberyards and home centers. Fill the cracks just slightly below the surrounding surface for the best appearance. Then cover the cracks for two days so they aren't damaged by traffic. Deeper cracks should first be filled to within ½" of the top with foam backer rods. These should be compressed in the crack with a screwdriver or a putty knife and then covered with crack filler. If the crack is over ½" wide, fill the gap in a couple of applications so everything has time to cure properly. Breaks along the edge are the hardest to repair, but with a little effort, you can help maintain that edge just a bit longer.

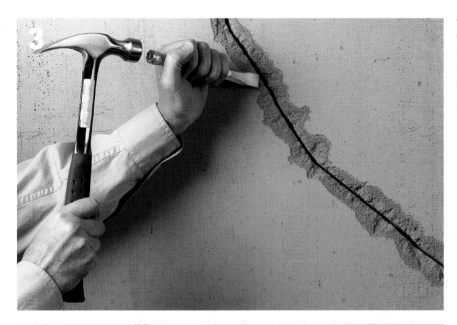

To repair a concrete pool wall crack, use a chisel to cut a keyed cut that's wider at the base than at the surface, and no more than ½" deep. Clean out the crack with a wire brush.

Fill wide cracks partway with expanding foam, working from bottom to top. Do not fill past the keyed cut. Smaller cracks do not need filling with foam.

Mix hydraulic cement according to the manufacturer's instructions, then trowel it into the crack, working from the bottom to top. Apply cement in layers no more than ½" thick, until the patch is slightly higher than the surrounding area. Feather cement with the trowel until it's even with the surface and allow to dry thoroughly.

How to Patch a Plaster or Stucco-lined Pool

To mix your own stucco or plaster patching compound, combine three parts sand, two parts portland cement, and one part masonry cement. Add just enough water so the mixture holds its shape when squeezed. Mix only as much as you can use in one hour.

Chip off the crumbled, loose, or deteriorated veneer from the wall, using a cold chisel and maul. Chisel away damaged veneer until you have only good, solid surface remaining. Use care to avoid damaging the wall behind the veneer. Clean the repair area with a wire brush.

Old metal lath

New metal lath

Clean up any metal lath in the repair area if it is in good condition. If not, cut it out with aviation snips. Add new lath where needed, using masonry anchors to hold it to the concrete pool wall.

Mix fortified sand-mix concrete (or specialty concrete blends for wall repair), and trowel it over the lath until it is even with the surrounding surfaces.

Apply a second, smooth layer of stucco. Build up the stucco to within ¼" of the original surface. Let the patch dry for two days, misting every two to four hours.

To re-create a rough surface texture, use a soft-bristled brush to stipple the surface. To blend in the repair, add pigment to the sand mixture or paint the repair area after it dries.

For a smoother surface, knock down the slightly hardened finish coat with a steel float. Dampen the patch periodically for a week. Let it dry for several more days before painting.

PROJECT: Maintaining Tile Walls and Decks

Much like interior tile floors, tiled pools, spas and pool decks are extremely durable, but they do require periodic maintenance. Accidents happen and although it takes quite an impact to break an outdoor tile, it is possible. Broken tiles or failed grout can expose the subbase to moisture, which will destroy a deck over time.

Major cracks in grout joints indicate that movement of the subbase has caused the adhesive layer beneath the tile to deteriorate. The adhesive layer must be replaced along with the grout in order to create a permanent repair.

Perhaps the biggest challenge with tile repair is matching the grout color. If you're regrouting an entire patio, just select the color that complements the tile; if you're replacing a tile, you have to blend the new grout with the old. A good tile dealer can help you get the best color match.

Any time you remove tile, check the subbase. If it's no longer smooth, solid, and level, repair, replace, or resurface it before repairing the tile. If the subbase contains cracks, install a liquid-based isolation membrane system—simply apply the liquid adhesive, lay the membrane over the crack, then apply the final coat over the top and allow to dry thoroughly.

Protect unglazed tile from staining and water spots by periodically applying a coat of tile sealer. Keep dirt from getting trapped in grout lines by sealing them every year or two.

How to Grout Outdoor Tile

Completely remove the old grout (if there is any) using a rotary tool or a grout saw. Spread the new grout over the tiles, using a rubber grout float. Force grout into the joints, holding the float almost flat, then drag the float across the joints diagonally, tilting the face at a 45° angle. Tip: Add latex-fortified grout additive so excess grout is easier to remove.

Use the grout float to scrape off excess grout from the surface of the tile. Scrape diagonally across the joints, holding the float in a near-vertical position. Patio tile will absorb grout quickly and permanently, so it is important to remove all excess grout from the surface before it sets. Note: It's a good idea to have helpers when working on large areas.

After the grout has dried for about four hours, use a nail to make sure it has hardened. Use a cloth to buff the surface until any remaining grout film is gone. If buffing does not remove all the film, try using a coarser cloth, such as burlap, or even an abrasive pad to remove stubborn stains. Seal the grout after it cures completely.

How to Replace Outdoor Floor Tile

Remove the grout from around the damaged tile, using a rotary tool, utility knife (and several blades), or a grout saw. Then, carefully break apart the tile, using a cold chisel and hammer.

Scrape away the old mortar with a putty knife. Make sure the subbase is smooth and flat.

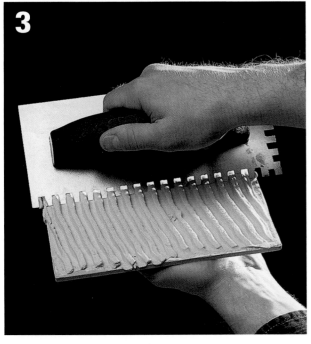

Use a notched trowel to cover the entire back of the replacement tile with an even layer of dry-set mortar.

Set the tile in place, and press down firmly to create a good bond. If necessary, use a carpet-covered 2 × 4 and a rubber mallet to tap the tile flush with the neighboring tiles.

(Continued next page)

Use a small screwdriver to remove excess mortar that has oozed into the grout joints, then wipe up any mortar from the tile surface. When the mortar has dried completely, grout around the tile.

Mix matching grout according to the manufacturer's directions and fill the grout lines, applying the grout with a grout float. Carefully wipe off excess before it dries.

Grout Sealer

Like the tile inside your house, exterior tile must be watertight. All the grout lines must be solid, fully packed and free of cracks or chips. Neglecting problems can result in damage to the subbase, and possibly the entire tile job.

Apply grout sealer to grout joints every one to two years to protect against water, wear, and stains. Use a sponge brush to spread the sealer and keep it off the tiles. If you do spill on the tiles, wipe it up immediately. Allow new grout to cure fully before sealing it.

How to Re-grout Wall Tile

Scrape out the old grout completely, using an awl, a utility knife or a grout saw (or all three). Brush out the joints with a grout brush.

Clean the grout joints with warm, soapy water and a sponge, then rinse and allow the joints to dry.

Mix the grout according to the directions and apply a liberal coat with a rubber grout float. Work the grout into the joints by holding the float face at a 60 degree angle to the tile.

Let the grout dry for about one hour, then wipe away the powdery residue from the tile face with a dry cloth. Let the grout cure for at least 24 hours before exposing it to moisture.

Upgrading Your Pool and Spa

A recent study found that there were approximately 8 million swimming pools and more than 5 million spas and hot tubs for private home use in the United States, the bulk of which were sold or installed after 1980. Every year, more than 350,000 swimming pools and 400,000 spas and hot tubs are added to those totals, according to the American Pool & Spa Association (ASPA, formerly the Pool & Spa Institute). Bottom line: there are a lot of pools and spas out there, most of them aging and to some degree in need of repair or remodeling in order to boost your property's resale value, suit new lifestyle needs or design preferences, and/or achieve greater energy efficiency and convenience.

Your ability to upgrade or alter the look, feel, and function of your pool or spa depends on several factors, perhaps the most critical being your budget, but also the shape and style of the pool or spa, the condition and capabilities of the existing equipment, and how much space near and around the pool or spa you are willing to dedicate to the project.

Pool and spa remodeling (as opposed to repair work) presents a gamut of options. You may simply want to replace the pool deck with a more fashionable or multi-leveled surface, or install new equipment that automates water balancing and cleaning chores or reduces energy use. You may want to integrate a spa into or near an existing pool, or create an outdoor cooking and dining area to get more value out of your backyard oasis. Perhaps you've marveled at the variety of playful water features, such as sprays and fountains, or the more extensive makeovers that showcase fire pits, rock structures, and landscaping to create natural settings, and wondered if your pool or spa can be similarly transformed.

Pool and spa remodeling is a burgeoning business in which almost anything is possible, but it's also vastly different from starting from scratch. Like a second-story addition or upgraded kitchen job, it requires careful consideration of existing conditions, especially from a structural and mechanical standpoint. Will the structure accept a new interior finish? Can your equipment handle the new and extended functions of the pool or spa? Most important, are you willing to spend the time required to manage the leaves and flower petals from poolside plants, the water from a flowing fountain or slide, the gas line for a fire pit, and another kitchen to clean up?

If you're convinced that remodeling your pool and spa is a worthwhile investment, as it is for an increasing number of owners, consider the projects described in this chapter as guidelines to starting down that road.

Project Planning

The types and styles of pool and spa remodeling projects are nearly endless, based as much on personal taste and style as they are on building materials and engineering technology. But increasingly, pool and spa owners aren't limiting themselves to just one project, investing instead in more comprehensive makeovers. While such ventures are certainly tempting, and support a truly architectural approach to a

Project Idea: Add a spa. While adding or integrating an in-ground spa to your existing concrete pool is certainly an option, there are more economical and equally stunning options for adding value to your water amenity.

pool or spa setting, they can become quite expensive very quickly, and likely require the expertise of multiple contractors.

Setting a Budget and Selecting a Contractor

Regardless of whether you decide to tackle a pool or spa remodel yourself or employ a professional contractor experienced in such work, it's critical to set a budget for the job and align it with the cost of what you envision.

Creating a project budget is simply a matter of determining your monthly disposable income—what's left over after necessary expenses such as the mortgage payment, various utility bills, car payments, and other debt or ongoing household expenses. This amount, in addition to any savings or other available funds, can be used to pay for your project in cash or to pay off a short-term loan or a line of credit on a monthly basis.

To determine a budget, simply keep track of all of your household and personal expenses for a few months, then average each line item to find what you typically spend per month. From there, separate each expense as "essential" and "non-essential," such as

Project Idea: Upgrade Mechanicals. Technologically advanced heaters, filters, pumps and motors, and automated systems and controls save energy and simplify pool and spa ownership; it may also be appropriate to right-size your pump or filter to optimize their respective functions.

Project Idea: Add a poolside structure. If you've got the space, building a new poolhouse or permanent shelter next to a pool can open up a world of new possibilities in dining and entertaining.

Project Idea: Replace an old deck. Even if your old pool or spa deck is in fine shape, and more so if it's showing a bit of wear from years of use, a new platform can be a simple way to boost form and function.

your monthly mortgage payment (essential) and your bi-weekly massage appointment (probably non-essential). Take the essential items out of the calculation, as that total amount is untouchable as money you can reliably spend on a pool or spa remodeling

Work with professionals to help you plan all aspects of your pool remodeling project, including (and perhaps most importantly) the financial ones.

project, leaving you with the total of all of your non-essential spending: your disposable monthly income.

Add in whatever savings or other funding sources you can tap for the project and check out loan programs that might "extend" your payment terms longer than the length of the project (which will need to be paid off at completion). The result is your project budget: the total amount you are comfortably able to spend on a pool or spa remodeling project.

Keep in mind that, unlike new construction (pools, spas, or buildings), remodeling occasionally exposes problems and issues that must be rectified before the "new" work or features can be built. It may be, for instance, that exposing the pool walls reveals a crack or leak that must be repaired, or a soil condition that will cause long-term and chronic damage if left unchecked. The point is, allocate some of your budget—perhaps 15 percent—as a contingency against such discoveries and necessary repairs, including using experts such as engineers, rather than spending your whole budget on dramatic features and having to scrounge for funds to pay for what's needed.

With your budget number in hand, and any loans or lines of credit secured (or at least pre-approved), be prepared to share your budget, along with your remodeling dreams and ideas, with a professional contractor who has a history of successful projects like the one you envision for your property. Rather than "bidding out" the project among three of more potential contractors, select one with whom you feel comfortable and confident, and work with him or her to negotiate a contract, scope of work, and detailed specifications that match your budget.

Respecting What You Have

Opinions differ among industry experts and professional pool and spa remodelers, but changing the shape and depth of an existing pool structure can be an expensive and extensive undertaking. That kind of investment demands careful consideration, not just regarding its cost and value, but also what a total transformation does to the look and feel of your overall property, especially in relation to your house.

There are schools of design thought that say a house and its surrounding environment should complement each other. A symmetrically designed house,

for instance, is best suited by a similarly formal outdoor area, including a classically designed and finished pool setting. A less formal house in shape and finishes, by contrast, can best support a natural scene for and around the pool or spa, while regional or strongly ethnic architectural styles, such as Mediterranean or Asian, suggest like-styled pools and gardens.

There are, of course, those that subscribe to the theory that opposites attract, and therefore insist that a formal house is best contrasted by an informal (or natural) pool setting as part of an overall outdoor aesthetic.

Regardless of which camp you place yourself, at least be aware of your circumstances. Transforming a rectangular, in-ground concrete or vinyl-lined pool to one with a free-form shape, beachfront entry, spillover spa, rock waterfall, vanishing edge, or other built-in feature is possible if you have the time, money, and an expert remodeler, but is it practical? That's a decision only you can make, but do yourself the favor of a comprehensive evaluation before diving in.

Project idea: Upgrade your landscaping by planting a beautiful garden in your pool area. Just make sure the new garden doesn't create any runoff into your pool or spa (and vice versa—the sanitized water will eventually kill plants).

Adding a Spa

Unless you live in a climate that enables year-round enjoyment of your existing pool (or nearly so), the option of structurally integrating a new, in-ground spa will necessarily limit the use of that new feature to the same seasonal use of your pool. In other words, if the pool and spa share water, both are open and closed at the same time—a scenario that often works counter to enjoying a cool dip in the summer and a hot soak in the winter.

If you're dead-set on integrating the two, however, or live in a climate in which that scenario does not seasonally conflict, know from the outset that such a project is arguably the most complex and expensive option for adding a spa.

Essentially, you are building a new in-ground (if smaller) vessel, but with the added requirement of tying it structurally to your existing pool. Assuming you have a concrete pool, the project will require extensive excavation to expose the walls and bottom of the pool where the new spa will be located, and well as the excavation for the spa itself and its underground plumbing lines.

Obviously, the pool deck will be destroyed (or at least temporarily displaced) and the pool drained of water, enabling workers to break through the pool wall to expose the steel reinforcement (or rebar). To ensure a reliable connection between the pool and

spa, the existing rebar must be connected at every point along the perimeter of the opening, including the floor, to the new rebar forming the walls and floor of the new spa. The entire remodeled structure is then encased in concrete—usually gunite or shotcrete—and then finished in plaster or another material, the entire area backfilled properly, and a new deck installed.

The process is similar for vinyl-lined, in-ground pools, with the exception of the rebar and new concrete. Still, the structural walls of the pool must be exposed and integrated with those of the new spa, and you'll have to replace the entire pool liner or, more likely, fuse two liners together to accommodate the oddball overall shape you've created.

Setting a fiberglass vessel next to an existing fiberglass pool is possible, but the two structures cannot be physically integrated; rather, they'll simply be in close proximity to each other, each likely operating on separate mechanical systems.

In addition to the construction process, a pool and new spa that share water necessarily changes the calculations that determine a properly sized water circulation, filtration, and heating system. While the new spa can rely on a dedicated equipment set, that scenario dictates finding a place for a second set (and probably shielding it from view), not to mention the time commitment required to properly maintain two systems.

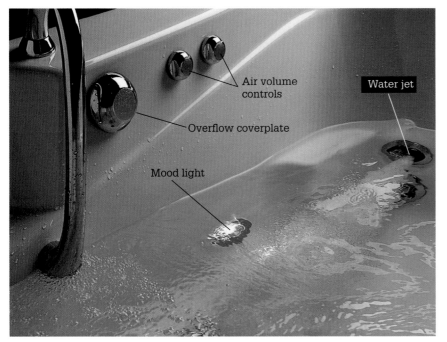

Project idea: Mood lights are sold as factory-installed accessories by many manufacturers. Most are available with several filters to let you adjust the color to suit your mood. Mood lights are low-voltage fixtures wired through 12-volt transformers. Do not wire mood lights or other accessories into the electrical circuit that supplies the pump motor.

Air volume controls

Water jet

Overflow coverplate

Mood light

It's more likely, then, that the new pool-spa combination will share a system (if perhaps with a separate heater and booster pump for the spa and its jets), which means that your existing equipment is probably inadequate and must be upgraded entirely to handle the increase in water volume, filtration requirements, and perhaps chemical distribution needs for the new, dual-use vessel.

Affordable Alternatives

A much simpler, less expensive but no less inviting or dramatic way to add a spa to your existing pool is with a portable spa unit. Though it's not recommended to set portable spas into the ground (thus burying the skid pack and making it inaccessible for service), such self-contained units can be set flush into a new or existing raised wood deck (providing access from below), surrounded by rock formations and/or landscaping to shield their skirts and appear built-in, or set on a concrete pad cut into a hillside to make the top of the spa flush with the pool deck but still allow relatively easy access to the mechanical works.

As discussed in earlier chapters, portable spas offer several advantages to in-ground spas, and especially so in a remodeling or add-on project. As self-contained units, they rely on properly sized equipment suited to the particular features of a spa, namely faster and higher heating capabilities and the ability to operate hydro-jets. The heater, for instance, might be electric, the most expensive fuel source for heating a full-sized pool but suitable for the water volume of a spa; the pump, meanwhile, includes a booster to power the jets, with a lower operating (and less costly) speed for normal circulation.

While it's true that a portable spa cannot share water with a pool, thus eliminating the drama of a spillover or waterfall between the two vessels, the advantages outweigh that dramatic effect. In fact, you can give the illusion of a shared-water scenario by having a waterfall built between them that spills water into both vessels. That is, assuming you accommodate the extra water volume in your circulation system calculations.

In addition, consider that the best place for a spa may not be near the pool—especially if that pool is located far away from the house—but rather closer to the house, such as on a rear yard deck or patio slab, so that it's easily and quickly accessible to bathers. A spa is also a year-round amenity, which the pool may not be depending on your climate; better to maintain a separate spa that's ready for a winter's soak than cover it up with the rest of the pool if or when you winterize.

Adding Amenities

As mentioned earlier in this chapter, the trend in pool and spa remodeling is to completely remake the look, feel, and function of these outdoor amenities rather than simply tackle one or two upgrades. As a result, the market for a variety of ancillary features, from full kitchens to fire pits, is on the upswing.

A portable spa is a quick and easy addition to your pool area that gives instant payback.

If you have the space, or can clear some footage for it, an outdoor kitchen and dining/lounge area adds immediate value to the pool and/or spa area, making it an even more desirable destination and extending its use beyond recreation and exercise. Replacing the rolled-out Weber kettle and picnic table and benches are built-in appliances—headlined by massive, multi-burner, propane-powered barbecue grills—and comfortable seating, ideally in a covered yet still open loggia or deck setting. That way, even if the pool is closed or not in use during some months of the year, the kitchen can still be opened for outdoor cooking (if perhaps not dining), especially if it is within close proximity to the house.

All of that function, of course, requires power. Instead of lighting a fire under a few coals in the kettle, you now need a gas or propane line to the pool area, as well as supply and drain plumbing for a sink and perhaps a dishwasher, and electricity for the refrigerator and other major and small appliances, grill ignition, ventilation fans, and lighting. In short, adding an outdoor kitchen is no less of a job than upgrading or building your home's kitchen.

Bringing all of those services to (or close to) the pool or spa deck requires professional and code-approved installation. You or your contractor will need to obtain a building permit and schedule peri-odic inspections to confirm its compliance with local building codes. It's likely that a new or supplemental service panel and/or meter is required, as well, to handle the dedicated circuits and utility lines.

The distance between the street or service panel and your pool or spa, and specifically where you intend to build your outdoor kitchen and dining area, can have a significant impact on the cost to install the various services you'll need; locating the new feature near the house, such as on an adjacent covered patio or wood deck, shortens the lines and might even allow you to branch off existing conduits or at least follow the same runs back to the service panel, thus avoiding constructing new trenches or chases.

Once "stubbed up" and ready to be connected, however, the various power lines and fuel sources for an outdoor kitchen simply need to be "plugged in" to their respective appliances and other amenities, which are often set into permanent cabinet and countertop structures akin to the kitchen inside.

Unlike the kitchen in the house, however, the finishes of an outdoor cooking area need to withstand the weather, specifically water. For that reason, materials such as brick and concrete, as well as quartz-surfacing materials, are often used for outdoor kitchens, as are stainless steel appliances and cabinets. The resulting look is often sleek and contemporary, but

A flagstone deck has beauty and charm that far exceeds plain concrete—especially failing concrete.

with a necessary toughness and durability to maintain its value and lessen maintenance chores and replacement costs. (Tip: If you insist on the look and feel of wood cabinets for your outdoor kitchen, specify woods such as teak, cypress, or mahogany that resist moisture damage, and finish them with several coats of paint or varnish to further protect them.)

Along the lines of a complete pool or spa makeover, folks who go to the expense of adding a full outdoor kitchen and dining/lounge area also might extend the project scope and budget to include a pool house, complete with a shower, restroom facilities, and changing area.

Such an amenity is especially valuable when the pool or spa is located some distance from the house, relieving bathers from having to hike back to use the restroom or change clothes. But for pools and spas located a hop-skip from the house, the owners might choose instead to upgrade or add a full bath inside

(perhaps with a small laundry set), with ready access to the pool or spa deck, to serve family and guests both inside and outside. In that case, a pool house might simply be built, without any services, as a shed for pool furniture, toys, and maintenance/cleaning equipment.

Replacing a Pool Deck

For many pool and spa owners, the traditional concrete slab deck has become a boring and outdated feature that detracts from their enjoyment and increasingly causes maintenance and repair headaches with every passing year. By far the easiest and most affordable decking option, concrete provides little dimension, interest, or color. As a result, the deck has become a target for remodeling jobs to help extend the design dynamic of the pool or spa.

Project idea: Poolside kitchens are convenient and fun. Creating one can be as easy as rolling in a grill and some outdoor furniture, or as complicated as installing a large gas grill with a built-in prep and eating area.

There are, of course, more practical reasons to replace the pool deck. Over time, the concrete can crack, usually by hydrostatic pressure or upheaval from the backfill underneath it or perhaps by intruding tree or plant roots from nearby landscaping features. Once it starts, that condition is worsened by water from the pool or spa being splashed or carried by bathers onto the deck and seeping through the deck to the dirt, thus adding to its moisture content.

In addition to increasing soil issues, which may eventually cause pressure against the pool wall, cracks in a concrete slab deck can be a safety hazard and replacing the deck will eliminate them.

Systems Upgrades

If there is one remodeling project that may not inspire or include any other aspects, it is upgrading or replacing the pool or spa's equipment set. Simply, such a project is a whole different animal than any

aesthetic changes made to the deck or vessel; rather, it's strictly an investment to improve the functionality of your pool or spa.

As with any appliance, the motor-pump, filter, heater, and other mechanical features of a pool or spa equipment set is bound to wear out to the point of diminishing returns. That is, when they become more trouble and costly to maintain than the price of a new replacement. Assuming proper maintenance and care, the typical "design life" of many pool and spa mechanics is about 10 years; if your pool equipment is approaching that age or is older, it might be time to upgrade the system.

Of course, there are other, equally legitimate reasons to replace various components in the equipment set. As mentioned earlier, adding a spa that will share the system with the pool almost always requires a recalculation and replacement of the pump and filter to handle the extra water volume and turnover.

Fire and water

As much as people are attracted to the sights and sounds of water, they're almost equally drawn to fire. Water and fire, in fact, present an intriguing, sensual contrast; putting them together in the form of a fire pit on the pool deck serves a variety of aesthetic and functional needs. Most fire pits or chimneas (tall, self-contained fireplaces with chimneys) are wood-fired, but an increasing number of them are direct-line gas or propane-fueled to reduce emissions, provide added safety, and offer convenience and greater flame and heat control. Regardless, they provide a pleasing look and a measure of comfortable heat, encouraging late-evening gatherings long after the pool and the kitchen (if not the adjacent wet bar) have been closed for the night.

In addition, recent technological advancements in pumps, filters, heaters, automatic in-line chemical feeders, and cleaning systems and controls that save energy, reduce maintenance chores, and/or lower chemical use and costs are often smart investments with fast returns, if perhaps simply in their added convenience and smooth operation.

As your equipment ages or causes you to maintain it more diligently and at increasing expense, consider the following mechanical upgrades to the system:

Switch to a DE filter. Replacing an aging sand or cartridge filter with a diatomaceous earth (DE) unit, which filters out finer particles than the other two types, can help lower your water balancing chores. It's also a good time to resize, and probably increase the capacity of the filter. Add a multiport valve and a sight glass to monitor the backwashing and priming process; the latest DE filter technology and design might require backwashing only once or twice a season, and for perhaps only 10 to 15 minutes—a far cry in terms of time and wasted water compared to older filters.

Replace the pump and motor. New pumps and motors are not only smaller in size, but run more quietly and more efficiently than those of just a decade ago. Combined, those qualities can enhance your pool or spa experience immensely, as the equipment is more easily concealed from view and less intrusive as an annoying background sound when the system is running. Oh, and a new pump and motor might save a you a few bucks on your energy bill as well.

Upgrade to a heat pump. Heaters, which are often appropriate even for the hottest climates (think cool desert nights in Las Vegas or Phoenix), use a lot of energy, especially to raise the temperature of a 30,000-gallon swimming even 10 degrees. In most markets, gas or propane is the preferred energy source, regardless of the heater. But if neither is available or is too expensive an option in your area, consider an electric heat pump.

Modern heat pumps for pools are dimensionally smaller, more energy-efficient, and more reliable in their operation than those of the past. Rated for their energy efficiency like other household appliances, heat pumps for pools operate like air conditioners in reverse. The unit sucks in warm air while exhausting cool air, then transfers that collected heat to the pool water. In addition, the heat pump's operation produces a condensate, which may add up to 10 gallons of heated water to the pool—not enough to overflow the edges, but providing some extra measure of heated water to help reach the desired temperature.

Heat pumps take about 1 to 2 days to boost the temperature of the pool by 10 degrees (about as much as you can expect from a pool heater, as opposed to a faster-heating spa unit), and will work like your furnace, on a thermostat, to automatically maintain that temperature for as long as you desire.

Supplement with solar. Solar water heating, like heat pump technology, has come a long way since its initiation in the late 1970s. Roof or ground-mounted collectors gather heat from the sun onto tubes and transfer it to water circulated through those conduits, then out to the pool vessel.

The obvious downside of solar heating is its inherent dependence on the sun; on cloudy and short winter days—when you most need the pool heated—the collectors aren't able to collect enough heat to warm

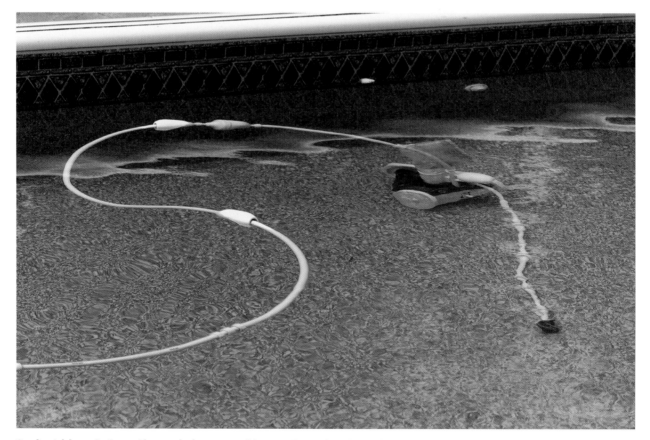

Project idea: Automatic pool cleaners, either suction units with their own pumps and collection bins or in-line blowers that push dirt and debris to the skimmers and main drain, are "on" during the pool's normal recirculation cycles, helping reduce manual brushing and vacuuming tasks and, in the case of the suction system, removing debris that can clog, or at least tax, the pool's filtration system.

Project idea: Build an addition for a spa if you don't have a good place for one in your home already. A kit-type three-season porch or solarium often is a good fit with a home spa.

the water. Solar is also an unreliable or impractical way to heat a spa, as the temperature in the tubes rarely reaches what you want for good soak.

The upside of solar, of course, is that you're using a "free" and clean energy source (the sun) and a system that requires little maintenance and has no moving parts to repair or replace. Modern solar collectors are less expensive and more efficient than their precursors, reducing the return on investment (or payback) considerably.

To balance the pros and cons of solar pool heating, consider using the system to supplement a more mainstream energy source to power the pool heater. This arrangement can occur two ways: first, as a traditional, heat-transfer system that overrides the mechanical heater when solar heat is available, thus reducing the energy that unit uses; second, as a source of free electricity that reduces your household's overall dependence on that energy source, including what it needs to heat the pool or spa.

In the second scenario, photovoltaic panels, or collectors, trap the sun's heat and convert it to electricity. Tied to the power grid, the system sends the electrical current to the service panel to power everything from your appliances and lights to the pool or spa heater; any excess energy is credited by the utility, so that even when you need electricity from the power grid, you're using power you've already "banked" with the utility, and therefore do not pay for until those credits are exhausted.

A third, completely passive solar heat source is the pool water. Left uncovered, the water will absorb the heat of direct sunlight to warm itself, reducing the need, or length and number of cycles required, to mechanically heat the pool. But the same solar gain that heats the water also evaporates it; combined with a summer breeze across the pool surface, an uncovered pool can lose quite a bit of volume during just one day, which needs to be monitored and replaced to maintain the integrity of the circulation system.

PROJECT: Install an indoor spa

Installing a spa or whirlpool bath in a master bathroom isn't as difficult as you might think. If you've ever installed an ordinary bathtub before, the process will be quite familiar to you once the rough-in of the spa deck structure is completed. Completing a rough-in for a spa requires that you install a separate GFCI-protected electrical circuit for the pump motor. Some building codes specify that a licensed electrician be hired to wire whirl-pools; check with your local building inspector.

Select your whirlpool before you do rough-in work, because exact requirements will differ from model to model. Select your faucet to match the trim kit that comes with your whirlpool. When selecting a faucet, make sure the spout is large enough to reach over the tub rim. Most whirlpools use "widespread" faucets because the handles and spout are separate, and can be positioned however you like, even on opposite sides of the tub. Most building centers carry flex tube in a variety of lengths for connecting faucet handles and spout.

5 ft. minimum

Grounding wire

Dedicated 20-amp circuit

▶ Anatomy of a Spa

A whirlpool circulates aerated water through jets mounted in the body of the tub. Whirlpool pumps move as much as 50 gallons of water per minute to create a relaxing "hydromassage" effect. The pump, pipes, jets, and most of the controls are installed at the factory, making the actual hookup in your home quite simple.

The electrical service for a whirlpool should be a dedicated 115- to 120-volt, 20-amp circuit. The pump motor should be grounded separately, normally to a metal cold water supply pipe. Most whirlpool motors are wired with 12/2 NM cable, but some local codes require the use of conduit. Remote timer switches (inset), located at least 5 ft. from the tub, are required by some codes, even for a tub with a built-in timer.

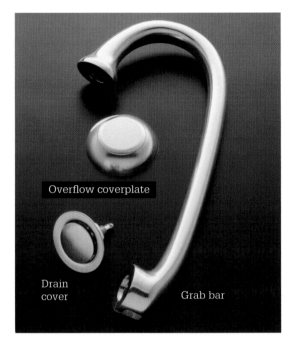

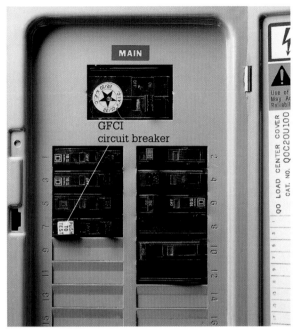

Trim kits for whirlpools are ordered at the time of purchase. Available in a variety of finishes, all of the trim pieces except the grab bar and overflow coverplate normally are installed at the factory.

A GFCI circuit breaker at the main service panel is required with whirlpool installations. Hire an electrician to connect new circuits at your service panel if you are uncomfortable installing circuit cables on your own.

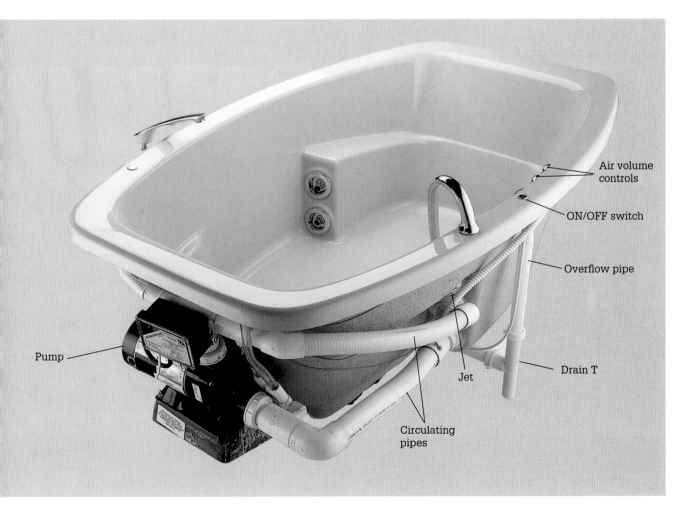

How to Install an Indoor Spa

Outline the planned location of the deck frame on the subfloor. Use the plumbing stub-outs as starting points for measuring. Before you begin to build the deck, check the actual dimensions of your whirlpool tub to make sure they correspond to the dimensions listed in the manufacturer's directions. Note: Plan your deck so it will be at least 4" wide at all points around the whirlpool.

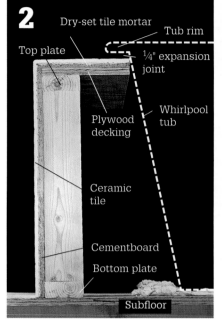

Cut top plates, bottom plates, and studs for the deck frame. The height of the frame should allow ¾" for the plywood decking, ¼" for an expansion gap between the deck and the tub rim, and 1" for cementboard, tile, and mortar.

Assemble the deck frame. Make sure to leave a framed opening for access panels at the pump location and the drain location. Nail the frame to the floor joists and wall studs or blocking, using 10d nails.

Cover the deck frame with ¾" exterior-grade plywood, and attach with deck screws spaced every 12". Using a template of the whirlpool cutout (usually included with the tub), mark the deck for cutting. If no template is included, make one from the shipping carton.

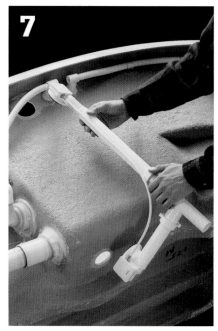

Drill a starter hole inside the cutout line, then make the cutout hole in the deck, using a jigsaw.

Measure and mark holes for faucet tailpieces and spout tailpiece according to the faucet manufacturer's suggestions. Drill holes with a spade bit or hole saw.

Attach drain-waste-overflow assembly (included with most whirlpools) at the drain and overflow outlets in the tub. Trim the drain pipe in the floor to the proper height, using a hacksaw.

Apply a layer of dry-set mortar to the subfloor where the tub will rest. Make 12" spacer blocks, 1¼" thick (equal to expansion gap, tile mortar, and cementboard). Arrange blocks along the edges of the cutout.

With a helper, lift the tub by the rim and set it slowly into the cutout hole. Lower the tub, pressing it into the mortar base, until the rim rests on the spacers at the edges of the cutout area. Align the tailpiece of the drain-waste-overflow assembly with the P-trap as you set the tub in place. Avoid moving or shifting the tub once it is in place, and allow the mortar to set for 6 to 8 hours before proceeding with the tub installation.

(Continued next page)

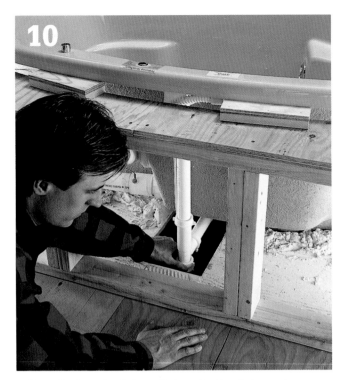

10

Adjust the length of the tailpiece for the drain-waste-overflow assembly, if necessary, then attach assembly to the P-trap in the drain opening, using a slip nut.

11

Inspect the seals on the built-in piping and hoses for loose connections. If you find a problem, contact your dealer for advice. Attempting to fix the problem yourself could void the whirlpool warranty.

12

With the power off, remove the wiring cover from the pump motor. Feed the circuit wires from the power source or wall timer into the motor. Connect the wires according to the directions printed on the motor.

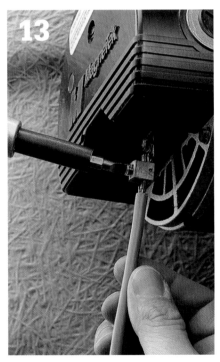

13

Attach an insulated 8-gauge wire to the ground lug on the pump motor.

14

Attach the other end of the wire to a metal cold water supply pipe in the wall, using a ground clamp. Test the GFCI circuit breaker.

15

Clean out the tub, then fill it so the water level is at least 3" above the highest water jet.

16

Turn on the pump, and allow it to operate for at least 20 minutes while you check for leaks. Contact your whirlpool dealer if leaks are detected.

17

Staple paper-faced fiberglass insulation to the vertical frame supports. The facing should point inward, to keep fibers out of the motor. Do not insulate within 6" of pumps, heaters, or lights.

18

Attach cementboard to the sides and top of the deck frame if you plan to install ceramic tile on the deck. Use ¾" plywood for access panel coverings.

19

Attach finish surfaces to deck and deck frame, then install grab bar, faucet, and spout. Fill the joints between the floor and deck, and between the tub rim and deck surface, with silicone caulk.

How to Install an outdoor spa

Building a hot tub into a deck is usually done in one of two ways. If you design your deck at exactly the right height, you can create a full inset by resting the hot tub on a concrete pad and building the deck around it.

But on a low-profile deck, or a tall deck, the most practical solution is to mount the hot tub on the surface of the deck and build a secondary platform around it, creating a partial inset. As shown on the following pages, the structural design of the deck must be modified to ensure that it can support the added weight of a hot tub filled with water. Make sure your deck plans are approved by the building inspector before you begin work.

Installing a hot tub usually requires the installation of new plumbing and electrical lines. When planning the installation, make sure to consider the location of plumbing pipes, electrical cables, switches, and access panels. For convenience, arrange to have the rough-in work for these utilities done before you install the decking boards.

Plan posts and beams to support the maximum anticipated load, including the weight of the hot tub filled with water. In most cases, this means altering your deck plan to include extra beams and posts directly under the hot tub.

Lay out and install the ledger, footings, posts, and support beams, according to your deck plans. Lay out joist locations on the ledger and beams, and install the joists, following local code requirements. Many building codes require joists spaced no more than 12" on center if the deck will support a hot tub. If your hot tub requires new plumbing or electrical lines, have the preliminary rough-in work done before continuing with deck construction.

3

Install the decking boards, then snap chalk lines to outline the position of the hot tub and the raised platform that will enclose the hot tub.

4

Lay out and cut 2 × 4 sole plates and top plates for the stud walls on the raised platform.

5

Mark stud locations on the top and bottom plates. Studs should be positioned every 16" (measured on center), and at the ends of each plate.

6

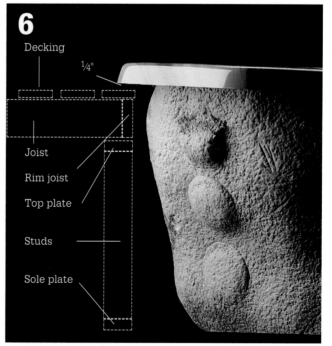

Decking

¼"

Joist

Rim joist

Top plate

Studs

Sole plate

Measure the height of the hot tub to determine the required height of the studs in the platform walls. Remember to include the thickness of both wall plates, the joists that will rest on the walls, and the decking material on the platform. The surface of the finished platform should be ¼" below the lip of the hot tub.

(Continued next page)

Construct the stud walls by screwing the plates to the studs. Position the walls upright on the deck over the outline marks, and anchor them to the deck with 2½" deck screws.

At corners, join the studs together with 3" deck screws. Check the walls for plumb, and brace them in position.

Blocking

Toenail a 2 × 6 rim joist along the back edge of the platform, then cut and install 2 × 6 joists across the top of the stud walls at 16" intervals, toenailing them to the top plates. The ends of the joists should be set back 1½" from the edges of the top plates to allow for the rim joist.

Cut 2 × 6 rim joists to length, and endnail them to the joists with 16d nails. At angled wall segments, cut diagonal blocking and attach it between the rim joist and adjoining joists with deck screws.

Cut decking boards, and attach them to the platform joists with 2½" deck screws. If your hot tub requires cutouts for plumbing or electrical lines, do this work now.

Set the hot tub in place, then build 2 × 2 stud walls around the exposed sides of the tub. Measure, cut, and install siding materials on the exposed walls.

Build platform steps to provide access to the platform, using siding materials to box in the risers. Where required by code, install railings around the elevated platform.

Wood decking creates a warm tones and nice pattern and texture around your pool. It will, however, require periodic maintenance and refinishing. It is one of the few options available for decking around raised pools.

Steps for removing a concrete pool deck

As with most demolition projects, removing a concrete pool deck is a fairly simple if often messy project. Consider the following steps whether you plan to do the work yourself or hire a professional to remove and dispose of the old material:

- Drain the pool, turn off the filtration system, and cover all skimmer, drain, and return outlets with rags or plastic sheeting to keep dirt, dust and debris from clogging the works.

- Rent a Dumpster or find out the best way to dispose of the material once it's removed, such as hauling it to the local landfill.

- Using a jackhammer, pick, and/or a sledgehammer, break up the slab and coping material into small, easy-to-carry pieces; remember to use eye and nose protection and wear work boots and gloves for the job.

- Once the big sections are gone, carefully police the area for smaller shards and pieces; collect them in a bucket and add them to the disposal pile.

- Now, you're ready to replace or upgrade the backfill, set a drainage system, automatic cover, or extra structural support, and install the new decking material.

Flagstone makes for an elegant yet informal pool deck. Flagstone can be set into mortar or laid onto a sand base. Flagstone is best purchased from local stone supply yards.

Precast stepping pavers are a relatively easy and inexpensive way to redeck a pool. They must be laid on a very flat, smooth sand base. They can be purchased at most major home centers.

Stone tile is a premium building material used to create elegant and formal pool decks. Although traditionally sold only at premium stone yards, stone tile has recently become available at the large home improvement warehouse stores.

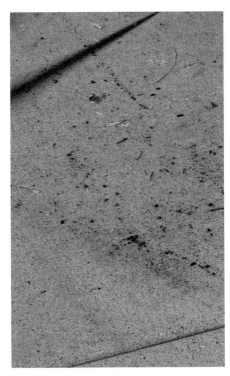

Brushed concrete is a relatively inexpensive pool deck surface, and perhaps the most common. To minimize slip hazards, it should be brushed or textured while still wet to provide a slightly rough surface.

Cobblestones or interlocking pavers offer a means for creating unique patterns and colors in a pool deck. These materials normally are laid on a sand base.

PROJECT IDEA: Automatic Pool Cover

Safety-rated automatic pool covers are made from reinforced fabric that can support the weight of several people at a time (although this is not recommended regular usage for the product).

Automatic pool covers are increasingly popular accessories that are normally installed at the time of construction, but can be easily retrofitted. The advantages of owning one are threefold: it is a great safety feature (you can keep your pool covered and accessible by key only); they reduce evaporation and heat loss; and they keep debris out the pool. Compared to a manual cover, they are much easier to roll out or roll up. You only need to turn a key that is mounted on a control panel that must be in clear view on the pool. The only real downside is that they cost a minimum of $10,000 installed.

When not in use, the cover is rolled up on a power-driven roller and is stored in a bunker in the pool deck.

When the keyed control is switched on, the automatic pool cover is rolled out or retracted. Better models will cover or uncover a standard size residential pool in about a half minute.

Start.

15 seconds.

30 seconds.

Seasonal Maintenance

If you own an outdoor pool in a cold climate, annual winterizing is likely to be on your seasonal schedule; similarly, closing your spa during an extensive vacation might also be a smart, money-saving option. Of course, anytime you close or winterize a pool or spa, you have to re-open it.

Regardless of your climate or vacation situation, you probably have some pool furniture and accessories to care for, as well. Upholstered loungers and chairs, tables, umbrellas and awnings, and an array of pool toys also need to be maintained to combat both extreme weather conditions and everyday use.

This chapter presents a step-by-step method for winterizing or closing a pool or spa, from adjusting the pH and chlorine levels to lowering the water volume (if at all), blowing out pipes, and protecting the integrity of the cover and accessory items.

Reopening a pool or spa is an equally systematic process, including a thorough cleaning, a careful restarting of the pump, filter, and other equipment, and a more extensive amount of testing and chemical balancing to achieve ideal water quality.

Together, the proper closing and reopening of a pool or spa not only helps ensure an easier, trouble-free transition between seasons, but also lessens the burden of routine cleaning and maintenance and reduces the potential for damage and costly repairs.

Relatively few owners will have the opportunity to close and reopen a pool or spa, at least on a seasonal basis. But knowing the steps to those processes comes in handy when that off-chance occurs. And, almost every owner has some furniture and toys to tend to, whether to ward off the weather or maintain against everyday use, and will likely at some point be faced with patching a crack or leak. Understanding the nuances of special and seasonal care is essential for long-term enjoyment of your pool or spa.

Closing or Winterizing

Truly closing or winterizing a pool or spa requires a step-by-step process for properly protecting the shell, skimmers, and various mechanical components from damage caused by freeze-thaw cycles, surface frost, and debris, among other environmental factors, as well as to safely guard against accidents, vandalism, and unauthorized use.

As with routine cleaning and maintenance chores, there are few differences between closing and reopening a pool versus a spa, or even between an in-ground or above-ground vessel; any distinctions are described in the steps outlined below.

Ask professional technicians about their approach to closing/winterizing and reopening pools and spas, and you're bound to find a few subtle differences, as well. As with any responsibility that comes with pool or spa ownership, it's important to gain a solid understanding of the basics, from a variety of sources, toward developing a routine that best suits your particular comfort level, circumstances, and budget. In the meantime, as long as you stay within the recom-

mended ranges of various chemical levels and water volume, you should experience few, if any, issues.

In that spirit, consider the following steps to closing or winterizing a pool or spa as a template or starting point for your own plan, whether it's something you execute on your own or negotiate with a professional service technician.

Chemical balance. Adjust the pH level of the pool to between 7.2 and 7.8 to help prevent algae growth, stains, and scaling while the water sits idle. Establishing a chemical balance among all water quality features is essential to the welfare of the pool surfaces and exposed components while it's closed, as well as making it easier to balance the water when you reopen.

Shock or superchlorinate. Adding three to five times the amount of chlorine as your usual, in-season treatment will raise the level of free or available chlorine in the water, providing plenty of sanitation while the pool is closed due to the fact that few, if

Tools and materials for opening and closing a pool, include (clockwise from left): Air pillows to support pool cover; wet-and-dry shop vacuum; air compressor for blowing out plumbing lines; lubricant for gaskets; a skimmer plug; a submersible pump; pool antifreeze.

Keep the pool covered once leaves start falling, and you begin preparations for the seasonal closing of the pool. You don't need to use your safety-rated winter cover if you're not ready for it yet. Any summer cover or solar cover will do.

any, organic materials will gain entry into the water during that time.

Add algaecide and/or antifreeze. Some experts also recommend adding algaecide to the water to specifically prevent algae growth that would be difficult to see, much less address, when the pool is closed and covered. Others also advocate adding antifreeze specially formulated for pools (not the same as car antifreeze) to lessen the depth or degree by which the water might freeze in extreme climates, thereby helping reduce the potential for surface damage and mineral staining. Antifreeze is also recommended if

you choose not to "blow out" or empty your pool's pipes and other components; however, leaving water in the system is not generally advocated in a freezing climate, even with antifreeze.

Run the system. You should run your recirculation and filtration system and conduct regular cleaning chores, as normal, before you winterize or close the pool—even if no one is using it—to help preserve its chemical balance. Once you're ready to winterize, run the system continuously for 24 to 48 hours to "clean out" any lingering organic matter in the pipes, outlets, skimmers, and filter so that the chlorine or

Tips for Seasonal Maintenance

- Decide early to winterize a pool and gather the right gear in preparation.
- Understand how the closing and reopening processes work together to ensure smooth seasonal transitions.
- Keep a watchful eye for cracks and leaks in surfaces.

- Conduct routine cleaning and maintenance when the pool or spa is open/in use to mitigate serious problems.
- Know your pool's construction and finishes to prepare for minor repairs.
- Schedule an annual professional check-up.

Shocking Your Pool

Pool shock is a chemical that you pour into the pool water to elevate the available sanitizer (usually chlorine) level (you can also buy nonchlorine shock). Adding shock at closing helps keep the water healthy while the pool is dormant. Read the label to make sure the shock is right for your pool and to find usage information.

Add shock directly to the water. Pour the prescribed amount of chemical into a glass measuring cup and then into the water, doing your best to avoid splashing. Make sure to do this when the recirculating system is on.

Backwash the filtration system to clean out the filter thoroughly (see pages 112 to 113).

other sanitizer can combat it before closure and last until reopening.

Clean the pool. Remove as much debris as possible from the pool surfaces by removing leaves and debris on the surface, brushing and vacuuming the walls and bottom and cleaning out the skimmer baskets and filter medium, lessening organic material in the water and mitigating clogs or corrosion that might occur while the pool is closed.

Shut off the system. After running the recirculation system (see above), shut off power to the equipment set at the service panel, removing the circuit breaker or fuse, if possible, to prevent any accidental restarts before you're ready to reopen the pool. Keep the fuses in a sealed bag or container with other parts you've removed so that they are all in one place and easy to find when the time comes. Also, shut off any other energy sources, including gas lines (setting the valve to "pilot only" or off completely) and solar panels used for heating or electricity generation.

Shut off power to your pool at the subpanel once you have run and winterized the systems. Some professionals recommend physically removing the breakers so the system is not turned on by accident. If you do this, store the breakers in a sealed bag in a cool, dry spot.

Backwash the filter. If you have a diatomaceous earth (DE) filter, backwash it until the sight glass (gauge) is clear, drain the tanks, and leave the backwash valve open to passively vent any lingering moisture so that it does not freeze and damage the works inside.

Protect the pump. Thoroughly drain and/or blow-out the pump housing and lubricate or replace the gasket or O-ring; do the same for the filter, heater, automatic chemical feeder(s), booster pump, and valves within the exposed sections of the plumbing system, as appropriate. In extremely cold climates, professional technicians and pool experts recommend removing the pump (and booster pump, if installed) and storing it in a dry place, such as the garage or basement. If not, all pumps should be wrapped in insulation or a heating coil to guard against freezing.

Store accessories. Remove slides, ladders, handrails, and diving boards or platforms, as practical or possible, as well as the hoses and heads for any automatic

Thoroughly brush and vacuum the pool walls and floor before covering up the pool for the season.

Lubricate gaskets on the pump and at any other seals that require lubrication prior to closing.

In most areas it is best not to drain above-ground pools for the winter. You will need to eliminate enough water that the water level is beneath the skimmer intake (weir) line so the pool water stays out of the plumbing, where it can freeze and cause damage. Above-ground pool covers have a cable that's sewn into the cover like a drawstring on a trash bag. One good way to install the cover is to start by folding it in half and lay it out over half the pool. You'll want a couple of helpers for this job.

Tighten the cable that runs through the hem to attach the cover. Make sure the cover is secure, but do not overtighten it.

Slip air pillows underneath the pool cover to keep the cover from sinking when it collects water. Then, flip the other half of the folded cover over to completely cover the pool. As another measure of safety, or vandalism prevention, consider removing the ladder or steps that lead to the pool deck.

Blow out the pipes to dislodge any clogs and clear out water so it does not freeze inside the pipes. You can use a leaf blower or a shop vacuum set on reverse for this job. Most professionals use an air compressor with a specialty fitting that attaches to the pump.

cleaning devices. Clean and store them in a covered or enclosed location. Store the diving board flat to prevent warping. For any exposed metal surfaces or components that cannot be removed but will be exposed to the air, grease their surfaces to protect them from harsh conditions and corrosion.

Drop the water level. Close the valve to the skimmer line(s) and drain the pool so that the waterline is just under the skimmer opening(s) and/or return lines, or below the tile border (as expanding frozen water might crack a tile surface). Do not drain the pool completely, as the water serves as an insulator and to balance the pressure being placed on the outside of the shell by the backfill material, thus mitigating

cracks and leaks. It's okay (and in some extreme climates, expected) if the pool water freezes; the slightly lower level will accommodate any expansion and, as long as the recirculation system is closed off from the water, won't allow the ice to migrate out of the pool shell.

Blow out the pipes. Like automatic lawn sprinklers, the pipes and outsets serving your pool need to be completely free of water; if not, any lingering moisture can freeze and expand, causing leaks in the lines. With the water level below the skimmer and return outlets, use the reverse flow of a pool vacuum or an air compressor to force the water out into the vessel. Remove the surface fittings and skimmer

Mild Climate Care

Mild seasonal climates may not require you to close or winterize you pool, but they will have an impact on your routine cleaning and maintenance chores. Simply, as pool use lightens as the temperature drops, your schedule can relax a bit. Instead of testing and balancing water quality every second or third day during the height of swim season, for instance, that chore might be reduced to once a week or more in the late fall, early spring, and throughout the winter; cleaning out the

filter medium or skimmer baskets and running the recirculation system may also be performed less frequently. Cooler temperatures also mitigate bacteria and algae growth, requiring less sanitization—all of which adds up to less time and cost to maintain a pool or spa. Your best gauge, however, is a watchful eye on the condition of your pool or spa; if it looks like it needs a cleaning or chemical balancing, regardless of recent use, it most likely does.

Winterize a Spa?

The hot, bubbling water of a spa or hot tub is the perfect antidote to a chilly night, right? But in extremely cold climates, when just going outside is a hassle or perhaps even hazardous (making it difficult to do much of anything, much less soak in a spa), the shell and mechanical equipment must be winterized to protect it from harsh conditions and freezing, which will cause damage and costly repairs. To winterize a portable acrylic-fiberglass spa, drain the vessel entirely and blow-out all of the pipes and skid pack components. Plug all openings and clean the surfaces thoroughly, then install and secure a foam-core cover. Never drain a wooden hot tub, however, which will cause the staves (or sides) to shrink within a day or so, perhaps to the point where they cannot recover and reseal once the tub is refilled. For in-ground spas, winterize the shell as you would an in-ground pool.

Unlike swimming pools, outdoor spas typically are drained to winterize them. It is important that the plumbing lines be blown completely clear of water or they will burst when frozen. Some spa technicians recommend filling the lines with antifreeze. And be sure to cover the spa completely so water cannot get into the shell.

Store accessories and chemicals in a dedicated area. Make sure any chemicals that should not freeze are stored in an insulated or heated area.

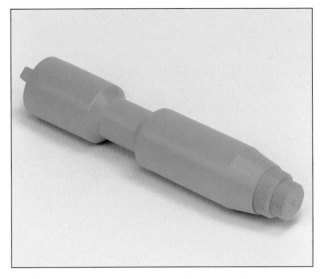

A skimmer plug is inserted into the opening in a pool skimmer to block the passage and insure that no water finds its way into the recirculation system during the winter months.

baskets and close off the outlets, valves, return lines, vacuum lines, and skimmer openings with flexible rubber plugs or Gizzmos (with Teflon plumber's tape on the threads) to keep water from intruding back into the system. Put the fittings, and any other loose parts and pieces (such as the bolts from the diving board or ladder) in the skimmer baskets and store them for safekeeping.

You can also "blow out" the main drain, protecting it as well. Hook up the compressor to the main drain valve in the equipment set and run it until bubbles flow from the main drain into the water. Then plug the pipe or close the gate valve, creating an air lock that won't allow the pool water to enter the drain.

Cover the pool. Install a safety-rated cover over the pool, anchoring it securely in place. In the case of an automatic cover, make sure it is totally across the surface, then lock it in place and shut off power to its operation at the service panel. During the winter or while to pool is closed, periodically make sure the cover is still anchored and taught, and diligently keep the surface free of standing water and ice; foam sheets, air pillows, or inflatable exercise balls or truck tire tubes are effective (and generally affordable) ways to keep standing water from freezing before you can remove it from the cover's surface. A small pump system for large pools is easier and probably safer

Pool cover options

Three types of covers are appropriate for a winterized or closed pool. The first is a domed structure supported by air above the water surface; its shape effectively sheds rain, snow, and debris from the cover and easing the reopening process. A second type is a loose, non-safety rated shield held in place by bags of sand or water or tied down to the deck or coping; it is adequate for keeping debris out of the water, but provides no safety protection and might tear or fly off in extreme storm con-

ditions. To create a "peaked" or domed shape for this type of cover, inflate a beach ball or two and let them float on the water, under the cover, which will also help keep the pool water from freezing completely. A third option is a true, safety-rated cover. Typically a thick, reinforced vinyl material that is stretched taut over the water and anchored to several hooks or snaps set flush into the deck or coping, a safety-rated cover also helps prevent off-season vandalism.

than using a long-handled broom to remove standing water on the cover.

Dispose of chemicals. By the time you're ready to reopen the pool, you'll want to use fresh chemicals instead of those that have been sitting around for months. If you know you're going to close or winterize your pool for a coming season, try to plan your chemical use during the rest of the year so that you won't waste a lot of open and unused material once the pool is closed. Follow the directions on each container for proper disposal.

Once you winterize a pool, there's really nothing to do until it's time to reopen it, except keep the cover clear of standing water and debris. That's the point, really, to closing a pool: to give you a break from the cleaning and maintenance routine you follow when it's open and in use.

Clean and store furnishings. If you own a pool or spa, chances are you have gathered a fair amount of gear to enhance your enjoyment of it, from deck chairs and roll-away barbecue grills to a variety of water toys and games.

Whether you plan to winterize your pool or simply expect to use it infrequently during the off-season, your investment in pool and patio furniture and other accessories need to be protected from the weather as well.

Whatever furniture and equipment you can move should be taken off of the pool or spa deck and placed either under cover nearby or inside a shed; if it's simply covered (instead of enclosed), secure a tarp over the top of it, allowing some air to flow from the bottom to vent any moisture. If possible, store upholstery, such as lounge and chair pads, as well as fabric awnings or umbrellas, in a shed or the garage, ideally encased in a plastic cover for protection.

If you truly have nowhere to store chairs, loungers, or tables, push them as close to the house as possible and weigh them down at their feet and seats with sandbags or something of similar bulk, then cover them with a secured tarp.

Similarly, stash your pool cleaning and safety equipment away in an enclosed shed or your garage; if you lack the room in either place, consider a garage storage system that attaches to the ceiling, enabling use of otherwise wasted vertical space—especially for the safekeeping of seasonal items. Telescoping poles can either be collapsed, hung vertically, or spanned across the exposed roof rafters of a garage or shed, out of the way.

Meanwhile, thoroughly clean and dry leaf catchers, life preservers, float lines, life rings, and rescue tubes, among other gear, before storage to minimize

Don't neglect the pool deck and outbuildings that support the pool activities, such as storage sheds and gazebos. Give them a good washing down so one season's grime doesn't become a permanent part of the surfaces (See Pressure Washing Pool Furnishings, next page).

mildew growth. Toys, too, especially those with metal parts that can corrode, need to be cleaned, dried, and greased against even mildly cold weather and moisture.

If possible, keep all of your pool cleaning, safety, and recreational equipment together, along with the components—such as the pump, skimmer baskets, and accessory items—that you removed from the pool deck during the winterizing process. That way, everything is in the same place, easily found and preserved, for when it's time to reopen the pool.

A gas-powered pressure washer is an invaluable tool for cleaning your pool and pool deck (see pages 52 to 53), as well as for cleaning outdoor furnishings prior to storage.

Pressure-washing Pool Furnishings

Through general use, winter storage, or simply exposure to weather, outdoor furniture and accessories can collect plenty of dirt, grease, and grime. A wash and rinse from a pressure washer can quickly revitalize furniture, barbecue grills, and other outdoor accessories for another season of enjoyment.

A high-pressure blast is often all it takes to clean surface dust and dirt from furniture frames and vinyl-covered seat cushions. Stubborn stains

on cushions should be spot cleaned, then rinsed with plenty of clear water to flush out any detergent from inside the material. Extremely soiled or stained items, such as barbecue grills, will require treatment with a multi-purpose cleaner or heavy-duty degreaser, followed by a high-pressure rinse.

Outdoor furniture is crafted from a wide variety of materials, including wood, wrought iron, aluminum, vinyl, and plastics. Each of these materials can be safely cleaned with a pressure washer, but caution must be taken to prevent damage to each material's particular finished surface. For best results when cleaning any furniture surface, always begin with a wide spray pattern at a distance; then move closer as needed to increase the effective cleaning power. A turbo nozzle can be used on wrought-iron and vinyl furniture frames.

To avoid unwanted cleaning of surrounding areas, clean your outdoor furniture on an open, durable surface, such as a driveway or patio. Remove all seat cushions from chairs and benches, and umbrellas from tables, prior to pressure washing.

Use a high-pressure, wide spray pattern to remove general dirt and grime from furniture frames. Use a multi-purpose detergent and a brush attachment to treat and penetrate heavy buildup and stubborn stains.

To clean vinyl-covered seat cushions, reattach the cushions to the furniture frame to hold them in place, then rinse thoroughly in high-pressure mode. Spot clean stubborn stains by hand using a utility brush and hot soapy water, followed by a high-pressure rinse with plenty of clear water to flush any detergent from inside the cushion.

The restoration of old patio furniture can go faster with your pressure washer. A tight spray pattern will strip old paint and finishes with ease, leaving you very little sanding and scraping work. However, use caution when stripping wood; concentrated blasts of water, such as that produced by the 0° spray pattern, can damage wood fibers.

A lonely diving board will tantalize you all throughout the long, cold winter, making it even more exciting when that eagerly anticipated time comes to reopen your pool for the swimming season.

Reopening

Reopening a pool after it's been winterized isn't simply a matter of following the closure process in reverse. Though many of the steps seem to follow that course, reopening has its own pace and procedures to mitigate damage to the vessel and its supporting parts and systems, ease water-balancing chores, and avoid extensive (and expensive) repairs.

One of the most important considerations is to make sure the water is completely free of ice, and that it is unlikely to freeze again until the next winter. Consult a local almanac, pool expert, or local garden nursery regarding what is historically the last day of frost for your climate to help set a date for reopening.

Buy new chemicals and testing gear. Restock your supply of chemicals and purchase new reagents or test strips in preparation for the upcoming swim season.

Prep your cleaning equipment. Gather and assemble, if necessary, your cleaning gear, and set it up near or on the pool deck for easy access. Pull out your safety equipment, as well, and check it for any damage or wear before putting it back in service. Review your safety plan, adjust it as necessary, and communicate it to your family and other users of your pool or spa.

Clear the cover. If you've been diligent about keeping your winter pool cover free of debris and standing water, there shouldn't't be a lot of either to remove right before reopening. If possible, brush or otherwise direct the debris and water to one side and off of the cover to help contain it and prevent it from getting into the water once you remove the cover.

Remove and store the cover. Carefully untether the cover from its anchoring system and fold or roll it off

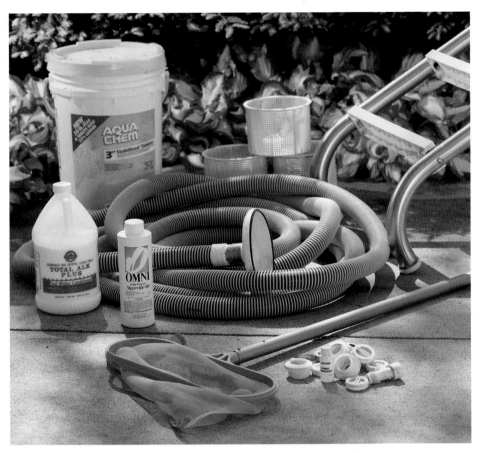

Gather up your supplies and materials and move them to a convenient staging area to make your reopening run as efficiently as possible.

of the pool surface. Unfurl it on a clean, flat surface, such as a driveway or patio, and clean and dry it thoroughly, using a stiff, nylon-bristled brush and non-abrasive detergent and soft rags; avoid air-drying it in direct or hot sun to keep it from getting brittle and cracked, and thus useless for the next season. Apply a dusting of pool-specific talcum powder (available at most retailers) to both sides before re-rolling or folding the cover and storing it in a cool, dry location.

Reconnect the system. Reinstall the pump and other components that you removed for the winter, hook up the pipes and hoses, and open the valves to the recirculation and filtration system in preparation for restarting the equipment. Lubricate gaskets, valves, and other parts, or replace them if they were damaged during the winter. Open or activate gas lines and solar-collection systems.

Clean up. Rinse out all skimmers and skimmer baskets and filter media, or replace them if damaged or worn, and put them back in place within the system. Remove winter plugs and replace the fittings on the outlets and skimmer openings along the pool's surfaces. Manually brush the pool walls and floor clean (there should not be much material to stir up) and fill

If you've been dutiful about policing your pool cover during the offseason, sweeping it clean prior to removal won't take long at all.

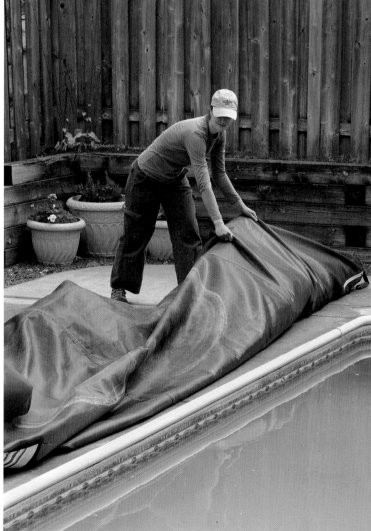

Start at the deep end when you're removing a safety-rated pool cover. The more straps that are removed, the more the cover will want to sink, so it's better to be in shallow water when it comes loose. Once the cover is removed, drive the strap screws back so they are recessed in the pool deck.

Spread the cover out in a driveway and hose it down thoroughly. Make sure it has dried completely before you fold it up and put it into storage for the season.

the pool to the waterline, just above the skimmer weir opening (or flap).

Check for cracks. Examine the pool walls and floor, as well as all pipes, hoses, and components of the equipment set and cleaning gear, for cracks or fissures. Likewise, look for and repair any surface damage to the waterline tile, coping, deck material, and perimeter drain system caused by frost heave. Patch or repair and refinish, as necessary or possible.

Reinstall accessories. Pull out slides, diving boards, and other accessory parts, check them for any damage or make any needed repairs, and reattach them securely in place.

Switch on the power. Reinstall fuses or circuit breakers or simply flick the breaker switches at your main electrical service panel to bring power back to the pool's pump and recirculation system. Switch on the pump and filter and keep a close eye on the skimmers, drains, and filters to make sure the system is running smoothly. Switch off the system or any component if it needs adjustment, then retest.

Vacuum the pool. With the system running, vacuum the pool walls and floor, beginning at the shallow end and from the tops of the walls to the floor, toward the main drain in the deep end.

Buff up the brightwork so your metal surfaces are gleaming when you return them to their appointed places.

Heat it up. Most likely, you'll want to jack up the heat in your pool so you can enjoy it in the early to mid-spring months, then back it off as the outdoor temperature rises in the summer and early fall.

Balance the water. Allow the recirculation, filtration, and heating system to run at least two hours, but no longer than a day, before testing the water quality for sanitation and chemical balance, then follow your normal routine for achieving the desired water quality.

If necessary, due to a low free chlorine reading, superchlorinate or shock the pool water to bring that level back to normal. The pool water may appear cloudy at first, but allow the filtration system to recirculate the water multiple times to see if it clears before addressing the issue with a professional or with chemicals.

Reset your furniture. As the weather permits, uncover or pull out your pool furniture, toys, barbecue grill,

Be prepared for a shock when you unveil your beloved pool. The ravages of time build up as the months pass. Even if you shocked the pool water the day of closing, you will very likely find a thick layer of algae and slime on the pool bottom. But the good news is, it will clean up pretty quickly and you should have your water balanced and swimmable in a week or so.

and other ancillary equipment and set it on the deck. Use temporary covers or roll/move it back under cover to protect it against fickle weather.

If you made a conscientious effort to close or winterize your pool, and done what little cleaning is required for the cover during that time, the reopening process should be relatively easy, allowing you to enjoy your pool again within a few days.

Understanding the fundamentals of closing and reopening a pool or spa, identifying and making minor repairs, and recognizing when more extensive renovations or replacements are required or warranted is a critical component of being a responsible owner. With the basics ingrained, you'll soon develop your own routines and systems based on those rules of thumb, or be able to intelligently negotiate service contracts with pool and spa professionals.

Using skimmer baskets to store small pool parts is a good way to help make sure you'll find them when you need them.

Hoping to avoid the labor of closing and reopening a pool or spa? There's always the four-season approach. This has its own set of issues, of course.

Pool and Spa Safety

The importance of safety in and around your pool or spa cannot be overstated. Simply, it is your primary responsibility as a pool or spa owner to make sure everyone who enjoys it, cleans it, keeps the water balanced, and peers at it enviously over a properly designed privacy fence or through a self-closing, self-latching gate is kept out of harm's way.

If you choose to accept that responsibility, just as you have to maintain your pool or spa to ensure its peak performance, you're well on your way to providing a safe and healthy experience for your family, friends, and neighbors.

Comprehensive pool and spa safety encompasses several practical measures. Ideally, your pool or spa was designed and built with safety in mind, including features such as a slip-resistant deck and coping, a secure perimeter fence and gate(s), the proper depth and other dimensions for a variety of activities, and provisions for a safety-rated cover.

Other protection recommended by the U.S. Consumer Product Safety Commission (CPSC) to maintain a safe and healthy private swimming pool or spa include: having life-saving and first aid gear close at hand, properly anchoring handrails and other accessory and accessibility features, and posting easy-to-read signs. A pool or spa safety plan may also include lighting schemes, thermometers (to ensure safe water temperature), and a variety of alarms.

A nonskid pool deck is a requirement for a safe swimming area. Broomed concrete is a very popular choice because it is inexpensive and offers great traction even when it's wet.

▶ Keys to Pool and Spa Safety:

- Take responsibility for it.
- Designate and educate a safety "expert."
- Set rules for safe behavior and enforce them.
- Take a comprehensive approach to safety.
- Review and refine your safety plan at least once a year.

Pool depth and slope are big factors in safety. Modern pools typically have a lightly sloping shallow end for safe wading, with a quick drop-off to safe diving depth in the deep end once the depth hits 5½ ft.

Safety also extends to how and where you store and use the chemicals needed to maintain a healthy water chemistry, as well as setting and enforcing rules of conduct in and around the pool or spa during times when it's open and when it's closed. Carrying an adequate level of homeowner liability insurance—and following the rules to maintain coverage—is a measure of safety as well.

Pools and spas are inherently unsafe, as evidenced by the thousands of unintentional injuries and deaths that the CPSC attributes to the use of private residential swimming pool and spa use every year. But if you approach your ownership responsibility with that understanding and then apply that respect with a variety of measures that lessen the risks and hazards, you'll greatly reduce the chances of experiencing an accident.

Whether you are thinking about adding a pool or spa to your home, or have purchased or want to buy a home with one or both of these amenities, a few basic features of its design help make it safe.

In fact, building codes regulating pool and spa construction and installation across the country often dictate many of these safety-related features, helping explain why the number of private pool and spa injuries and deaths have gone down (but still happen!) while nearly 800,000 pools and spas are added each year to the several millions already in place.

The pool floor. An important safety design feature for a swimming pool is the slope of the pool's base or floor. Most codes mandate that the base descend (or slope) at a gentle one foot in depth for every 7 ft. in length until the depth reaches 5½ ft. That 1:7 ratio of depth to length enables small children, especially, to better judge the depth of the water before they literally get in over their heads.

Between the shallow-end slope requirements and the rules regulating safe water
depth and clearance for a diving board, a
finished pool designed for both recreation
and diving needs to be about 50 ft. long.
The shrinking size of an average new-
home lot these days perhaps partially
explains why fewer new pools accommodate diving boards; simply, there just isn't
enough yard space.

Older swimming pools were often designed with a
minimum depth of 12" and typically were accessed
by a single, slip-resistant step built in to the shallow
end. Today, some pools feature a shallow end akin to
a beach, in that the entire base gently slopes up to
the pool deck; users can enter the pool from any
place along the poolfront, which also allows their
bodies to more easily adjust to the water temperature. In other designs, the traditional step down into

the water spans across the entire width of the shallow
end, enabling safe entry at any point.

Once the depth of the pool reaches $5\frac{1}{2}$ ft., it can
descend deeper at a more severe slope, which is prudent if you want a diving board at the deep end of the
pool and you're running out of real estate in your
yard. Prevailing building codes require a minimum
$7\frac{1}{2}$ ft. depth for safe diving from a deck-mounted
board; that depth also must be maintained at least 8
ft. in front of the board (which itself must extend
over the water from the pool deck at least 3 ft.) and 6
ft. on either side of it to provide enough safe clearance for divers.

The deck. In addition to a properly sloping pool base,
other safe design features include a slip-resistant
deck and coping on at least three sides of the pool or
spa. "Slip-resistant" is defined loosely as a semi-rough
surface you can grip with your bare feet. The deck
should extend at least 5 ft. from the edge of the pool
(and 3 ft. from a spa's edge) to provide plenty of
space to approach and enter the water and get out
safely and completely.

Like the gutter system in your house, pool decks
are designed with a slight, almost imperceptible slope
to drain splashed or rain water away from the surface

Safe pool decks don't need to be unattractive. Many popular landscaping products used for patios and other
outdoor surfaces also make beautiful, nonskid pool decks. These textured concrete pavers are a good example.

Steps near a pool should be broad, shallow and covered with material that is not slippery when wet. If there are more than two steps you should also have a grippable hand rail on at least one side.

to mitigate puddles and stagnant water, thus keeping the surface safe and clean. Some pool decks slope to an integral drain system set flush to the deck that carries incidental water away from the surface even more efficiently than a sloped deck alone.

Slip-resistant surfaces for pool and spa decks and coping are commonplace materials, and are regulated by building codes related to swimming pool and spa construction or installation. Though designed to last several years, a slip-resistant pool deck may become worn (if perhaps only in areas of heavy foot traffic),

but can be resurfaced easily and inexpensively to match the rest of the deck and restore its measure of safety. Traditionally a slab of concrete with a pebbly or roughed-up surface treatment, pool decks today are built using a wider range of materials, all within the code, including interlocking concrete or brick paving stones, flagstones, and engineered wood-polymer lumber, among others, to create a distinctive and more pleasing (and still safe) pool deck.

Accessibility. To be safe, a pool or spa must provide properly designed, slip-resistant, and adequately anchored access into and out of the water. These points of access (or egress) should be placed at opposite ends of a pool, if not in more places along its length, and on two sides of a spa.

Bright metal ladders that arch over the pool deck and into the depths of the water leap to mind as traditional points of access into and out of a pool, but accessibility has become more sophisticated in recent years. Stylish handrails and built-in step designs, beach-like shallow ends, and more fluid transitions between pools and integral spas have become popular safety measures as well.

Drain suction fittings. Below the surface of the water lurks another safety hazard: the drain. More specifically, its powerful suction that helps circulate and

▶ Define your deck

Most of us might think of a "deck" as something built out of wood planks that extends from the back door into the yard. But in pool and spa lingo, the term "deck" refers simply to the flat, solid surface leading up to and around the pool or spa, more so than any material from which it might be built. Wood, in fact, often makes a poor pool deck because it can get dangerously slippery when wet.

A sturdy ladder with slip resistant rungs or steps needs to be well-anchored to provide safe access.

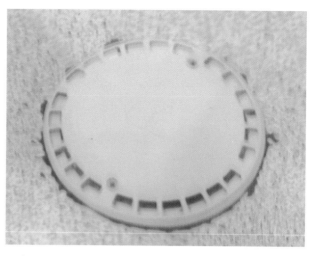

A dome-shaped drain cover keeps objects and limbs from getting drawn into or snagged on the drain.

refresh (or treat) the water in the pool or spa to help keep it healthy. An improperly covered drain can easily entangle long hair or even suck in skin and body parts and hold a person (most often a child) underwater, unable to escape its grip.

Safety standards regulate the cover (or fitting) that allows proper water circulation without sacrificing safety. In the last 15 years, the CPSC has helped develop more stringent standards for spa manufacturers (including a requirement to provide two drain outlets per pump instead of one, thus reducing each drain's suction power), as well as a dome-shaped cover design for spa drains that can be retrofitted over older spa drain openings.

Drain covers should meet and show the certification label of the American National Standards Institute's (ANSI) A112.19.8M standard. Consult a pool or spa professional to make sure you not only have the proper drain covers, but that they are the right size and are securely attached.

Safety Equipment

Like the works that run a pool or spa, there is a basic set of equipment for safety and water rescue. At a minimum, you should keep a life (or toss) ring, shepherd's hook, and rescue tube in good repair and within a few steps of the water. For longer and larger pools, double the set and keep each one at opposite ends of the pool.

Specifically, each life ring should have a securely tied rope that measures the same width as the pool, allowing it to be tossed out to a swimmer in distress anywhere in the water. For similar reasons, each shepherd's hook pole should measure at least 12 ft. long, with a hook on one end that is strong and secure enough to enable a swimmer to grasp it and be pulled to safety; the hook can be removable to accommodate a net that serves as a manual debris catcher/strainer.

Though typically associated with lifeguards, a foam and vinyl-coated rescue tube should feature an integral shoulder strap and a section or closed circle

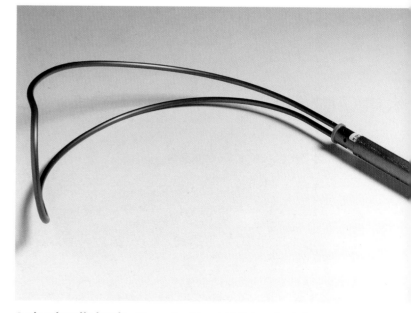

A shepherd's hook with a pole at least 12 ft. long is vital as a tool for reaching a distressed swimmer.

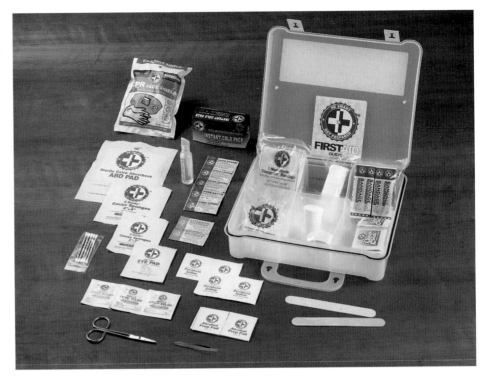

A well-stocked first aid kit should be on hand and easily accessible. Inspect it periodically to make sure everything is up-to-date.

of rope at one end to help keep a swimmer's head above water during a rescue.

While life rings and shepherd's hooks are made to resist most climate conditions, and therefore can (and should) be left out on deck while the pool is open, the vinyl coating of a rescue tube can become brittle and crack if exposed to extreme changes in climate; as such, consider storing it in a weather-resistant box or shed on or near the pool deck and having it on hand only when people are using the pool.

A full set of safety gear doesn't end with these three items; ideally, the following equipment is also on deck whenever someone is in the water:

Life preservers or jackets. As cute as they are, water wings and similar flotation devices aren't as safe as certified life jackets for young children and non-swimmers. Keep a few child-sized jackets on hand, as well as an adult-sized model, so that everyone can enjoy the water safely.

First aid kit. A complete first aid kit for a pool and spa includes pressure and a variety of adhesive bandages, a gauze roll and pads, an antiseptic spray or pads and/or an antibiotic gel, 30 SPF or higher-rated sunscreen, waterproof medical tape, tweezers, cold pack, latex gloves, cotton swabs or pads, and a first aid instruction book. There are several sources for complete kits, most in the $50 price range, situated in wall-mounted, waterproof containers perfectly suited for a pool or spa setting.

A wood fence near the pool area is a handy spot to mount a waterproof first aid kit.

Telephone. Today's cordless and cell phone technologies allow you to take a phone with you on deck when there are people in the water and not have to leave them unattended to answer a call. That said, sketchy cell service or an undercharged cordless phone battery might hinder your ability to make an emergency phone call. Instead, consider extending a land line out to the pool deck, with the phone encased in a waterproof, wall-mounted housing and/or under a protective cover or overhang to shield it from the weather.

Rope and float line. Once the depth of the pool reaches 5½ ft. (per building codes, mentioned earlier) and begins to more steeply descend toward the deep end, a rope with decorative floats along its length lying across the pool at that juncture provides a visual reference to a more radical change in water depth and serves as an effective "do not cross" barrier for young and/or inexperienced swimmers. The rope and float line can be easily removed and stored close by when it's not needed.

CPR and first aid training. Your designated safety expert (and perhaps a backup for that person if they're unavailable) should be trained and certified in cardiopulmonary resuscitation (CPR) and basic first aid to react quickly and with confidence in the event of an emergency. Local hospitals and healthcare clinics, YMCAs, fire and rescue departments, the Red Cross, and other civic groups in your area offer CPR and first aid classes, usually for free; the YMCA or a health club may offer lifeguard and water safety classes, as well.

Thermometers. An easy-to-read thermometer designed for underwater use is a great measure of safety for a spa, where water temperature exceeding 104 degrees F. (40 degrees C), or lower for young soakers, can be dangerous. Check the thermometer before each use.

In a swimming pool, a thermometer is handy to know if and how efficiently the heater is working, or to make sure the temperature is where you or other swimmers want it to be for different activities (e.g., cooler for lap swimming, higher for recreation or in cooler months). To get the most accurate gauge of the pool's overall temperature (as opposed to one specific spot in the water), consider a thermometer that's built-in to your pool's skimmer.

Lighting

Lighting brings beauty and romance to a pool or spa setting, but it also enhances safety and usability.

Today's pools (and some spas), as well as the landscaping around them, are adorned and enhanced by a variety of lighting products and design schemes. But lighting also plays an important part of pool and spa safety, specifically if you plan to use the pool or entertain on the pool deck at night.

The most common pool lighting system is a series of underwater lamps or sconces encased in waterproof fixtures and set tight and flush to the inside wall in niches around the perimeter of the pool. These floodlamps create a ring of light that help indicate the water's edge, as well as illuminate the water's depth in case someone or something falls in and needs to be rescued or recovered. They also add to the ambience of the pool.

Replacing underwater lamps

1. If a light fixture or lamp looks cloudy or has a black, soot-like substance behind the front cover, or otherwise isn't operating properly, replace it.

2. Use only replacement parts, including lamps, designed for the fixture and its use, ideally from the same manufacturer.

3. Turn off power to the lighting system at the service (or circuit) panel, not just the switch.

4. Remove the fixture (housing) and place it on the pool deck, out of the water.

5. Remove the damaged lamp and replace it with a new one of the same size (dimensions) and wattage recommended for the fixture.

6. Turn on the power and quickly test the lamp to make sure it works. Do not leave the light on for more than a few seconds, as it can get extremely hot. Turn off the power again.

7. Install a new gasket (about $3 from a pool supply outlet) and reseal/close the waterproof housing.

8. Hold the fixture underwater for several minutes to expose any leaks; a few air bubbles at first are common, but a continual stream of bubbles indicates a leak.

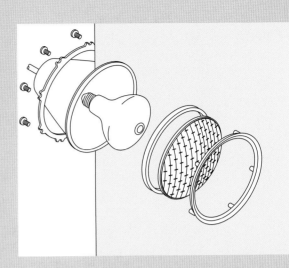

9. If the fixture passes the leak test, turn on the power and retest the lamp on deck. Turn off the power again.

10. Reinstall the fixture in its niche within the pool wall, then turn the power back on.

While all lighting and other electrical work around the pool requires the skills of a trained professional for safe and code-compliant installation (such as a ground fault circuit interrupter, or GFCI, to mitigate electrical hazards), lights that are installed underwater are especially sensitive, for obvious reasons. As with all lighting, there are wires leading to the lamp housing from a junction box on deck that must be kept away from water; special gaskets, seals, and waterproof lenses and covers designed for underwater lighting ensure that water does not get into the fixture. In fact, the bulb (or lamp) is the only component that isn't permanently sealed against the water, allowing you (or a pool-savvy, professional electrician or technician) to change out a blown bulb.

If you've ever touched a bare bulb or even an enclosed lamp cover when the light is on, you know it can get quite hot. Today's quartz and halogen bulbs, which deliver more light (or lumens) than a standard incandescent flood lamp, can get especially dangerous in a sealed environment, such as a sealed underwater light fixture. However, they are cooled by the temperature of the water; as such, they should never be turned on above the water level, except perhaps for a few seconds to test them when you (or someone) changes out a bulb.

In addition to underwater lights, a safe pool or spa lighting scheme can also include fixtures mounted flush to the deck, also around the edges of the water to outline the location of the pool or spa. Similarly, low-voltage or solar-powered landscape lights along the steps, stairs, or path from the house to the pool or spa add another measure of safety.

Motion-sensitive, wall-mounted floodlights—with enough range to reach the edge (and ideally the middle) of the pool or spa—can be an effective indicator that someone or something (like a small animal) is on the pool deck or in the water without permission, signaling a potential problem.

Regardless of the extent of your pool or spa lighting scheme, consider installing one light switch inside the house and another near the pool. That way, you can turn on the lights to the path and pool or spa before leaving the house for a swim or soak, and turn them off again upon your return; the

Rules and Signs

Clear signs placed in prominent places serve as constant reminders that reinforce important safety messages. A pool must be at least 7½ ft. deep for deck-diving off the deep end. Diving boards require even greater depth.

Party Rules

Consider these safety tips for a poolside party:

- Put someone in charge of supervising the pool and/or spa during the party.
- Keep non-swimming activities, including games, cooking and refreshments, and general seating, away from the pool or spa.
- Keep the pool or spa deck free of clutter; store or hang up safety equipment and pool furniture, which can be tripping hazards (especially at night).
- Unless using the pool is part of the party, consider covering it with a reinforced mesh cover so that no one or nothing falls in during the party.

switch near the deck allows you to illuminate your pool and spa (and the deck and other outdoor features) when the sun goes down rather than having to tromp back up to the house to do it.

Most pool and spa accidents happen because someone is acting unsafely in or near the water. Rough-housing, horseplay, call it what you want, but it often leads to minor or severe injury.

As a pool or spa owner, it is your responsibility to set and enforce rules of behavior for yourself and others using the water. These rules, as well as life-saving, CPR, and first aid instructions, the location and operation of power shut-off switches, and maximum occupancy (generally, one person per 15 square feet of surface area) should be posted on large signs in clear view of the pool or spa so that everyone can see, read, and follow them; many health and safety codes regulating pool and spa use require these signs, often in specific maximum distances from the water's edge. Make sure every user reads the signs and understands the rules before they go for a swim or a soak and that the fun will stop if they don't adhere to them.

Some standard rules of pool and spa conduct include mandatory adult supervision, hours in which the pool or spa is "open" or supervised, no swimming alone (kids and adults), no running, pushing, holding people under water, or other rough play, no alcohol or glass containers in or near the pool or spa (and certainly no swimming, diving, or soaking while intoxicated), only one person on the diving board or slide at a time, and no excessive bouncing or running dives from the board.

To be most effective, rules dictating the use of specific features, such as the diving board or slide, should be posted at or near those accessories, while more general rules and emergency instructions can be posted on signs around the perimeter of the pool or spa deck. Emergency numbers, for instance, might be best posted near the telephone.

Signs can also be inlaid into the edges of the pool deck or in the coping around the pool or spa, traditionally to indicate the depth of the water at given intervals and also to warn against diving directly from the pool deck. Posting and/or inlaying a "no diving" sign, even in the deep end, is essential if you have a diving board, so that two divers (one on the board, one on the deck), don't dive in at the same time and collide underwater. Pools without a diving board but a safe diving depth of at least 7½ ft. can allow diving directly off the deck in the deep end.

In addition, make sure all floating pool toys and furniture are removed and stored away after each use, removing temptation from young, curious eyes and imaginations as well as helping extend the useful life of the toys, games, and furniture.

Enforcing rules of conduct and other safe behavior can be an exercise in tough-love; no one wants to stop the fun or be the rules cop. But proper and consistent pool and spa safety is too important not to enforce the rules every time they are broken. Warnings are a good intermediate step, but allow too many without real consequences and they become white noise.

Signs are even more important for visitors to your pool than for regular users. It is useful to have one sign that covers most of the safety rules so it can be easily referred to.

For the best results, even if it's initially difficult to do, set and clearly communicate the procedures for how you'll enforce the rules; for instance, the first time merits a warning, the second time earns a 15-minute time out, and the third time bars the offender from the pool or spa for the rest of the day. Once you formulate a plan within your comfort level and for your situation, stick to it. Doing so will not only earn you respect, but help ensure a safe and healthy—and enjoyable—experience for everyone.

A solid fence on all sides provides privacy for swimming and sunbathing, and it also keeps neighborhood children from venturing into danger. In fact, most local codes require fences or walls around pools and outdoor spas.

Fences and Gates

Fences and gates are an excellent measure for safe pool and spa ownership; they are among the primary "levels of protection" promoted by the CPSC and required by both building codes and homeowner's liability insurance policies to maintain compliance.

Simple, properly designed, built, and installed fences and gates for pools and spas effectively block access to the water, greatly reducing the chance that a curious neighbor's child, or your own, will wander onto the deck and fall into the water unsupervised. Pets, too.

The specifications for an effective fence and gate (or multiple gates) for a private residential pool and spa are very precise. A fence or solid wall at least 4 feet high should completely enclose the pool. The walls of your house qualify as such barriers, but the open ends and sides must also be enclosed.

Other fence design specifications include leaving no more than a 2" space between the bottom of the fence and the ground and no openings of more than a half-inch within 18" of the gate latch, so that it can't be reached between the vertical slats or another opening in the fence. The fence should also not obstruct any view of the pool or spa from the house.

Avoid the "ladder effect." In addition, the design or construction of the fence or wall should not create a "ladder effect" that allows outsiders to use the structure of the fence or wall to climb over it. For instance, the horizontal braces set between the posts of a common wood privacy fence should be 54" apart, with the bottom brace no more than 4" off the ground; ideally, the braces should face the pool side of the fence, so there's no chance that anyone from the outside, child or adult, can climb over it.

For the same reason, the face of the privacy fence should feature vertical (not horizontal) pickets or slats, which can be spaced no more than 4" apart to filter a soothing cool breeze across the pool or spa.

Chain-link fences, which are less expensive than wood fences or concrete privacy walls, should

The "Ah-Ha" Solution:

On some of today's custom-designed pools featuring a disappearing (or infinity) edge and/or a spectacular view beyond, pool designers and homeowners might employ an age-old French livestock trick to avoid placing view-blocking fences along the back edges of their pools, and still comply with safety codes and liability insurance policies. Called an "ah-ha," the technique requires a lot that slopes away from the back of the pool or spa area, enabling the construction of a four-foot minimum-height retaining wall in which the top of the wall is flush (or even) with the pool deck or water's edge. If there are steps down to the area behind the pool or spa, that access must be blocked by a self-closing and self-latching gate that meets pool and spa safety specifications, thus completing the design.

include plastic slats installed diagonally through the openings to reduce the ability to climb up and over the fence. Portable fences that temporarily isolate the pool or spa when children are present, also are allowed as long as their vertical poles, spaced 15 ft. apart, can be secured into the pool deck to create a secure barrier. Even a thick row of shrubs, or a hedge, can serve as a barrier if allowed by the local code enforcement agency.

The ladder effect also relates to landscaping and furniture on either side of the fence; if you can help it, avoid planting climbing trees along the fence line, or trim the lower branches high enough to discourage people—especially curious and active kids—to climb them. Decorative planters, benches, or other features should be avoided for the same reason.

Gates within a properly designed fence, wall, or other pool or spa barrier must be self-closing and self-latching to ensure safety and comply with building codes and most insurance policies. In addition to a spring-loaded closer that operates the gate away from the pool (so that it closes if pushed from the outside), the latch on the inside of the gate structure should be located at least three inches from the top and 54" from the ground to keep small children from reaching over or up to the latch and opening the gate.

Above-ground pools. Generally, the design of above-ground pools and elevated spas creates an adequate safety barrier to the water. Usually at least 48" high (or deep), an above-ground pool or spa creates its own fence, and may also be topped with a shorter fence around its perimeter to keep swimmers or soakers from falling off the deck.

A self-closing gate latch automatically catches and secures the latch when the gate swings shut.

That said, getting up to the deck of an above-ground pool or elevated spa requires steps or a ladder. In other words, a potential safety hazard and an access to the water that needs to be blocked. If possible, the ladder or steps should be temporary so that you can disassemble or remove them when the pool or spa is not in use or open. If they are permanent fixtures of the pool's or spa's design and structure, at least the top or the bottom, and ideally both, should have a self-closing, self-latching gate.

In addition to secure gates in pool and spa fences or walls, the CPSC also recommends similar locking mechanisms for the doors and windows of your home that lead or look out to the pool or spa to keep small, curious children from getting on deck and falling into the water. Multi-point locks, hinge pins, swing arms, and other retrofitted security measures for doors and windows are easy, affordable, and effective safety provisions against intruders.

Pool and Spa Covers

Outdoor spas and swimming pools should have a safety rated cover that won't collapse or give way if someone steps or falls onto it.

Previous chapters mentioned the myriad benefits of a pool or spa cover as a way to heat the water, or at least help longer preserve a desired temperature, lessen the burden on the heating system, reduce water balancing chemicals, and slow evaporation, among other benefits. Some pool and spa covers also offer a significant measure of safety.

Pool safety covers feature a thicker vinyl material than standard covers that is reinforced with high-strength polymers to bear at least 400 pounds per square foot. They are designed to provide a continuous connection between the pool and the pool deck, leaving no gaps into the water. A certified pool safety cover meets the F1346-91 (2003) standard established by of the American Society For Testing and Materials (ASTM).

Be Very Alarmed

Pool alarms that automatically signal an intrusion onto the deck or into the water, or when a locked gate is opened or a fence line breached, can be effective pool and spa safety measures. A variety of alarms specifically designed for pool and spa use, or for general security and safety, include:

- **Pool alarms.** Placed in the water and triggered when someone or something breaches the water surface when the pool or spa is supposed to be closed.
- **Child alarms.** Also called "personal immersion alarms," these devices are secured to a young child to signal when he or she goes beyond a safe distance from a supervising adult or the house, or falls into the water. A clip-on transmitter sends a signal to a remote receiver in the house and/or on the pool deck.
- **Exit alarms.** Home security devices that signal when a door or window (in this case, directly out to a pool or spa) is breached.
- **Gate alarms.** Like door alarms, these devices alert the owners when someone not authorized to enter the pool or spa area opens a locked gate.
- **Infrared detectors.** A narrow beam of light is cast across an opening or area of the pool or spa; when breached, it triggers an alarm. These hard-wired or wireless systems are an unobtrusive supplement to a perimeter fence or wall.

No matter which alarm or combination of alarms you select, purchase those that meet ASTM standards for pool and child alarms and offer remote receivers so that the signal can be heard in your house or elsewhere besides the pool or spa deck.

Pool alarms are considered supplemental or backup safety measures rather than stand-alone precautions or protection against pool and spa hazards. They can be, however, an effective first line of defense, alerting you to (and perhaps scaring off) intruders on your pool or spa deck.

Some pool safety covers are stretched and secured over the top of the water, latching to hooks built flush to the pool deck or coping at three-foot intervals around the pool's perimeter. Such covers can be cumbersome, however, in that they must be rolled or folded up manually and stored somewhere near the pool when there are people in the water, a heavy chore. They also are difficult to secure, requiring at least two people to hold and stretch the material to reach the hooks in the coping. Those chores may cause a lapse in your safety plan, leaving the water open to accidents when the pool is not in use or is unsupervised.

For that reason, among others, the CPSC recommends a motorized safety cover that is rolled up either at one end of the pool or in a concealed area under the deck. In the case of the above-deck placement, you still have to secure the cover to the coping, while concealed systems automatically secure the cover in tracks located just above the water line. A motorized system can be activated manually, remotely, or automatically, so long as there is no chance of someone getting trapped under the cover as it is closing or when it is closed. Newer systems feature motion sensors that automatically stop and retract the cover when triggered, similar to an automatic garage door system.

Regardless of the type of safety cover you have or select, make sure to keep standing water from pooling on top of it, typically when the pool is seasonally closed. Use a pool or wet-vacuum, push-broom, or similar means to remove standing water that can become a drowning hazard itself if left unchecked.

Spa Covers. Even pools that feature integral spas often have a separate cover for the spa, allowing soakers to use it without removing or exposing the pool; certainly, stand-alone spas and hot tubs need covers to keep them safe, among other benefits mentioned in previous chapters.

Unlike pool covers, spa covers typically provide several benefits, including safety. Featuring an insulating foam core wrapped in a thick vinyl shell, spa and hot tub covers are lightweight and, because of the typically small opening of most spas, easier to remove, set aside, and replace—even by one adult—than a full-size pool cover. Most fold over and feature straps to make handling them easy.

Though standing on a spa cover is not recommended, its foam core is thick and rigid enough to withstand the weight of an adult. They completely cover the opening and feature latches along the perimeter that enable you to lock the cover in place so that children or unauthorized users can't gain access to the water.

Keep chemicals and equipment safely locked up

Chemicals for achieving and maintaining balanced water quality, even organic and non-toxic alternatives, need to be stored and handled with extreme care as part of your pool and spa safety plan. Not only is unbalanced or unsanitary pool or spa water a health and safety hazard, but the chemicals themselves also pose risks.

For the sake of efficient storage and handling, most pool and spa chemicals are sold in concentrated forms that are mixed with water to deliver their intended effect. As such, they can be highly volatile if consumed or perhaps even just exposed, especially directly from their containers, by a curious child or due to negligent handling by an adult. All chemicals should have labels with instructions regarding what to do if they are consumed, come in contact with the eyes or skin, or in case of some other kind of accidental exposure.

To keep and handle them safely, pool and spa chemicals should be kept in a locked or otherwise secure shed or cabinet in a cool, dry place. If you have or build a pool shed to store furniture, safety equipment, covers, and other gear in the off-season or when the pool or spa is not in use, design a place for chemical storage, as well. If not, a high shelf or locked cabinet in the garage are acceptable alternative locations. It's also important to keep them away from the metal components of accessory features, such as ladders, to avoid corrosion from chemical fumes.

Before using any pool or spa chemical, make sure it has a complete and legible label, shows no signs of leaking or moisture intrusion, and has not exceeded its expiration date; if any of those criteria aren't met, safely dispose of the container and the chemical at a designated hazardous materials disposal site and replace it.

When handling any chemical, make sure to follow the use instructions on the label, including any safety gear such as rubber gloves or eye and respiratory protection to guard against excessive exposure or accidental consumption. Use only one chemical at a

time; put the container securely away before using the next one, and use clean, separate scoops or other tools to measure and disperse each chemical. Wash your hands thoroughly after using each chemical to avoid any dangerous or volatile reactions among them. It's also a good idea not to let children or pets "help" when you or a trained professional technician are treating or balancing your pool or spa water.

As you apply the chemicals, either in concentrated or water-mixed form, into the pool or spa water (always add chemicals to water, not water to chemicals), take care to keep splashing to a minimum so they won't come in contact with your skin, eyes, or mouth, or even the deck, to which some chemicals may cause surface or aesthetic damage. Finally, make sure the pool or spa is closed to swimmers and soakers not only while you apply the chemicals, but also for the recommended time after application to allow them to evenly and completely dissolve and disperse in the water.

Resources

A•Pro
Hot tubs, pools and supplies
Lindstrom, MN
800-937-2776

Beachcomber Hot Tubs
www.beachcomberhottubs.com
800-663-6557

In the Swim
Pool and spa chemicals and supplies
(catalog and on-line)
800-288-7946
www.intheswim.com

The Hot Tub Dude
Used/reconditioned hot tubs
www.hottubdude.com

Photo Credits

PHOTOGRAPHY CONTRIBUTORS

The Association of Pool and Spa Professionals
www.theapsp.org
703-838-0083
pages 10, 12, 17, 20, 26, 27, 29, 31, 34, 37, 38, 41, 43, 75,
159 (top), 174, 177, 178, 183, 185, 224

Beachcomber Hot Tubs
www.beachcomberhottubs.com
800-663-6557
pages: 14, 62 (top), 76, 219, 227, 233

California Pools and Spas
www.californiapools.com
Front Cover, pages 4, 6 (top, both), 8, 73, 175, 181, 227

Coleman Spas
www.colemanspas.com
page 219 (bottom)

Endless Pools
www.endlesspools.com
800-233-0741
page 32

FAFCO, Inc.
www.fafco.com
530-332-2100
page 128 (bottom)

Gran Associates Architects and Planners
Pool house by Architect-David Kriegel.
www.granassociates.com
page 42

Heliocol Solar Pool Heating
www.heliocol.com
800-7-SOLAR (797-6527)
page 128 (top)

Intex Pools
www.intexpools.com
page 30

Marquis Spas
www.marquisspas.com
800-275-0888
page 13

Softub, inc.
www.softub.com
800-711-5382
pages 36, 180

Trex Company, Inc.
www.trex.com
800-BUY-TREX
Pages 176 (top), 231

VERSA-LOK Retaining Wall Systems
www.versa-lok.com
651-770-3166
page 223

PHOTOGRAPHERS

©Brand X Pictures/ Royalty-Free: page168 (top).

© Todd Caverly: page 177.

©Corbis/ Royalty-Free: page 182.

©Derek Fell Horticultural Library: page 16.

©ImageState/ Alamy: page176 (bottom).

©Jerry Pavia: page 172-173.

Index

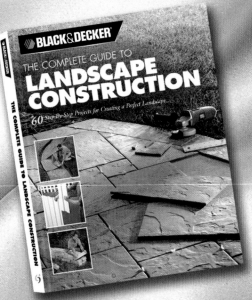
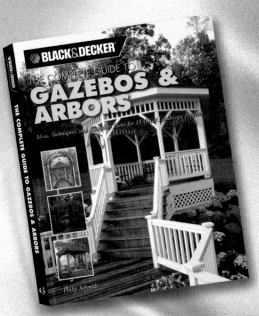